INVERSIONS

INVERSIONS

Writing by Dykes, Queers & Lesbians

Edited by Betsy Warland

PRESS GANG PUBLISHERS

VANCOUVER

Grateful acknowledgement is made to the following for permission to reprint copyrighted material: Jane Rule, "Lesbian and Writer," from *A Hot-Eyed Moderate* (Tallahassee, Florida: Naiad Press, 1985); and (Toronto: Lester & Orpen Dennys Ltd., 1985) copyright © 1985 by Jane Rule. Irena Klepfisz, "Forging a Woman's Link in *di goldene keyt:* Some Possibilities for Jewish American Poetry," from *Dreams of an Insomniac: Jewish Feminist Essays, Speeches and Diatribes* (Portland, Oregon: The Eighth Mountain Press, 1990); copyright © 1977, 1990 by Irena Klepfisz.

The editor wishes to thank Frances Wasserlein and the Vancouver Lesbian Centre for their support of this project. The publisher acknowledges financial assistance from the Canada Council.

Canadian Cataloguing in Publication Data
Main entry under title:
InVersions

Includes bibliographical references.
ISBN 0-88974-036-4

1. Lesbians' writings, Canadian (English).* 2. Lesbians' writings, American. 3. Canadian essays (English) — Women authors.* 4. American essays — Women authors. 5. Canadian essays (English) — 20th century.* 6. American essays — 20th century. 7. Lesbianism — Literary collections. I. Warland, Betsy, 1946-
PS8365.I58 1991   C814'.5408'0353   C91-09160-2
PR9197.7.I58 1991

First Printing September 1991
1   2   3   4   5   6   95   94   93   92   91

Design and cover art by Valerie Speidel
Editor for the Press: Barbara Kuhne
Typesetting and production by V. Speidel
Typeset in Bodoni; Linotronic output at The Typeworks
Printed on acid-free paper by Friesen Printing
Printed and bound in Canada

Press Gang Publishers
603 Powell Street
Vancouver, B.C. V6A 1H2
Canada

CONTENTS

II
Head Wind

III
Site Reading

Inventing InVersions

BETSY WARLAND

W hen my mother pours out her real emotions and perceptions in an un-
guarded way she "vents." *InVersions* vents and invokes the various ways in
which dyke, queer and lesbian writers are inventing with the written word.
"Necessity is the mother of invention," as the saying goes. So, this book is
also about how our literature has grown to such an extent as to create the
necessity of inventing a book in which we, the writers, reflect on our experiences, beliefs and writing practices.

When I trace the beginnings of my motivation to address the scarcity of
exchange among us as writers, I think back to the Women and Words/les
femmes et les mots conference which we held in Vancouver in 1983. Eight
hundred women involved in creating, producing, teaching and selling
women's books gathered together for the first time in Canada at that ground
swell event.

There were many conference firsts, among them a panel on lesbian writing
with panelists Beth Brant, Nicole Brossard, Mary Meigs, and myself. The
room was packed and the energy was electrifying! Ever since, I have longed
to bring more dyke, queer and lesbian writers together to talk about our work
and thinking.

In the fall of 1989 I participated in a Women's Studies conference where I gave a paper investigating the ways my lesbianism has informed the content, language, and form of my books (an excerpt of this paper, "moving parts," is reprinted here). Shortly after, I came across Mary Meigs' essay "Falling Between the Cracks" (also reprinted here) in *Trois*, a Montreal literary journal. I felt very stirred by Meigs' essay, which was uncompromising in its contemplations of what it has been like for her to be a lesbian writer in Canada. I realized how utterly rare it was to find such a text and how much I needed to read it. I also recalled how many of the women who had heard my paper at the conference responded with considerable pent-up emotion. The intensity of these responses within myself and others convinced me that it was up to us to initiate an exchange among ourselves as writers, which would be of benefit to us as well as to readers, teachers and critics of our work.

By April of the following year (1990) I sent out the first round of invitations soliciting texts for *InVersions:*

> As a lesbian writer, you have no doubt felt that aspects of your work have either been frequently misinterpreted or ignored by reviewers and critics. These oversights and mono-sights can be maddening, laughable, or discouraging. They can persist within lesbian and feminist circles (which tend to focus on the content of our work and our social obligation as writers) and they persist within the mainstream literary circles (which tend to either ignore our writing, or focus on it formally to the exclusion of the content, or become obsessed with our lesbianism to the extent that it obscures the actual focus and intent of the writing).

Why reclaim the word "invert"? I'm attracted to the way the very word itself indicates a radically different position from which we see, experience and speak life — that it's not simply a matter of "sexual preference." "Invert" seems to have first been used in England in an anonymous (". . . was a woman"?) review of a paper that was published in 1871 in the *Journal of Mental Science*. In 1897 Havelock Ellis managed to publish, against considerable odds, *Sexual Inversion* (part of his *Studies in the Psychology of Sex* series) which was the first book on "the subject."[1]

This, in turn, helped give Radclyffe Hall the courage and the public context for writing *The Well of Loneliness*, which was published in 1928.[2] The public scandal, trial, and resulting ban on the book did not deter it from becoming "the lesbian bible" for several generations of European and North American women. The few passages in the book that are, given our general awareness today, clearly racist and classist, are off-putting to say the least. Internalized homophobic prejudices are also evident. Yet, having finally read the book recently, I was struck by how many insights Hall had about being an "invert," despite living in a repressive, isolating era which allowed for no possibility of collective self-defined political thought.

Invert, To turn, bend. Shape-changers. The turn of a phrase, the page, the mind. *Inside-out and upside-down.* Coming out turning us inside-out revealing the world upside-down: things aren't what they seem. Every writer in this book has learned this from the depth of her being.

The words **verse** and **prose** originate from the same Indo-European root as **invert**, as do the words **subvert** and **convert.** Through our prose and verse we subvert the his-and-hers monogram version and convert readers to new ways of seeing and being.

Conversation, *com- with* + *versari, to live.*

We "live with" one another through the writing, reading and reflecting process documented in this book, for it is with these words that we are making an intimate home *and* a public culture that has never existed before. That *InVersions* is the first collection of its kind in North America attests to this fact.

The making of a public culture is a complex process. External resistances from those of the dominant culture (or from those wishing to be part of the dominant culture) can be quietly brutal. To complicate the matter, we don't have a unified public persona to automatically present to protect ourselves. As a queer culture, we are not rooted in a particular geographical location; as lesbians, we have not been able to preserve much of our history and art; and as dykes, we are part of other cultures and races with profound differences among them. In her text "To(o) Queer the Writer — *Loca, escritora y chicana,*" Gloria Anzaldúa's critique of the common usage of the word *lesbian* as inclusive and representative is an example of our fundamental differences. The book's subtitle, *Writing by Dykes, Queers and Lesbians,* was chosen with her analysis in mind. Inverts in versions. *InVersions:* not one but many *versions* we must learn to live with-*in*.

Although my central motivation for editing this book was to expand the rapport among us in North America, it soon became clear that I had to narrow the focus to what I knew best — poetry and fiction. I couldn't extend an open invitation for submissions as I knew this might have resulted in an encyclopedic book.

I selected a number of fiction writers and poets who have published at least one book in which their sexual identities clearly informed their writing, and who have experienced public response (or lack of response) to this work. Still, within these two genres I now see that I have not been truly representative: the absence of lesbian romance and speculative fiction writers immediately comes to mind.

A page limit for the book necessitated further choices. Did I want a collection with as many writers as possible who would only be allowed a few pages each, or did I want fewer writers who had more room in which to investigate their thoughts? Since this was our first opportunity to exchange ideas and experiences (in this form and to this extent) it seemed important not to do this in a cursory way. Consequently, fewer writers were invited to participate.

It was important to me that the diversity of our age, class, cultural background, race, publishing experience, political/literary beliefs and practices be represented. So, the book you hold in your hands has been shaped by all these decisions as well as by each writer's personal decision to participate (or not).

It was crucial that women writers of colour be in the conversation of *InVersions*. Like so many readers and writers, I, too, have often been sparked and influenced by their perceptions and writing, and this companionship means a great deal to me. Most books that are being published still diminish or deny their integral part in our conversation. And though I appreciate all of the writers' trust in my editing of their texts, which were on a topic that many of them had not addressed in such a public way before, I particularly value this willingness on the part of each of the writers of colour.

The excellent French to English translations by translators Marlene Wildeman and Lou Nelson have enabled the inclusion of Quebec writers Nicole Brossard, Anne-Marie Alonzo and Gloria Escomel in this English language conversation. They, along with a number of other Francophone feminist writers, have not only shaped Quebec literature and theory but have also influenced the evolution of English Quebec and English Canadian feminist writing and theory. Because the translators' identities by necessity are submerged in their translations, I have asked both to write autobio-statements [see "Translators' Autoportrait(e)s"] to make their presences more evident.

During the process of making *InVersions*, the necessity of providing publications lists became apparent. Obtaining basic information about the body of the work of even the better-known writers in the book is difficult. This creates a frustrating deterrent for writers, readers and researchers alike. In order to compile these publications lists each writer was asked to list her books (authored and co-authored), edited and co-edited books and journals, selected work published in anthologies and journals but not in her books, selected interviews, and several longer critical articles and/or reviews on her work. These lists are selective and by no means comprehensive. Several of the writers have not kept detailed records over the years, while for a number of others complete lists were edited for space considerations. Nevertheless, the foundation of the writing life is documented here, and this is an important addition: information is indeed power.

During the months of re-reading and editing these twenty-four dynamic texts, I became very aware of the resonances and resistances among them, and I wanted the order to reveal (rather than conceal) these connections and contradictions. For me, these texts constellate around four basic places of speaking. The quest for an intact personal presence in which the writer's sexual identity and related life-experience can freely inform her writing is the central focus of the texts in "Embodying Our Words." "Head Wind" brings together the texts which essentially reflect on personal, literary and political external resistances to this intact, articulated writing presence. The texts in "Site Reading" are concerned with reading (as in sight reading music or an archaeological site) cultural, political, creative and philosophical practices generated out of our particular embodied voices. And the texts in "Questions Beyond Queer" give presence to other vital aspects of writers and their work which lesbian and/or feminist predominant thought and practice often denies, subsumes or fails to notice.

Now, when you, the reader, experience a surge of excitement at seeing the names of the writers you want most to hear, and then disappointment at the absence of those writers who are not included, so I, too, am aware of both the vitality and the incompleteness of *InVersions*. Yet, it is the combination of these very responses which creates the desire to generate more books of this kind. We need them and I look forward to reading them.

InVersions is a beginning, and with that in mind I find this gathering of voices remarkably honest, disturbing, passionate, angry, tender and thought-provoking. I was struck over and over again by the emotional and intellectual integrity of these writers as I worked with their texts. I found myself saying "I love these women!" Although many of us have never met and perhaps we wouldn't all necessarily like one another, there is a strong-spiritedness among the writers of *InVersions* which is very compelling.

Living with these writers during the past year and a half of editing *InVer-*

sions has not always been easy, but it has always been revealing. Even though most of us live within, or on the borders of, more than one writing community, it has been very exciting for me to feel the tangibility and the endless possibilities of the queer, lesbian and dyke writing communities.

Invert. The turn of a phrase, the page, the mind.

NOTES

1. Havelock Ellis, *Studies in the Psychology of Sex* (New York: Random House, 1942. Reprinted edition).
2. Radclyffe Hall, *The Well of Loneliness* (London: Virago, 1982).

I

Embodying our Words

To Be or Not To Be Has Never Been the Question

BETH BRANT

My first work was published in 1981, the year I turned forty and the year I began writing. By first work I mean just that — the first pieces of writing I had ever done. I was not a diary-keeper or a journal-doodler. I lived my life, I talked my stories to friends, to lovers, to family. This was the way it was.

Then I saw Eagle. He swooped in front of our car as we were driving through Seneca land. He wanted us to stop the car and so we did. I got out of the car and faced him as he sat in a tree, his wings folded so gracefully, his magnificent head gleaming in the October afternoon sun. We looked into each other's eyes. Perhaps we were ten feet away from one another and I was marked by him. I remember that I felt in another place, maybe even another time. He stared at me for minutes, maybe hours, maybe a thousand years. I knew I had received a message and that message was to write.

Sinister Wisdom was my first publisher, the feminist journal that at that time was being edited and published by Michelle Cliff and Adrienne Rich. The two pieces I submitted, *Mohawk Trail* and *Native Origin*, were raw and unformed. Michelle wrote me a letter and in a few sentences helped me with the forming. The rawness I wanted to keep. Perhaps because to me, rawness was synonymous with honesty. And I believed, and still do, that honesty is what writing is about. Was this work lesbian-identified? Yes, because that's who I am. And in my bio I stated very clearly and proudly who I was — a Mohawk lesbian. These two identities are mine and they are one with me. I have always felt in these ten years I've been writing, that betraying who I am would be a betrayal of the grandmothers and sisters who came before me. And it would be a betrayal of the daughters and granddaughters who are to follow me. This is not altruistic — it is Indian. It is not naive — it is Mohawk. It is not self-aggrandizement — it is lesbian. Eagle brought that gift to me, *to the me that I am*.

In my community, the Native community, questions of self-identity are usually left to white people who will spend too much time agonizing over them and use up too much breathable air discussing them. In other words, self-identity crises are an exercise for those who have no community or history of that community. We're all Indians, so what is good for one will ultimately benefit the community. At least, that's what I was taught. Yet, I have been hurt and ostracized by some Indians, men and women, who have made it clear that being a lesbian, or **saying** it out loud is not good for my community. I think what they're really saying is — you embarrass me by your sexuality, therefore you embarrass our people, and **white** people will think even less of us than they already do. I do not say that my people are looking for approval from white society. But there are some individuals who may have something invested in the white society — whether it be a good job working for the government, a place in literary circles, or an enforced belief in the white stereotype of what Indian women should be — and are frightened by what can be taken away. And why shouldn't they be? Everything else has been stolen, why not the small niches that keep a roof over our head and food on our tables? Yet, I want to say that homophobia is the eldest son of racism and one does not exist without the other. Our community suffers from both — inside and outside.

If I have been hurt by some heterosexual Indian people, I have been moved and energized by others. I gave a reading at a university and in the audience was an elder, a Yankton Sioux woman whom I admired and greatly respected for her work in getting Indian skeletal remains rightfully returned to their people for proper and honoured burial. I was very nervous about being in the same room with her, let alone reading the story I had planned, one about a lesbian mother whose son has died. I read my story, finding, as I do, that I was lost in the words and the telling, forgetting about externals. After the reading, the elder came up to me, a big, commanding woman. She touched the False Face I wore around my neck, "Very impressive," she said. Then she smiled, "You sure write purty." I took her hand and said, "Thank you, Grandmother," and that was that. Later I fled to a quiet place to have a cigarette and a cry. She approved of me. And what's more, she liked the way I told a story. Surely, the finest praise I could receive. These kinds of encounters have happened much more frequently than the other kind.

And yet. . . and yet, I earn my living by my writing. That Indian elder cannot, by herself, pay the mortgage and feed my stomach, even though her words fed my writer's soul. So there comes the time when I can't ignore being ignored by those whose reviews would mean the difference between getting royalties on a hundred books or ten thousand. And I **would** prefer the ten thousand, there is no doubt about it. But what would that mean? Do I really want my work reviewed in the *New York Times Book Review?* Sometimes, yes. But knowing how the system works and who controls that system, I would no doubt be reviewed by some white man who once wrote a half-assed article about Indians and is therefore the resident "expert." His opinion doesn't matter to me or my people. The reviews I have had about my books have been good ones, but it is interesting for me to see what is ignored by reviewers. Take this quote from *Booklist,* a review catalogue sent out to booksellers in the U.S.: "Beth Brant's book, *Mohawk Trail* is impossible to classify simply." The review ends by saying "Highly recommended for Native-American literature collections," but in between, leaves out the fact that I am a lesbian, that I am urban, that I am Mohawk. Instead, I am described as "part-Indian." True enough that I am a half-breed, indeed much of my work centres on that state of being, or as LeAnne Howe, Choctaw writer puts it, "You're torn between wanting to kill everyone in the room, or buying 'em all another round of drinks." I guess the reviewer couldn't classify my writing (why does an act of creation **have** to be classified?) because I don't write in pleasant racist stereotypes and I write about queers.

Frankly, the fewest number of reviews about my books have been in the feminist presses. *Mohawk Trail* was reviewed by one feminist newspaper, *Sojourner,* and that review was written by Joy Harjo, someone hard to ignore. The review was a wonderful one, not because of the good things she had to say about my writing, but because she **understood** where I was coming from. The feminist presses must subscribe to the theory (or the wish) that Indians are dead and gone. And that is where the rage overcomes me. I have been a working, marching, demonstrating participant in the women's movement for twenty-odd years, steadfast in my belief that feminism is the saving

grace for the world's people — women, men, children and those people of the
air, the sea, the land and the cosmos. Native women's books are **rarely**
reviewed in the feminist media, but I notice that Lynne Andrews' books are
steady best-sellers in the women's bookstores which still carry them. I have
never been a civil-rights feminist. That is, I believe, along with Audre
Lorde, that "the master's tools will never dismantle the master's house." And
writing for the masters or the mistresses of the house will not be the tool that
destroys racism. I do want to be reviewed and I want to be reviewed in my
many complexities as a human being — lesbian, Indian, woman, mother,
feminist, working class, mammal and on and on.

This makes me think of one of the longest reviews I received about
Mohawk Trail, by a white, gay male. The review was terrific, coming from a
working-class perspective and from a man who understood the conflicts and
triumphs of being gay. The reviewer had spent some time among Indians, as
a neighbour in Detroit and as a lover, and this was evident in his writing. I
realized, with that review, that no one discusses the issue of class in the
same breath with Indian writers. Just as we are perceived to be invisible, so
are we not considered in the context of where we work, what we do to work,
what we have to endure to bring a pay cheque home. My dad worked on the
line putting parts on cars. He also painted houses, worked in a salt mine,
worked construction, planted trees during the Depression, bartered physical
labour for venison, and did what he had to do and wanted to do. And this is
where I came from — an urban Indian, working-class home. We were poor
sometimes, but Daddy always worked and so did Mama. Sometimes, being a
writer, I feel like I'm not really working and there is a sense of guilt surrounding that. I probably never will resolve that guilt and I'm not sure I want
to anyway. It gives me a nice edge I'm comfortable with; keeps me angry,
gives me a sure nose for pretension, in myself as well as in others. I can spot
a phoney a mile away and I like that about myself.

I do not know where this writing of mine comes from. It is not a separate
entity. I **do** know that it is a gift and like most gifts, requires an interchange
to take place. When the writing-spirits call me (I do not write every day,
although I think about writing every day) I respond. My body responds, my
heart responds, my racial memory responds. I do not censor myself when
writing. I will not make a character heterosexual if she or he is not. In sending out my vita I will not excise those anthologies or journals that have the
words lesbian, gay, dyke or queer in them. I may as well excise those journals and anthologies that have the words Native, Indian or woman in their

titles. In my bio notes I usually say I am a lesbian mother and grandmother. It is always interesting to see who will accept my work and what they will do with it and me. Editors who wouldn't change my stories without permission feel they can change the contents of my bio. Suddenly I find myself a mother and grandmother who lives in the States. These omissions used to anger me; now I find them oddly amusing. I figure by now that most readers know me as "that Mohawk lesbian" or "that nice, Indian Granny that lives in the States." Both are true. And I know who I am — a statement I couldn't have made years ago when I was a battered woman, a self-hating half-breed, a woman who self-destructed at every turning, before I acknowledged my lesbianism and before I began to write. And anyway, most of my stories are about lesbians and gay men; all are about Indians.

It would be an untruth to say that coming out as a lesbian set me free. But it would be true to say that writing put me on the path to freedom. And I don't mean "personal" freedom. I mean the freedom to be a loving, useful member of my community. I have used this analogy before, but I will use it again here — the Sun Dance. The Sun Dance is a ceremony of Plains Indians where the participant endures hours and even days of dancing into the sun to make a communion with the Creator. While to white-European eyes it may seem a dance of the individual, in actuality it is a dance for the community. I never felt this so forcefully as when I was editing *A Gathering of Spirit*. Each Native woman who contributed to that anthology was making her dance. All of us, together, made a dance for each other. Our community. Our communion. That is how I feel when I am writing and the writing-spirits are singing to me. I am making communion with my people, with the Creator, with myself — all those parts of me becoming one. All working together. All dancing and feasting together. It is **why** I write. To make a whole. To take these splits that were forced on me by racism, classism, homophobia, colourism, and baste them together.

Through the years the threads have become stronger and that is due to the many lesbian and gay Indians I have met and corresponded with since *A Gathering of Spirit* and *Mohawk Trail* were published. These brothers and sisters have helped hold me together. And my give-away to them is to be a stronger writer and member of our family. I do not write out of isolation or a longing for the Muse — that European entity that mysteriously appears to white men. I have imposed a solitude on myself. The room where I work is a hermitage of sorts. But I am never alone here. My senses are fired up and ready to communicate. There may be music — from Lou Reed to Kiri Te

Kanawa. There are pictures on my walls — from grandchildren to friends and relatives. There are objects to touch — from a piece of old brick found at a Mission graveyard to a pine cone that reminds me of the trip where a lover and I made love on the earth, the open sky and sun caressing us as we caressed each other. There is tobacco and sage burning, to bring good spirits to the room. My candles are lit to remind me of the fires of my People. No, I am not alone here.

Native peoples have always told stories. And among those storytellers were lesbians and gays. This I know, despite the attempts of Jesuits, missionaries and other infiltrators to "white-wash" us and make us invisible. I am just continuing a long tradition, only this time around using a computer. And stories are meant to be spoken — that part of tradition never changes. The written becomes the spoken whether by mouth or hands, the spoken enters the heart, the heart turns over, the earth is renewed. In the end, this is what matters to me. "I write because to not write is a breach of faith." I believe that now as surely as I did in 1984 when I wrote those words. I must have faith in the power of a Mohawk lesbian to make a difference through writing. I do have faith in the power of Native lesbians and gay men to make that difference through beading and weaving words into life. Because we do our work with love.

SELECTED PUBLICATIONS

BOOKS
Mohawk Trail. Ithaca, N.Y.: Firebrand Books, 1985; Toronto: The Women's Press, 1990.
Food and Spirits. Vancouver: Press Gang Publishers, 1991; Ithaca, N.Y.: Firebrand Books, 1991.

EDITED BOOKS
A Gathering of Spirit: A Collection of North American Indian Women. Montpelier, Vermont: Sinister Wisdom Books, 1984; Ithaca, N.Y.: Firebrand Books, 1988; Toronto: The Women's Press, 1988.

ANTHOLOGIES
"Recovery and Transformation." In *Bridges of Power: Women's Multicultural Alliances,* edited

by Lisa Albrecht and Rose Brewer. Philadelphia & Santa Cruz: New Society Publishers, 1990.

JOURNAL PUBLICATIONS

"Grandmothers of a New World." *Woman of Power*, no. 16 (Spring 1990).

ARTICLES, REVIEWS AND INTERVIEWS

Catherine Daligga. Review of *A Gathering of Spirit. Gay Community News*, December 1983.

Dorothy Allison. Review of *A Gathering of Spirit. Native New Yorker*, January 1984.

Gloria Anzaldúa. Review of *A Gathering of Spirit. Conditions* 10 (1985).

Joy Harjo. Review of *Mohawk Trail. Sojourner*, January 1987.

Kerrie Charnley. Interview. "Beth Brant: Telling the truth for each other." *Kinesis*, September 1989.

Cora Hoover. Master's Thesis. "The Making of *A Gathering of Spirit*." Yale Univ., April 1991.

Christian McEwen. Interview. "Beth Brant: Native American Writer." *Visibilities*, May/June 1991.

When the Words Open Into
Some Not Yet Open Space†

MINNIE BRUCE PRATT

Last Friday I cleaned out Miss Brown's apartment, full of old newspapers, roaches, leaking canned goods, empty tubes of zinc oxide for bed sores, greeting cards from the women she'd once clerked with at Lansburg's. I saved some of the cards, her brush and comb, underwear, a few dresses; she can't keep much in a two-foot wide closet in the nursing home. I found letters that she'd written last spring when she'd been so worried about money: the same sentence, written over and over, instructions to Social Security on how to send her money to her home address, not to the bank, she was ninety-two, couldn't go out anymore to the bank, couldn't get her money unless they'd send it to her home address, 518 Ninth St., #203, she was ninety-two, not strong enough to go out, wouldn't be able to get her money unless they sent it to her at home, not the bank, not strong enough to go out, she was ninety-two... Pages and pages of the same letter, stuck in old phone books, in a dictionary, in her kitchen cabinet in piles of folded wax paper, between

---

†Excerpted from *Rebellion: Essays 1980-1991*, Firebrand Books, 1991.

paper plates with quarters and pennies in case of an emergency. Pages of pleading messages, never mailed, but written over and over, a prayer, a magic incantation, the words willing that some action be taken, that help appear: the words calling up action.

Back in town at the end of last spring, after a long absence, I heard from Mr. Cox that Miss Brown was distraught. I went to her and settled how she could get her money. The written word had not brought me; but she had fixed her need inexorably in her fading mind by writing over and over, by repeating to herself and then to others what was necessary, until something was done.

Now her piles of old newspapers, clippings of celebrities and atrocities, remind me of my own boxes of yellowed papers, cut from the newspaper of any town where I've lived, and saved as notes for some future poem or essay. I finger her desperate letters to the authorities and think of the book of poems that I've just finished, the poems where I tell over and over the story of my life, my love for another woman, the loss of my two boys to their father: anger, injustice, grief, almost unendurable pain, isolation, joy, reconciliation, defiant laughter, poem after poem. But was my writing the same as hers? A shout to someone to do something; a reminder to myself of what I needed to remember, words to center me in a hostile and chaotic universe; a prayer, a justification of need; a repetition to keep my sanity; a stubborn clinging to what I needed in order to go on with my life on the edge, on the margin of power. I shudder with recognition at the repeated phrases, at her grip on the centrality of her own need, her life.

———————

After a poetry reading at a small new women's bookstore, a woman approaches and says to me, "I feel that if I said what you just said, lightning would strike me." I had just read some poems that were explicitly sexual and lesbian; I'd talked about my children, my lover, my mother; I'd said the word *lesbian* several times. Her reaction to this wasn't uncommon: sometimes after I read my work, women are silent or shrink back from me as if there is some scorched smoking circle of dirt around me, as if I'd been struck, for my sin, with lightning by god; as if I might be struck down, for my rebellion, by some unseen power.

During this reading, as I spoke I had a flash, a jump of my heart, that I was saying the word *lesbian* too many times. After all, it was a new bookstore; perhaps this first reading would give it a reputation as "too lesbian" and women would be afraid to come. And the program for which I was in town as a resident writer was a community program: maybe it would damage them somehow that I and my poems were being so unmistakably clear. A flash of doubt, though I didn't change anything I was saying or reading, a flashback on other moments when I opened my mouth and *lesbian* came out in one form or another; and I feared the blow. As if my word might vaporize my children, my mother, the person offering me a job I needed, might obliterate me and my lover in a public place. The power of my own word turned against me.

After the reading, I talk to another woman who comes up to thank me. I speak of my fear of saying too much, of being "too lesbian." She is surprised that I still worry about this, surprised that I would hesitate. She thinks of me as "brave," as "strong," as "beyond" that fear. I don't think of myself as brave or strong. The only way to understand that I exist from one day to the next, one year to the next, is to write down my life, and in the end, send this out to others. The poems sent or read aloud: like someone writing an obscure sacred document. Is this power? It does not feel like power, but necessity.

Yet there are moments when the words open into some not yet open space. Then I feel I am stepping into power. And perhaps it is then, hearing those words, that others think, "This is the moment she will be struck down."

———

When I was thirteen I began keeping a journal in spiral-bound flimsy notebooks. But I never promised myself that I would be a writer. Instead I said: *I'll learn to fly a plane, I'll travel around the world*. Escape, escape. I quit writing in my journals when I left home for college, though I wrote a few poems during my first two years at the university.

Finally, I married the man who was the editor of a literary magazine, a poet. (I joke bitterly sometimes that I wanted to be a poet and married one instead, the same way my girl cousin who wanted to be a veterinarian married one.) Not long after we married, at a party at our house in the middle of a smoldering cloud of cigarette smoke and a fog of alcohol, our philosophy professor pointed at me and declared: "You'll go to grad school; you can have an academic career." Laying his hand on my husband's arm, he said: "You will be the poet."

I stopped writing poetry after I married at twenty, had a child at twenty-one, and another child eighteen months later. For a long time after I married and bore my two sons, I heard nothing inside me, nothing at all, as if a door had closed on some inner voice, a heavy wooden door, thick, impenetrable. Perhaps I had closed it myself.

Ten years later, I began a new poem, one about my husband trying to kill me in various ways — with a homemade bomb, by handing me over to men who shot me, by turning me over to the police. A poem with images of him rising from pond water, a dead man "glowing yellow-green/bloated with invitation." A poem about my running away from him with the children, across the South "on Greyhounds, in strangers' cars."[1]

A poem in which I leave out the reason I fear him: I have fallen in love with another woman, am mad for her, mad about her, and he knows. I drink power from her body and mine, sexual power that opens and unfolds into another future, an ecstatic vista, unseen, unknown, taken on faith. I'm afraid he will pursue me down that mysterious way, coming after the power I take away from him; my sex, my secret, my words, my need, my key to the door he has not yet entered himself.

————

A few weeks after the beginning of my first love affair with a woman, I attended with her a conference where, one night, Robin Morgan read. I admired her work as ambitious, I envied her rolling lines, her weightiness; yet now I can't remember a single word she spoke. But I have carried with me since then the words of the other poet who read that night, Audre Lorde. She was the first writer, and the first poet, I heard speak publicly as a lesbian. That night she began with the revelatory words of her love poem to another woman: "Speak earth and bless me with what is richest."[2] Words praising her life, my life, spoken out loud before thousands of other women.

I was blessed, as a lesbian poet, that I could turn to Lorde's writing for hope in the flesh; and to Judy Grahn's poems for her answer to those who would try lesbians with a bitter judgment, condemn us to suffering and death. I was blessed to begin my life as a writer when women who loved other women were creating a world of politics and culture from their lives. I think I began to live as a lesbian and work as a poet only because other lesbians asserted that there *was* an *us* to listen to, to talk to. Slowly, I began to write poetry and to think of myself, not yet as a poet, but, in Grahn's words, as "a woman who believes her own word."[3] These two women, close to me in age, but seemingly separated from me, one by class, one by race, gave me the clearest answers to the question, "What would happen if one woman told the truth about her life?/The world would split open."[4]

When I turned for guidance to the woman who had asked this question in her own poetry, a woman of my mother's generation, Muriel Rukeyser, I learned that she also was a lover of women. I looked in her work for this love. But in the few possible poems the pronoun was *you*; there was no *she*; and the most explicitly lesbian poem (about nonprocreative sex) was "The Conjugation of the Paramecium," which described a slow "inexplicable" exchange of "some bits of nucleus" between two of these simple one-celled animals. She did assign "renewal/strength another joy" to this process, but this was hardly the grandeur with which she expanded on the life of Kathe Kollwitz, wife, mother, artist, who was the inspiration for her lines on truth and the splitting of the world. I could find in Rukeyser's poetry no similar nakedness of truth about a lesbian life. I felt a huge anger, a condemning anger, the anger of betrayal: why had she not told her *own* life clearly?

I felt the same anger when I turned to the words of Lillian Smith, who was, like me, white and Southern-born, also of the generation before me, whose work I had leaned on, who knew how each person had within her "a poet and a demagogue," one creating, the other attempting to destroy. And I learned that Smith had loved Paula Snelling for forty years, and had lived with her, and was her lover for at least some of this time, but that she could not bear the word *lesbian*, and with despisal had denied her own name.

In her essay, "The Role of the Poet in a World of Demagogues," Smith speaks of "the beats and the smokers of pot and the kids in high school who are now drug addicts and the young homosexuals flaunting their deviations and the young heterosexuals flaunting theirs. So few thinking in terms of the *quality* of relationships. . . "[5] But what of the quality of her relationship with Paula, denied for all those years?

Smith said in this same essay: "It is the omissions, *the absence of context*, that so dangerously distorts things." Did she think she would be struck down, blown up, if she spoke of her love for another woman? Did she think she would lose everything she loved, beyond what she lost by speaking out against segregation in the South? I say angrily to myself and to her, dead now twenty years: *What about the omission of "the deep truths" of your life with Paula? What about* this *distortion?* Angrily, because I needed her life as a way of understanding how to live my own.

I am angry because now I have to do, as a lesbian, the work she did not do — the splitting of the self open, over and over, the telling of the story, the risk of condemnation, the risk of loss. But I know that Lillian, and Muriel, did not have an *us*, and that I can write of my lesbian life only because a circle of women has been created to speak into.

————

As I work at my desk, under my window, two floors down, the next-door church is having Sunday morning service, and the day vibrates with gospel song, handclaps, the beat of drum and tambourine, crying out to God. At home on Sunday mornings when I was little, I could hear through the silence our church bell clanging, flat, brassy, calling us to come hear the voice of God in his Word. Three times a week I sat and listened to those beautiful and terrifying words, spoken by men who firmly believed in leading me down their way.

I had no place to go, three times a week, to hear a lesbian voice. How have we ever found each other? For a long time we sought each other only through the wordless look: searching for the other woman who was also looking, *really looking at you*, and seeing you, the woman who was the other lesbian. For a long time there were no public words for us, no definition for *lesbian* in the dictionary that described our life, no books in the library that named us other than "sick," "unnatural," "kin to thieves, murderers, and liars," and those books usually kept behind locked doors where perverted books belonged.

How did we find each other? We made a political movement and a culture; we taught ourselves to speak, to write, to sing; we heard each other and we found each other. Travelling one winter after I had left my husband, I went to a solstice ritual in Atlanta, held in a house the lesbian-feminist alliance had opened there, and I met Mab, a lesbian, a writer, also heading home to Alabama. I gave her a ride, and a friendship began that led to a decision: we couldn't wait for the world to name us writers, we must create ourselves. Mab asked me to work on the editorial collective of *Feminary*, literary journal for lesbians in the South, based in North Carolina; a publication rooted in a local women's liberation newsletter. We each self-published our first chapbooks of poetry. With other lesbians, we went on to organize a yearly writing conference for lesbians in the South, WomanWrites, also collectively run, with the firm rule that no "stars" were to be paid and brought in to teach us how to write: we would teach each other.[6]

And that is how I learned to be a lesbian poet: other lesbians taught me how. I learned by driving through the South in my VW bug to do the poetry readings that lesbians organized at a conference against domestic violence in Little Rock; at a women's health club in Fayetteville, Arkansas; at an abortion clinic in New Orleans; at a gay Metropolitan Community Church in Jackson, Mississippi; at someone's home in Gainesville, Florida; at a women's salon in a Quaker meeting house in St. Petersburg; at a women's bookstore in Birmingham; at a Women's Studies program in Tuscaloosa. I learned in writing groups with other lesbians; I learned from the comments and encouragement of lesbian editors and publishers.

They gave me the hope to keep on writing, the faith that there is another energy, another being, alert, looking for me, looking back. The faith that the words will find someone, not as a prayer to a god, but as the vibration of a sound that calls sound from another.

In the warm steam of us cooking supper together, I sat talking to other women, gathered by Susan and Betty, from all across the South: lesbians, poets, talking at once. I said loudly that I had vowed always to put something in my writing so people would *know* I was a lesbian. At the corner of the table, one of us leaned forward to speak out of the bitter experience of years, "No matter what you say, they'll always deny it."

Years later, Joan and I, holding hands, were catcalled and harassed by a bunch of young white men, the usual ridicule and shouts and the car speeding by. From a friend, some weeks after, I heard that a print artist was looking for poems inspired by specific locations in D.C. I wrote a poem about that night as if to a passerby, "To Be Posted on 21st Street Between Eye and Pennsylvania."[7] I wrote about being a lesbian; about being hated because of how I love; about trying to open my life into places not yet open to me. The man rejected my poem, because it was "too long for the printing format," and also, he said, "Is it *really* a poem? It's so *direct*."

Unless I write explicitly of how I am a lesbian, I will be denied my identity, my reality. When I do write explicitly, I am denied art.

I could choose an aesthetic of indirection, like a flash of lightning, white, on blank white paper, a subtle illumination of nothing that can be named. Instead I keep trying to write poems that hold, in some way, the idea of *lesbian*.

In a literature seminar this past winter, a student asks, "Why do you *need* to describe yourself as a *lesbian poet* on the back cover of your book?" Sometimes I feel like I'm writing a letter, the page covered with scrawled words like a prayer, the same letter over and over, without knowing who will read or understand it.

But I have been answered. Sometimes the listener raises her hand to still my words because they clash with her life. Sometimes her hand and her voice send her own words back to me:

> In the very beginning Donna and Lucy in our living
> room: making me recite poems out loud to them,
> over and over, shaping my meaning, tone,
> phrasing, so I could go to my first public
> reading as a lesbian, "So you won't disgrace us."

> The woman who wrote from prison to say:
> "I have sincerely enjoyed your poems —
> In your writings, you have expressed
> so many of the walled-up feelings that
> women have had in their hearts, and
> many of your poems brought tears to
> my eyes. — You said so many things
> that we carry locked up inside from
> generation to generation passed on
> from mother to daughter, from a
> grandmother! Sisterly, I remain, Helene."

> At a conference on battered women,
> the lesbian who walked out while I was reading,
> who later told me she couldn't bear the splitting
> images of violence which offered her no relief from
> her work every day.

> The woman who wrote to say that as a
> lesbian she'd been unable to look at her past, the

forced sex with men which she had always named
"not-rape," until reading some of my poems
she began to remember, and remember.

The young sorority women, reminding
me of myself twenty years before, who
chatted loudly as I read of the rape of
a woman lover; who were silenced by the cold
fury of my look; who walked out in the middle
of the next poem when I spoke, with a sacred
meaning, the word *cunt*.

The women friends who told me they kept my poems
by their bed and made love after reading them;
the dyke who said she read the love poems in
her bathtub; the university colleague, a lesbian,
who said uneasily that she felt like a voyeur
listening to me read erotic poems.

The woman who came up after a reading and said,
"I don't usually like poetry; it seems too
distant; nothing to do with me; but I like your
poetry."

The woman reviewer who, after finding me lacking
in comparison to Milton, said my work wasn't
poetry: I should simply stop writing.

The friend, a writer and a lesbian, who heard me
read some of the poems about my children; who
gave me nothing afterwards but a hug and a burning
look; who told me later she went home and started
a new short story; who said, "I kept thinking of
all the *work* in the poems."

My mother, sitting at the kitchen table,
who said of my work, "I can't be proud of you;
I want to be, but I can't." My acceptance of

that statement, as both rejection and love,
with my reply: "I know that; but I'm proud
of what I do." Admitting this moment as a
flash of truth between us, painful, intense;
my mother's honesty travelling with me
into my work.

The first time I read my poetry publicly
and as a lesbian, the woman who said to me,
"Write more. I want to know what happens next."

ACKNOWLEDGMENTS

I thank Betsy Warland for her suggestions about how to edit early drafts of this essay. I thank Mab Segrest, Cris South, and the women I worked with on the *Feminary* collective for my education as a lesbian poet. My grateful thanks to the lesbians who have organized and attended WomanWrites over the last fifteen years.

NOTES

1. The nightmare poem was "But Cato Said: Attach No Importance to Dreams," in my chapbook, *The Sound of One Fork* (Durham, N. Carolina: Night Heron Press, 1981).
2. "Speak earth. . . " is from "Love Poem," in Audre Lorde's *The New York Head Shop and Museum* (Detroit: Broadside Press, 1974). Her other books of poetry include *From a Land Where Other People Live* (Detroit: Broadside Press, 1973); *Coal* (New York: W.W. Norton, 1976); *The Black Unicorn* (New York: W.W. Norton, 1978); *Our Dead Behind Us* (New York: W.W. Norton, 1986). Some of her essays and speeches are collected in *Sister Outsider* (Freedom, Calif.: The Crossing Press, 1984).
3. Judy Grahn's classic poem "She Who," included in *The Work of a Common Woman: The Collected Poetry of Judy Grahn, 1964-1977* (New York: St. Martin's Press, 1978).
4. From "The Conjugation of the Paramecium," in Muriel Rukeyser's *Collected Poems* (New York: McGraw Hill Book Co., 1978).
5. Lillian Smith's essay appears in a collection of her prose, edited by Michelle Cliff, *The Winner Names the Age* (New York: W.W. Norton, 1978).
6. Information about WomanWrites, held yearly for Southern lesbian writers, can be obtained from the Atlanta Lesbian Feminist Alliance (ALFA), P.O. Box 5502, Atlanta, GA 30307, U.S.A.

7. "To Be Posted. . . " appeared in *Sinister Wisdom* 35 (Summer/Fall 1988). The address for *Sinister Wisdom: A Journal for the Lesbian Imagination in the Arts and Politics* is P.O. Box 3252, Berkeley, CA 94703, U.S.A.

SELECTED PUBLICATIONS

BOOKS

The Sound of One Fork (poetry chapbook). Durham, N. Carolina: Night Heron Press, 1981.
We Say We Love Each Other (poetry). San Francisco: Spinsters/Aunt Lute, 1985.
Crime Against Nature (poetry). Ithaca, N.Y.: Firebrand Books, 1990.
Rebellion: Essays 1980-1991 (autobiographical essays). Ithaca, N.Y.: Firebrand Books, 1991.

CO-AUTHORED BOOKS

With Elly Bulkin and Barbara Smith. *Yours in Struggle: Three Feminist Perspectives on Anti-Semitism and Racism.* Brooklyn: Long Haul Press, 1984; Ithaca, N.Y.: Firebrand Books, 1988.

ANTHOLOGIES

"Waulking Song: Two" and "Not A Gun, Not A Knife." In *Naming the Waves: Contemporary Lesbian Poetry,* edited by Christian McEwen. London: Virago Press, 1988; Freedom, Calif.: The Crossing Press, 1990.
"The Child Taken From the Mother." In *Gay and Lesbian Poetry in Our Time,* edited by Joan Larkin and Carl Morse. New York: St. Martin's Press, 1988.

JOURNAL PUBLICATIONS

"Red String," "Out of Season," "Shades," "A Cold That Is Not the Opposite of Life," "Walking Back Up Depot Street." *Conditions* 8 (1982): 106-118.
"To Be Posted on 21st Street, Between Eye and Pennsylvania," "Parked Down By the Potomac." *Sinister Wisdom* 35 (Summer/Fall 1988): 35-37.

INTERVIEWS

R.M. Kim. "Writing Poetry to Make Things Happen." *Windy City Times,* 18 May 1989, 13.
Jennie McKnight. "Explaining in a Way That People Can Hear." *Gay Community News,* 13-19 May 1990, 8-9.

The Everyday Life of Black Lesbian Sexuality

CHERYL CLARKE

to work to the end of day
to talk to the end of talk
to run to the end of dark
to have at the end of it all: sex

the wish for forever
for more often
for more.

the promises
the absurdity
the histrionics
the loss of pride
the bargaining
the sadness after.

in wakefulness wanting
in wakefulness waiting.

from "living as a lesbian at 35"
in *Living as a Lesbian*[1]

How does the writer make use of the energy of the erotic? How much a part of everyday life is it for the poet, even as she denies it, even as she resolves to be monogamous or celibate because of its danger. The erotic has always been risky for Black women, and poets no less. Promising to reject the lurid uses it is put to by capitalism or masturbating while writing becomes boring. What is its source in my life? Where do I go for it?

I first learned my sexuality is an endangered sexuality as a child growing up in a lower middle-class Black family with a secret. I learned there was a secret when no one would tell me why my older sister and brother had a different surname than my younger sister and I. My mother's sexuality was the secret — she was married previously and pregnant before she married. Later I learned that this secret was subterfuge for another more compelling secret — she killed a jealous admirer in self-defense before she married my father and before she divorced her first husband. So, the messages I received about my sexual self were: above all else, suppress it, control it, confine it. Besides, "Love," as the character Nanny says in Zora Neale Hurston's *Their Eyes Were Watching God*, "is the very prong the colored woman gets hung on." The secrets and the pretending not to know them made me risk the ironies of poetry.

I learned early that "love" (read *sex*) was something I had best not mess with. Love was best left to Hollywood and television. My mother consumed movies, television, and books. She let me have plenty of all three, hoping to distract me from the inevitable urge, which, of course, she presumed would be heterosexual. My earliest concept of how I wanted my sexual self to be was free from obligation to a partner, namely a husband. My father secretly advised me not to get married, "You see how much trouble *it* can cause. Make your own living before you get into *it*." The *it* was not marriage but sex. According to my mother, neither was supposed to happen before I was ready to commit myself to monogamy and permanency, even though this equation has produced nothing but contradictions in her life.

The suppressed erotic intrigued me as well as all the secrets hiding it. In spite of how she denied its importance and denied it in herself and tried to turn me against it, my mother's erotic was all over the place: in how she made herself up, in the way she dressed — the high heels, the fitted suits, and tight, low-cut evening clothes. And then there were the reactions of men on the street. My mother's best friends were women and they were the recipients of her erotic energy, her infinite versatility. Women filled our house one Sunday a month. I grew used to women, their ways, their stories, their excitements over one another's infrequent victories, their denials, and their ambivalences. They were pretty in my mother's dining room. If not pretty, they were talkative and always full of wit. Each had her forte. They wore wide skirts and colorful blouses, always high heels. They relied on one another. I longed for those Sundays once a month. I wanted their devotion and had my favorites.

Though she taught me how to suppress my erotic, my mother taught me that the enjoyment of female friendships is the enjoyment of female sensuality. And from a very early age, I decided I wanted to be in the company of women. Then began my dreams of being the lover of women, and those dreams would become poetry.

My mother and her women friends taught me an unsparing and sexual humor, a hallmark of the oral tradition of African-American women. African-American women's humor holds everyone and everything up to scrutiny and contempt, and self is never exempt. They allowed themselves the tutelage of the blues and the advice songs of Dinah Washington, popularly tagged, during the fifties, queen of the blues:

> I've got a secret way of loving
> and I own the copyright.
> I'm gonna put it on the market
> and do all my business right.
> Yes, I'll thrill you, baby,
> I can really satisfy your soul.
> I can really thrill you, baby,
> because I can satisfy your soul.
> I've got a secret way of loving
> that never has been told.

from "Mellow Mama Blues"[2]

My mother and her friends talked mainly politics, money, and day-to-day race relations. Sexuality was addressed in asides. Because I began to grow breasts early, someone would occasionally forget and speak directly about somebody's man's infidelity. I overheard one of them commiserating with my mother once over the fact that I would soon be pressured into having sex (with men), because I was "big for my age." And she was correct. Compulsory heterosexuality.

My mother did not push heterosexuality on me any more than she denied homosexuality. Her message, delivered anecdotally, was, it's safer just not to be sexual. Once you realize how pleasurable lust can be, you won't be able to control yourself. Or the other. Then, after the lust, there's pregnancy; then, the baby; and possibly a coerced marriage or giving the baby up for adoption or a guilt-ridden single-parenthood. If not that script, then a worse script: an illegal abortion, continued promiscuity, venereal disease, cigarettes, alcohol and other drugs, or coming to any number of other bad ends. Much better to be in school or working, and a virgin in either case.

> I will not sell it,
> I will not give it away.
> I will sit on it the rest of my days.[3]

My older sister inherited my mother's erotic and she, too, was unmarried when she became pregnant. This pregnancy and my sister's ostracism from our family were major events in my life, emblems of the danger of the erotic. I believed my mother's admonitions. These events inform the fiction of several poems: "fathers" and "Ruby the runaway" in *Narratives: poems in the tradition of black women*, "funeral thoughts" in *Living as a Lesbian*, and "Ella Takes Up The Slack" in *Humid Pitch*. My father had no decision-making power in our family, but he was a buffer between us and my mother's overwhelming authority.

In my article, "The Failure to Transform: Homophobia in the Black Community" in *Home Girls: A Black Feminist Anthology*, I tell of the first time I saw Black lesbians:

> I was walking down the street with my best friend, Kathy. I saw two young women walking together in the opposite direction. One wore a doo-rag, a Banlon button down, and high-top sneakers. The other wore pink brush rollers, spit curls plastered with geech, an Oxford tailored shirt, a mohair sweater, fitted skirt with kick pleat... I asked Kathy, "Who are they?" "Bulldaggers," she answered. "What's that," I asked again. "You know, they *go* with each other," Kathy tried to explain. "Why?" I asked still confused. "Protection," Kathy said casually. "Protection?" I repeated. "Yeah, at least they won't get pregnant," Kathy ended the querying.

I was given a Roman Catholic education, which placed on my shoulders the burden of keeping the secret of my mother's erotic. Pre-marital sex (fornication) and divorce are major sins and lust is a cardinal sin. My adolescent relationships abounded with girlfriends who became pregnant and whose lives changed radically; and others who were having sex, using birth control pills, and living with quantities of guilt. I was reading James Baldwin's *Another Country*, which introduced me to the homoerotic. And women were my best friends. I began to wonder why I was expected to give up, avoid, trivialize the acceptance I felt from women in order to pursue the tenuous business of getting a man. Could I resist the draft?

I did suppress the erotic and the lesbian in me until I was twenty-six and four years away from Washington, D.C., the mecca of predatory heterosexuality and the place of my birth. Heterosexuality never inspired a single poem in me, not even when I was practicing it.

That other black lesbians existed and were willing to be out made me embrace lesbianism as a politic. For many years, I said that lesbianism is a political identity not *just* a sexual identity. I was part of a generation of lesbians who struggled against the past stigma of sexual perversion/inversion and, in so doing, discarded some of the pleasure along with the dominance-subordinance of compulsory heterosexual relationships. With the publication of my second volume of poetry, *Living as a Lesbian*, I quarreled with this dismissal of sex. As long as my freedom to be sexual with women is endangered and under attack, as long as lesbian sexuality is the most invisible sexuality, politically, my poetry must be a medium for the sexual politics of lesbianism:

bump the supreme court and edwin meese
i'll read anything, do anything to be sexually aroused
i'll be a lesbian, queer, whore, a sleaze
and it won't be a peep show i ain't caroused.

from "committed sex," *Conditions* 16

My everyday life as a Black lesbian writer is marked by the struggle to be a (sexual) black lesbian, the struggle for the language of sexuality, and the struggle not to be the "beached whale of the sexual universe."[4] So, I created several black lesbian archetypes in my poetry that I might have a mythology, among them the women of "Of Althea and Flaxie" and "The moon in cancer" in *Narratives*, "Vicki and Daphne" in *Living as a Lesbian*, and "The Day Sam Cooke Died" and "Bulletin" in my most recent work, *Humid Pitch*.

Bulletin

Disguising her vigilance with passive stance, she read the bulletin stealthily, with
some difficulty and great understanding.

> The General will esteem it as a singular favor if you can apprehend a mulatto
> girl, servant and slave of Mrs. Washington, who eloped from this place yester-
> day. She may intend to the enemy. Her name is Charlotte but in all probability
> will change it. She is light-complected, about thirteen years of age, pert, and
> dressed in brown cloth westcoat and petticoat. Your falling upon some method
> of recovering her will accommodate Mrs. Washington and lay her under great
> obligation to you. A gentle reward will be given to any soldier or other who
> shall take

A spray of brown fluid splashed upon the publishing. She tore it down from its
post and ground it into the dirt.

"I bootblacked my face and hands
and any other parts that shows.
Ain't answerin to Charlotte, nigger,
nor no other name they give me.
I'm wearing a westcoast and pants,
left the petticoat in a cornfield.
I'm sixteen. Thirteen was a lie the owner told
the auctioneer.
I'm evil, mean, and will use my knife.
I dips snuff, chews tobacco, smokes a pipe.
Ain't no son of satan gon fall on me lessn
he want his tail curled.
Won't be intendin tward no white folk
—all of ems enemies.
I'm headed West.
I'll swim any river—maybe the Ohio—
follow any star.
And whoever try to take me up
may be ketchin his guts as he run."

Black women's sexuality is still an endangered sexuality. The experience
of slavery and the sadistic practices of that institution as it was applied to
Africans in North America still mark us in the expression of our sexuality
and the erotic. Our sexuality is further endangered by AIDS, compulsory
heterosexuality, racism, class oppression, and the ever-present threat of

rape. While I am privileged to write openly as a lesbian and to have my work appreciated and to sleep with a woman, I am reminded daily that this ain't no place to love a woman.

NOTES

1. I titled this paper after a panel I spoke on in 1984 at the National Women's Studies Association Conference which was entitled "The Everyday Life of Lesbian Sexuality." The title gives sexuality a dailiness and seeks to extend Audre Lorde's essential speech and article, "The Uses of the Erotic," which encouraged women, especially lesbians, to allow their sexuality, their erotic selves to exist in life.
2. "Mellow Mama Blues." Wise Woman Blues: Dinah Washington, 1943-1945. Rosetta Records, 155 W. 6th Street, New York, N.Y. 10011, 1984.
3. Ibid.
4. Hortense Spillers, "Interstices: A Small Drama of Words," in *Pleasure and Danger: Exploring Female Sexuality*, edited by Carol Vance. (Boston: Routledge and Kegan Paul, 1984).

SELECTED PUBLICATIONS

BOOKS

Narratives: Poems in the Tradition of Black Women. Latham, N.Y.: Kitchen Table: Women of Color Press, 1983.

Living as a Lesbian. Ithaca, N.Y.: Firebrand Books, 1986.

Humid Pitch. Ithaca, N.Y.: Firebrand Books, 1989.

CO-EDITED JOURNALS

Co-editor of *Conditions*, a feminist magazine of writing by women, with an emphasis on writing by lesbians.

ANTHOLOGIES

"Lesbianism: An Act of Resistance." In *This Bridge Called My Back: Writings by Radical Women of Color*, edited by Cherríe Moraga and Gloria Anzaldúa. Watertown, Mass.: Persephone Press, 1981; Latham, N.Y.: Kitchen Table: Women of Color Press, 1984.

"The Failure to Transform: Homophobia in the Black Community" and "Women of Summer" (short story). In *Home Girls: A Black Feminist Anthology*, edited by Barbara Smith. Latham, N.Y.: Kitchen Table: Women of Color Press, 1983.

"palm leaf of Mary Magdalene" (poem). In *The Leading Edge: Anthology of Lesbian Sexual Fiction*, edited by Lady Winston, 141. Denver: Lace Publications, 1987.

"Living as a Lesbian Underground" and other poems. In *Serious Pleasure: Lesbian Erotic Stories and Poetry*, edited by the Sheba Collective. London: Sheba Feminist Publishers, 1989; Pittsburgh: Cleis Press, 1991.

"Of Althea and Flaxie" and other poems. In *Bluestones and Salt Hay: An Anthology of Contemporary New Jersey Poets*, edited by Joel Lewis. New Brunswick, N.J.: Rutgers Univ. Press, 1990.

JOURNAL PUBLICATIONS

"Black Women on Black Women Writers: Conversations and Questions" (a five-woman discussion with Jewelle Gomez, Evelynn Hammonds, Bonnie Johnson, Linda Powell). *Conditions* 9 (1983).

"Leavings" (short story). *13th Moon* "Narrative" issue (1984): 133-141.

"Indira" (poem). *American Voice*. (Summer 1986): 20-22.

"The Homoerotic Other/Gay Voices, Black Voices." *The Advocate* (February 1991): 42.

"*Making Face, Making Soul/Haciendo Caras*, edited by Gloria Anzaldúa" (book review essay). *Bridges: A Journal for Jewish Feminists and Our Friends* 2, no. 1 (Spring 1991/5791): 128-133.

ARTICLES AND REVIEWS

Calvin Hernton. "The Tradition."*Parnassus* (1986): 518-550.

Barbara A. Caruso. "Book Review of *Living as a Lesbian*." *Obsidian II: Black Literature in Review* 2, no. 1 (Spring 1987): 94-100.

Margaret Randall. "Lesbian Poet Has Many Voices." Review of *Living as a Lesbian. Guardian Book Review Supplement* (Summer 1987).

Gary Indiana. "1988: Some Thoughts from 15 Artists." *Village Voice* 33, no. 3 (1988): 95.

Stephanie Byrd. "The Outer Limits of Commitment." Review of *Humid Pitch. Lambda Rising Book Report* (October/November 1989).

Rose Green Alone

SUNITI NAMJOSHI

A few years ago I wrote an article called "Snow White and Rose Green,"[1] which focused on how sexism and racism affect me as a woman writer. Then when I was asked for an article centring around the lesbian experience[2] I thought I could use the old article, perhaps revise it slightly; but it isn't that simple. The stresses fall differently. The relationship of a heterosexual woman to a heterosexual society is different from that of a lesbian to a heterosexual society.

In the old article I made the usual points:

> A writer is dependent on her audience. The words in a poem don't just mean what she wants them to mean, they also mean what her readers understand them to mean. The writer herself has some control in that she is using them in a particular context. If the writer doesn't share a great many of the ideas, assumptions and experiences of her readers, then there is going to be a problem. If, furthermore, the very language she is using is saturated with ideas she wishes to question and with experiences different from her own, then the problem is going to be compounded.

In my opinion these points are still valid both for the heterosexual woman and the lesbian, but the technical problem that the lesbian faces in dealing with heterosexist language is a far more radical one.

In the original article, I then asked what the woman writer was going to do, but in the attempt to re-write that article I suddenly realized that some of the options I had put down come across as mere mockery when directed exclusively at the lesbian writer. For example, "She can establish her own frame of reference." Or, "She can assume that an audience exists to whom she will make sense." Or again, "She can decide not to worry about an audience." Asking a lesbian to do these things is not the same as asking a heterosexual woman to do them. What is even more disturbing is the realization that I, a lesbian, did not really make this distinction when I wrote the original article. In other words, I had written an article about myself as a writer in which I had more or less assumed for the purposes of the article that the heterosexual woman was central and the lesbian peripheral. There's a frightening, though subtle, alienation from my own experience there.

The idea that for a lesbian writer the lesbian might be central, I owe to Gill Hanscombe. She suggested it to me. It seems astonishing that the idea had to be suggested. Feminists have got used to knowing that the equation of "man" with "human" excludes women. I don't think that we lesbians have fully realized that the equation of "heterosexual woman" with "woman" excludes lesbians.

In "Snow White and Rose Green" I listed the obvious similarities between sexism and racism in the matter of who does the defining, who is defined and so forth. Looking at it again from a solely lesbian perspective it becomes obvious that it is nonsense to subsume "lesbian" under "heterosexual woman." To put it very simply, in heterosexual English "lesbian" is a dirty word; "woman" isn't. And though I think that it is still true to say that heterosexual "women have (often) internalized the definitions and values (the language) of the definers, as have the colonials," I now feel that it's more important to say that in some fundamental way no lesbian ever has. The heterosexual tradition has no use for us. For lesbians to continue to exist is to defy its essence.

I added that there is one big difference, however, between women and foreigners: foreigners do not occur frequently in English literature; women do. "Either way we're faceless (not maskless) and I'm not sure which constitutes the greater technical problem: being defined out of existence, i.e., being over-defined, or hardly being defined at all, i.e., being vaguely defined as 'foreign'. " But it seems to me that the situation is even worse for a lesbian. She is saying, "I matter, what I have to say matters," in a language which says, "You are hateworthy in that you matter, and irrelevant in that you don't."

Next I made a few observations about the difference between the dilemma of the English Canadian writer and the Indian writer writing in English, and concluded with the obvious feminist statement: "Women have not been the legal inheritors of the 'civilization of man' in Canada or in Britain or in India." I failed to add that lesbians have been outcasts.

My central point in the original article was that women writers dealing with a recalcitrant language have to compromise with it, but that they must subvert it. But it's only now that I am becoming conscious of just how subversive it is to write as a lesbian.

The second half of the article consisted of examples from my own work which I thought were illustrative of the struggle with language and of the gap between intention and achievement. What is odd is that even when I thought I was illustrating the difficulties of writing as an Indian and as a woman, the examples themselves testify more eloquently to the difficulties of writing as a lesbian. I include three here.

Aphrodisiac

Being wedded and bedded
And not pig-headed,
He sought the horn
Of the white unicorn,
For the world is an ugly woman.

from *Poems*

My comment on this: "I wrote this 15 years ago. . . but the consciousness is so irredeemably male-centred and heterosexist that I really didn't see how I might salvage the poem." Fair enough, but what I'm painfully aware of now is that the "error" in the poem is a peculiarly lesbian one, or at least one that is peculiarly dangerous to a lesbian consciousness.

From the Travels of Gulliver (revised edition)

And I fell in love with a woman so tall that
when I looked at her eyes I had to go star-gazing.

Tall treasure-houses, moon-

maidenly silence. . . Someday I'll teach you
to smile on me. She sways, sighs,
turns in her sleep. Did a feather fall?
Thor's hammer blow makes no effects.
       I'm told that it's unnatural
to love giantesses.

       In the mornings small dogs bark.
Giantesses strut, fell trees like toothpicks,
while we just stand there, gaze up
their thighs, foreshortened, of course,
but astonishingly pretty.

       One day she picked me up off the floor and set
me on her nipple. I tried to ride, but consider my
position — indubitably tricky.

       To sleep forever in my fair love's arms,
to make of her body my home and habitation. . .
She keeps me about her like a personal worm.
She is not squeamish.

                                        Once,
the giddy and gay were gathered together.
Then she brought me out, bathed me
and kissed me. She put me in a suit
of powder blue silk and set me to sail
in a tepid cup of tea. There
I fought out the storm of their laughter.
I performed valiantly.

I love to hear her laugh,
              would not see her grieve,
but a teacup of brine would have seemed
more seemly. I could sail in such a cup,
be swayed by her sighs.

She gluts me on the milk
              of healthy giantesses:
"Poor little mannikin,
              will nothing make you grow?"
I grow. I am growing. You should
              see me in her dreams.

from *The Jackass and the Lady*

About this one I said rather naively: ". . . it grieves me that I had to use a heterosexual framework. I'm not equating 'lesbian' with 'feminist.' But if there's a difference between a man writing a poem about a woman, and a woman writing about a woman, then it should be made clear. And if there is no difference, then that should be make clear too." I said nothing at all about the questions of presentation and perception when the writer is a lesbian.

The article took its title from the following prose poem.

Snow White and Rose Green

Once upon a time there were two sisters and one got married and one didn't. Or once upon a time there were two piglets and one went to market and one didn't, or one was straight and one wasn't. The point is, whatever they did or failed to do, they were a great disappointment to their poor mother. Luckily for them, the two sisters loved one another. When they saw that their mother was growing more and more unhappy, they proposed to her that she cut them in half and out of the two good halves make one splendid one. Their mother refused in high indignation, but she was so wretched that the dutiful daughters went to a surgeon. The surgeon obligingly sawed them in half, then interchanged halves and stuck them together. But there were still two of them. This was a problem. So they went back home and said to their mother, "Now choose the good one." But their mother was furious that they had even thought of such a scheme. "You did it to mock me," she told them angrily. "You are both bad children." When the two sisters heard her say this, the Good One wept, but the Bad One smirked.

From the Bedside Book of Nightmares

In the comments I waffled on about how "the irony, the malice and the bizarre sense of humour are characteristic of Marathi," the language spoken in Maharashtra, which is where I grew up, and went on to remark, "but then I don't know that Marathas are too comfortable with lesbian feminists." True enough, but what prevented me from making "lesbian" the noun?

I'd like to conclude these notes with a few examples from more recent work and a bit of speculation about the struggle for a more specifically lesbian awareness.

From the Bedside Book of Nightmares was published in 1984. I thought I was tackling the bloodier aspects of women's liberation and gay liberation, but I think now that I may have also made some headway in taking the lesbian feminist perspective as central. I don't think that this can be done without the consciousness of an audience to whom such a view would make sense. I suspect, though, that in *The Bedside Book* the stress is on "feminist" rather than "lesbian," and that there is an underlying longing to convince everybody that we're all human really. In *The Conversations of Cow*, I think the longing to convince has decreased and there's a greater willingness simply to state. Certainly, I hope this is so.

One question, of course, is of what possible interest can a book by a lesbian, for lesbians and about lesbians be to anyone else? Are the peripheral heterosexuals supposed to learn from the peripheral heterosexuals in the book what it feels like to be peripheral? Besides, heterosexuality is hardly a peripheral concern for any lesbian in the world today. We have to deal with it, and what's more we have to deal with our feelings when confronted with it. I think that's what I'm trying to do in the following poem from *The Bedside Book*.

The Creature

I was in the garden, at the edge
                        of a wood.
I knew she would come, the light
                        gliding
across her shoulder blades, down
                        her back,
her eyes reflecting the surrounding green.
I crept a little closer.
                        I think she saw me.
I came out of the bushes
                        and stared at her.
She seemed to be pleased.
                        She settled on the grass,
leaning her back against a tree-trunk.
                        I knew she was waiting.
When she stretched out an arm,
                        I let her touch me.
I licked her throat, I cropped the grass
                        between her feet.
But then he appeared.
                        She looked up and laughed.
                        He looked down and smiled —
                        from a monstrous height.
I skittered off fast.

Then I came back
        and watched them at it.

The usual argument can be made that all poems are specific, deal with particulars and contain a universal element. Or I could beg the question. I could say, "I don't give a damn whether my work is of any interest to heterosexuals or not." But perhaps I do give a damn. It depends on the extent to which I have to compromise with their assumptions in order to be heard. Perhaps the service one renders them — if such service is required — is precisely this questioning of heterosexist assumptions.

What is even more interesting to speculate about than the particulars, the "content," is the effect on form. Take the ordinary love lyric as the basic poem. The persona, "I," says to the other, "you:" "I love you" or "I do not love you" or "Why are you so unkind to me?" or "Oh, how splendid, you are not unkind to me." Now, as is well known, in the heterosexist tradition, "I" speaks, defines himself, defines her, defines the relationship, while "you" keeps quiet. "You" presumably has ears and the intelligence to understand "I's" words, but she is not a poet, she is the object of the poet's attention. The poet is speaking *for* his other readers — it's a miracle that all women readers aren't lesbians — and *to* this particular woman. Her answer, if she makes one, is outside the bounds of the poem, and presumably also outside the bounds of art. There is a distinction between the "I" and the "other," the lover and the beloved, the male and the female, and also between the "you" in the poem and the readers of the poem.

But when the "I" is a lesbian, is she not saying, "I, a woman, address you, a woman, and since you are like me, presumably you have a mouth as well as ears; and what is more, what is true for me may be true for you, we can exchange roles." This is the notion I am playing with in the first of "The Lion Skin" sonnets.

The Lion Skin

That in some dream I might be a lion
walking nobly and happily through a wood,
and that some lady, who has had her eye on
me, might say to me I am both great and good.
And then in this dream may this lovely lady
ruffle my yellow mane and trim my claws
and lead me to a spot green and shady,

but here the dream fails. I'm forced to pause.
For what do we say, this lady and I?
What happens next? Do I remove my skin?
And what does she do? Is she shocked and shy?
Or civil, and removes her own clothing?
I've never had the courage to dream the dream through,
but I think she says, "You be me, and I'll be you."

from *The Blue Donkey Fables*

Does this alter radically the very conventions governing lyric poetry? Or is it only a gimmick? But there's another change that occurs when the writer is a lesbian. The real woman behind the "you" is being spoken *for* as well as *to*. She is not singled out from the other lesbian readers. The poet is speaking for them as well as for her, and they do not have to assume a different identity for the purpose of reading the poem. But isn't the real woman's reply still outside the bounds of the poem? Yes, but it is not necessarily or by virtue of history outside the bounds of art. The poem produced in reply now creates a space around both poems and that most I-centred of forms, the lyric poem, suddenly has a dual centre. Or perhaps they write a poem using "we," not "I," and "you" refers to the listeners and readers who are actually listening or reading. The notion that the lyric is somehow "private" or "personal" makes no sense in a context in which there is no distinction in kind between the person addressed in the poem and the eavesdroppers or listeners. There are many possibilities. Here, for instance, are two poems which are obviously connected, one of which is by Gillian Hanscombe.

Narrative Distance

Climb up here on this readymade mountain,
sit beside me, and watch the two women
walking on the beach, observe their relation,
mood and emotion, each connected to each.
One of them laughs, the other smiles; they appear
uninhibited, careless, carefree;
but our function is to watch — that is quite clear —
from our position of vantage we can see
into things. They are digging in the sand,
then they stop, consult one another, then proceed.

And now they are walking hand in hand;
they are picking up pebbles, sea-shells, sea-weed.
I feel they are deeply absorbed in making
something. I glance at your face. Would you agree?
What a lot of notes you seem to be taking.
I look back again, and to my dismay
the two of them have gone — just walked away.
Suddenly I'm reckless, "Let's go and see."
We scramble down the slope, but there's nobody
there, just the two of us, anxious, unready . . .

Reply to your poem of the same . . .

Yes they walked and watched and
wound arms when they weren't thinking about it and
wavered when they did. And yes the
two they watched
disappeared without permission.

What to make of it? Did
the oily sun have relevance or not?
And must the watchers quarrel about
who started it all and why?

The teaching says it is good to be puzzled:
it postpones confidence and inflates decisions;
and anyway, the watchers — being poets —
know each other's weakness, that they
observe only themselves (as is the
custom of their profession).

But we may, nonetheless, return to the narrative.
The women are unable to disappear. They must be
tumbling under the sleek surf,
tumbling between the dunes. Must
kiss lightly, touch briefly, gather shells.
At this distance, they must feel no pain.

We have dismissed them, says one watcher, suddenly troubled,
with a lie.
No, says the other; as a lie.

Perhaps, says the first, gravely, it's the sun after all;
it can drain away the colours.
And they can't have gone, says the other, peering out to sea.

from *Flesh and Paper*

What happens next when the individual "you's" respond with their own poems, and when this response in turn forms a whole, I do not know. One writes the poems first, theorizes afterwards. We are all just beginning to come into existence together. Whether or not we'll be able to survive is still in question. It's worth saying that this is the first time I have deliberately and consciously written anything at all specifically for us.

NOTES

1. In *Canadian Woman Studies* 4, no. 2 (Winter 1982).
2. In 1985, which is when this article was written. The project for which it was originally commissioned fell through.

SELECTED PUBLICATIONS

Books

Poems. Calcutta: Writers Workshop, 1967. Out of print.

More Poems. Calcutta: Writers Workshop, 1971. O.P.

Cyclone in Pakistan. Calcutta: Writers Workshop, 1971. O.P.

The Jackass and the Lady. Calcutta: Writers Workshop, 1980. O.P.

Feminist Fables. London: Sheba Feminist Publishers, 1981, re-issued 1984; re-issued with five new fables, 1990.

Dutch translation by Annet Planten: *Feministiese Fabels*. Amsterdam: Xantippe, 1983.

The Authentic Lie. Fredericton, Canada: Fiddlehead Poetry Books, 1982. O.P.

From the Bedside Book of Nightmares. Fredericton, Canada: Fiddlehead Poetry Books, 1984. O.P.

The Conversations of Cow. London: The Women's Press, 1985.

Dutch translation by Rita Gircour: *De onthullingen van Koe*. Amsterdam: Saara Publishers, 1986.

Aditi and the One-eyed Monkey (children's book). London: Sheba Feminist Publishers, 1986; Boston: Beacon Press, 1989.

CO-AUTHORED BOOKS

Translated and co-authored with Sarojini Namjoshi. *Poems of Govindagraj*. Calcutta: Writers
Workshop, 1968.

With Gillian Hanscombe. *Flesh and Paper*. Charlottetown, Canada: Ragweed Press, 1986;
Devon, England: Jezebel Tapes and Books, 1986.

JOURNAL PUBLICATIONS

"Snow White and Rose Green or Some Notes on Sexism, Racism and the Craft of Writing."
Canadian Woman Studies 4, no. 2, (Winter 1982); reprinted in *Kinesis*, September
1983.

With Gillian Hanscombe. "Who Wrongs You, Sappho?" In *Out of the Margins* (forthcoming),
edited by Jane Aaron et al. London: Falmer Press, 1991.

ARTICLES, REVIEWS AND INTERVIEWS

Mary Meigs. Review of *Feminist Fables, The Authentic Lie* and *The Jackass and the Lady*. *Room
of One's Own* 4, no. 1 (February 1984).

M. Travis Lane. "I and my Creature." Review of *From the Bedside Book of Nightmares* and other
books. *The Fiddlehead* 45 (Autumn 1985).

Kathleen Jamie. "Female-Centred Fables." Review of three books by Suniti Namjoshi. *Times
Literary Supplement*, 14 September 1990.

Diane McGifford. Article on Suniti Namjoshi. In *Writers of the Indian Diaspora: A Bio-
Bibliographical Critical Source Book*, edited by Emmanuel Nelson. Forthcoming [no
place of publication].

SOUND RECORDINGS

With Gillian Hanscombe. *Flesh and Paper*. (audio cassette) Devon, England: Jezebel Tapes
and Books, 1986.

FILMS

Flesh and Paper, The Life and Work of Suniti Namjoshi. Directed by Pratibha Parmar, produced
by Hyphen Films for Channel 4 Television (England). Broadcast on 3 April 1990. Distributed in the U.S. by Women Make Movies, #212-225 Lafayette St., New York, NY
10012.

The Freedom to Explore†

MARG YEO

Dear Friends,

Since we agreed to start a writer's group, or workshop, or whatever we're going to call it, I've done a lot of thinking about what I want from it, and more broadly, about why I feel one of my prime commitments as a writer is to work with other women, writing women, to share the process as well as the product with them.

It's not simply that, as a lesbian, I'm wanting a context that's safe and protective, though I'd be kidding myself if I tried to tell you that I don't need just exactly that. I want the freedom in my writing to explore what lesbianism and feminism might mean, to find forms and cadences that fit **my** content. I work hard at writing, and it matters terribly to know that I can count on criticism that comes not just from the shared politics of our feminism, but also from anger, and from a clear belief in the purpose of our writing, that it is **for women** first above all.

---

†In late 1990, two other lesbians and I decided to try meeting as a writers' group. It seemed a good idea to put down on paper what **I** was after, so the other two wouldn't get any surprises.

After all, here we are in pretty much uncharted territory once again, as women so often are. The history of women's writing teaches us that the literary establishment will put our writing down any way it can: we've all heard the "confessional, therefore sentimental, therefore worthless" brand of judgement. I believe we should try very hard indeed not to reproduce what writing men have done: the literary world is, with few exceptions, a stage on which competition and ego play big parts, and I can't see the virtue in our playing out the same selfish and destructive patterns when we have a chance to redefine the terms.

I confess that a lot of what I've learned about writing came from reading men: I could write sonnets with the best of them by the time I was sixteen, and then I discovered e.e. cummings and my whole life changed. But the most important things I've learned as a writer came from women, and it's those that have given my voice as a writer its real shape and substance. And nothing delights me more than women's writing.

I want to tell you about my history in writing workshops, because it's there that my real voice, my voice as a lesbian and a feminist, began to come clear. This all started for me in England, in 1977, at The Women's Arts Alliance. The WAA was a small gallery, performance space and bookstore, run by an unpaid collective, in a second floor warehouse in Cambridge Terrace Mews, just beside Regent's Park. When I first discovered the Arts Alliance in the autumn of 1977, it was by joining a poetry workshop run by an American woman named Harriet Rose. Two of the women in that workshop were to become my dear friends, and it was because of them that I got involved in the Women's Festival that ran in London for three weeks that November. Kay and Sara and I staffed a bookstore on the third floor of the Drill Hall, and we went to plays, concerts, dances, discussions, and a writer's forum with so many women — 200 maybe — that our whole day of reading and talking was just so clearly skimming the surface, was such a small drop in a huge bucket. We were higher than kites, though, and it was after that forum that we decided we wanted to start a new workshop, completely open and unled, in which we'd all have equal responsibility and equal voice.

The workshop that grew out of our enthusiasm that day ran for two years, first at the Women's Arts Alliance and then in the café above Sisterwrite, London's first women's bookstore, that Kay and two friends started on Upper Street in Islington. Because it was an open workshop, advertised weekly in *Time Out* and the *Women's Place Newsletter*, the faces in that workshop constantly changed, and we were visited by many women writers passing through

London. Of course, not everyone liked our fairly unstructured proceedings: I recall particularly one woman who spent the evening in a flurry of impatient sighs, and after treating us to a poem no one without a Ph.D. could have made anything at all of, told us we needed a Chairman and slammed the door on her way out. Without a chairman, we ran two very successful writing weekends, did readings, argued among ourselves, did more readings, and finally bogged down and gave up.

What I remember most, though, apart from what seemed to be the constant cold (so that I recall us as almost always huddled round a single paraffin heater and wearing all our clothes, hats, coats, scarves, mittens, though I know it must sometimes have been summer) — what I remember most are the words: Pat's poems about food, about her mother; Rosemary's wonderful dragon; Anne's million myths about women; Sara's dream poem in which her mother (or her stepmother, was it?) got down on her knees and scrubbed the motorway; Kay's strong lush descriptions of growing up Australian, of her mother's garden; the poem of Sue's, who was the youngest of us, that began, "Give me my grey hairs, I want my wisdom. . . "

Those women's words changed my writing, and opened doors and windows into worlds I'd never have known without their good sense and sensitivity to music and language and politics. When that workshop ended, Kay and I found Barbara, through *One Foot On The Mountain*, an Onlywoman Press anthology we were all in, and with Mary we started a monthly workshop, with a set theme to read and talk around at each meeting. That was more structured, perhaps, but it was fun, exciting, instructive, and again I have the strongest memories of Stef, Viv, Judith, Gill, Jan, Irini, Mary — I can hear their voices now. That group was intended only to last a year, and when it ended, Kay and Barbara and I began meeting fortnightly, on Fridays, for the next four, or maybe it was even five, years.

Being in a very small group can be both rewarding and extremely difficult, and our group was no exception. We became closer and closer, shared much more of our lives than simply the writing. We had very good times and pretty bad times, but to my mind the good times were better than the bad times were bad. The time that I remember as best of all was the stretch that led to a reading we did in September 1981. We worked harder preparing for that reading than I've ever done for another before or since, because we wanted it to be a whole, interwoven, a conversation in a way like those we had over dinner and poems in the Sisterwrite café, in which each poem would resonate, have some link to what came before and to what followed. We spent several Fridays reading each other poems, setting them together in such a way that we made a dialogue, a conversation, that we hoped would reflect something of the way we worked together, and we had such a good time doing it that on the last evening, as we walked together along Upper Street to the tube, we found ourselves dancing out of sheer good spirits and pleasure in each other's company, each other's words. The reading was wonderful fun too — we had managed to share some of the pleasure and the energy we got from working together.

That workshop ended, not because we quarrelled, though we did argue from time to time, but because both Kay and Barbara moved in new directions and we simply became less and less useful to each other. In the following years I found other workshops, though none gave quite the satisfaction that I'd found with Kay and Barbara, perhaps just because the levels of commitment never seemed to be as high — or maybe it was just that life was busier for all of us, Thatcher's Britain being what it was. What really stirred me up again was a quite wonderful lesbian reading series that a group of London lesbian writers started in the late eighties. It wasn't a surprise, really, that there were so many lesbians writing in a city the size of London, but it was still terribly exciting to head off on a Saturday night knowing that I was bound to hear at least one new voice, if not more, and to see the context in which I had written so long made concrete.

The planning group, of which I was a part, worked very hard indeed to make the readings a safe forum for discussion of the issues which often threaten to split our community. It has to be said, we were not always successful. The woman whose writing several women found racist never came back, and I heard other women say that they wouldn't read in a context in which they might be challenged. That seemed a great pity to me — one of the advantages of the intimacy Kay and Barbara and I shared was the secure space it gave us to discuss the contentious issues our writing sometimes raised. Not that we encountered every issue — our small numbers in that workshop meant of necessity some narrowness of view. I'd hoped to see in the breadth of the reading series an equal breadth of discussion. We worked hard to make the space a safe one, but it was soon clear that the readings, in their very diversity, were not a place in which most lesbians felt secure enough to open themselves to challenge, though those evenings were in so many other respects a great success.

It's that experience, more than any other, that has led me to want a return to a small group, not just for the intimacy and friendship, though I value that greatly, but for the freedom to explore what lesbian writing both is and has the potential to be. We will of course be limited, but we will each bring what our years and experience have taught us, and there will be without any doubt things we can learn from each other.

I wish I had a dime for every time I've heard someone say she envied another writer because of a poem, or a book, or because she was especially prolific or getting better — I just don't understand envy like that. I admire good writing (which is why I'm keen on working with both of you) — I am enriched by it as a writer and as a woman. When I read your new poem, your new book, and it's good, I want to dance in the streets. I want you to get better and better, and if I can help by being a good critic, or a good listener, I'm even more delighted.

In my twenties, I thought that one really good poem might change the world. Now I'm not so naive, and I know what a terrible, intractable place the world is, but I guess you can't keep an idealist down. I know one poem won't do it, but you'll never convince me that we won't do it together, even though I know very well the obstacles we face, not least of which are the barriers which threaten to divide us as lesbians and as women.

There are so many ways for us to enrich each other — I know I learn with every new poem I read, and I take strength from criticism that has heart and head clear about motives and meanings. The world that men own will not support us, and so it is even more important that we support each other. We can help each other find the way beyond rhetoric and polemic to a language that belongs to women, a language we can all speak. We can give each other strength to stand up to the publishers and the critics who will always want to rewrite us according to some man's ethics, some man's voice. We can ask each other the questions that must be asked about the language we have grown up with, taken for granted, and the version of it in which we must now choose to speak. We can create that language together; we can make it our own.

In my experience, the best way of getting this workshop, this endeavour, off the ground is to work hard at knowing each other — not just hearing but really understanding each other's voices. It won't do you a lot of good for me to show you how I might have written your poems — I need to know your voice so well, hear it so clearly that, as friends have said to me, I'll never be able to read a word of yours, wherever we may go, without hearing your voice and knowing exactly how you'd pause, and where you'd push at it. My grasp of the music of language and the cadences of the way **we** speak has been refined and redefined as many times as I've heard another woman's words, in a new voice. I can't help believing that, together, we make a voice so complex and vital that we will change the nature of poetry utterly, to suit ourselves, and have the best time in the world doing it.

Some of the happiest and most satisfying evenings of my life have been spent in writers' groups, laughing and crying over one good poem after another. I can't tell you how much I'm looking forward to this one.

Much love,
Marg

WRITER'S NOTE

This letter prompted a heated series of discussions in my group, and when we explored whether our differences around politics, and particularly around whether we wished to be challenged on and to discuss difficult issues, were so great that they might effectively prohibit our working constructively together, we decided that we three were not cut out to work together in that way. Indirectly, I was led to a new poem, which is appended here.

my muse

i.
5 am   everything's shut
down   wrapped up tight for the
night
        the snow
falls without a footstep from my window clear
out to arcturus   the wind has almost
ceased to breathe   the cat   dreaming
tips to her back   eyes tight   paws
padding the air in chase or
flight   and sighs   and settles
back to a black rhythmic and circular
zero on the bed
and me   i'm drifting

around my desk   waiting
for the next word to waltz in   like the
lover who never arrives till you've
given her up
                    (perhaps you don't tell her how
glad you are to see her   but you
should   in case she gives
you up   and
doesn't come again)
                    without
her   i am   not just alone   and
lonely   i am an un
broken code   thin wisp   a whisper   lost in the
wind   i am a whole
language   intricate   lyrical   inflected   and
spoken by no
one at all

ii.
my muse is a tough   tendentious
truthful woman
                    don't think of
wings
        she walks
everywhere   in and
out of my life   up and down my
apartment   pacing and thinking and issuing
instructions
                    today she comes
whistling   pulls me out of the
shower   tosses me a towel   orders me to get
on with it   *like*
this she says   tapping the beat of her
breath along my bones
                    and *can't you do*
anything without me?
                    she'd like me to be more
independent when i whine about
missing her   though she goes for
years and i never know when
she'll be off again   to

rio or the greek islands i
suspect   and always
without me

iii.

if i had my life to live all
over again   i wouldn't change
much   in spite of the pain   the loneliness   the wrong
decisions   in spite of the bad
years
    i have all the
women i've loved in
her   i have
my muse

14-17 February 1991

SELECTED PUBLICATIONS

BOOKS

game for shut-ins. Fredericton, Canada: Fiddlehead Poetry Books, 1971.

evolutions. Fredericton, Canada: Fiddlehead Poetry Books, 1973.

the custodian of chaos. London, Canada: Applegarth Follies, 1975.

something about silence. Fredericton, Canada: Fiddlehead Poetry Books, 1979.

unnatural acts. Devon, England: Jezebel Tapes and Books, 1987; Charlottetown, Canada: gynergy books, 1987.

getting wise. Charlottetown, Canada: gynergy books, 1990.

ANTHOLOGIES

Poems. In *One Foot on the Mountain*, edited by Lilian Mohin. London: Onlywomen Press, 1979.

Poems. In *Beautiful Barbarians: Lesbian Feminist Poetry*, edited by Lilian Mohin. London: Onlywomen Press, 1986.

Poems. In *Dancing the Tightrope: New Love Poems by Women*, edited by Barbara Burford, Lindsey MacRae and Sylvia Paskin. London: Women's Press, 1987.

Poems. In *Naming the Waves: Contemporary Lesbian Poetry*, edited by Christian McEwen. London: Virago Press, 1988; Freedom, Calif.: The Crossing Press, 1990.

Co-authored with Berta Freistadt. "A Cruel Trick: Menopause/Aging." In *Out the Other Side: Contemporary Lesbian Writing*, edited by Christian McEwen and Sue O'Sullivan, 30-38. London: Virago Press, 1988; Freedom, Calif.: The Crossing Press, 1990.

Poems. In *In the Gold of Flesh: Poems of Birth and Motherhood*, edited by Rosemary Palmeira. London: Women's Press, 1990.

SOUND RECORDINGS

My Buzz Kisses: The Evettes in Consort, 27 September 1981 (audio cassette). With Barbara Zanditon and Kay Stirling. London: RSL Records, 1981.

unnatural acts. Accompanied by Juliet Davey and Lucy White. Devon, England: Jezebel Tapes and Books, 1987.

Cave Canem!

Look Out: I Am About to Sing!

C M   D O N A L D

The story of my first poem. I stood in my grandmother's front room, the one we used for best, that is to say, hardly at all. The coal fire wasn't lit, and it was cold and damp and eerie, but I was on my own and not in with the family mêlée in the living room. I was about eight years old. I was looking out of the window at the sunset, feeling pretty numb, as usual. From nowhere, a line at a time, I composed:

The setting sun is over there.
Oh what a lovely sight.
The colours—yellow, pink and blue,
Not to mention white.

There was a pause during which I didn't think anything at all, then I soared to greater poetic heights.

The setting sun is beautiful,
Its colours oh so bright.
I love to see the setting sun
When it's nearly night.

Well, hell. What to do with that? I went back into the living room and told it to the family. Approval. Approval? Well, then, I'll do that again. And I did. And that, my dears, is how I came to be a poet.

My mother says that she used to read me a lot of poems when I was little, and to this she attributes my being a poet. (For my being a lesbian, she doesn't want any credit at all.) It's true that I was most attracted to strict rhythm and rhyme schemes. They seemed to me very satisfying; also you could let the direction of the poems be dictated by the range of rhyming words you could find. I took to Gilbert and Sullivan, at age twelve, like a duck to water.

I embarked on a career as a comic versifier. Poems were published by the class magazine, rejected by the girls' comic *Bunty*, published by the school magazine. One I remember was about breaking my arm (I did this three times, so I got to be an expert—and just look how many good rhymes there are for "bone"). I got As in English class. On several occasions, I shirked essay topics I would otherwise have had to think about by writing verse.

Sexuality didn't enter into this. I didn't really let it enter explicitly into anything. It is true that, when I was eleven, I fell in love with my best friend, Julie Ervine. That was 1962, the year we discovered D. H. Lawrence and had a fretful time trying to work out what the phallos were. That, needless to say, meant nothing to me. But at the point I distinctly felt the urge to stroke the ginger down on Julie Ervine's forearm, I was so scared I shut down the whole subject.

I was established in the role of clown by the time I was fourteen. It seemed to me the best deal so far. You made people laugh, so they liked you, and often they thought you were clever, too. But they didn't take you seriously, and you didn't ask for anything, seriously.

Several things happened at the same time after that. I was fourteen and starting in on adolescence. We moved from the midlands to the south of England: culture shock. But I was still persevering—I knew you had to work to be liked. From "Ten Little Vandals" (written when I was sixteen):

Ten little vandals standing near a cafe
All had flick knives, didn't look safe.
One got kettled on a bottle of wine.
Then there were nine.

.   .   .   .

Three little vandals, got no loot,
So One pawned the leather jacket from his leather suit.
The pawnbroker patched it up with a pot of glue
But number One was still inside, so then there were two.

I went on writing poems, but I didn't use them for classwork, partly because I was getting past the age where it was acceptable and partly because this school was more interesting. I had a best friend, Glenys Davies, who I loved (still do) and she used to give me subjects to write about. Here is a valiant attempt at the thoughts of a fly in a church (verse two):

I flew three times around the altar
A choirboy hit me. Did I falter?
No! I flew ahead undaunted.
My brethren say this place is haunted:
A fly was swatted—just for fun—
And he comes back to haunt the one

Who swatted him. . .
[and so forth]

But a sympathetic school enabled me to let up on clowning. There was no great impetus now I thought most of my teachers liked me. Poems became a more private issue, mostly between me and Glenys. Form had taken over: what I wrote was cheerful, rhyming, and aimless; poems maundered on, pieces falling into place like a jigsaw but no picture emerging.

Serious English essays gave way to serious poems. One was about a knight, very pale and cold and sad, who had done Something (Unspecified) Wrong. He was in love with a Lady but it was Impossible. But he was very noble really, though his critics couldn't see it.

I countered this new trend, since I found it a bit disconcerting, with funny poems and mistranslations for the school magazine:

Cave canem: beware, I am about to sing!
Ce vin doit être bu frappé: this wine must be knocked back.

And also false derivations, which, let's face it, I still do love:

decadent: having ten teeth;

ingenuous: having no knees.

And I am proud to have added recently a genuine Hebrew feminine plural:

mammoth: a gathering of mothers.

I fell in love with my Latin teacher, Cynthia (be still, my beating heart) Radcliffe, and added to my repertoire verse translations of the classics: the love poets Catullus and Propertius, of course. Studying languages was a great help: I was able to write more content-free verse in German and Latin.

But I went on writing miserable poems. I showed my mother one or two of this new style, but she didn't like them at all. She said they were horrible and miserable and she didn't want to see any more. So I kept them to myself and knew that I had been Wronged (remember adolescence?). Mind you, mine must have been pretty muted. I hadn't liked the Beatles because they seemed to signal the onset of heterosexuality among my classmates, and I didn't like the Rolling Stones at all, because they were rude. I did what I could with Beethoven and Schubert.

I wrote several angry poems about god, though as far as I can see they were just a vehicle for anger and not the result of any genuine concern for god, with whom I had never been in touch. A lot of the poems seem to me almost incomprehensible. Try a bit from this one about the sky:

Immortal wastes of wonder, a webwork whirling on,
A meaningless controversy which comes, is here, is gone,
An all-important entity, an independent whole,
A groping selfish sympathy, an ever-searching soul.

I mean, you can see I was upset. Though I still quite like the ending of the one about a girl who spent Too Much Time in Her Room, pined away, and died, while the parents:

. . . looked perplexed, then at each other, then
resolved themselves into one personality while
they tried to solve the problem.

Glenys was still staunchly reading the poems and liking them, and I developed a new ally in the form of my headmistress. Miss Hardwick had me for tea some Wednesday afternoons (when I should have been playing hockey) and gossiped with me, which shocked and delighted me. And she sang me Flanders and Swan's elephant song: "I'm suffering from amnesia, me mind's a perfect blank. Now life is very much easier, amnesia's to thank . . . "

This was my last year at school. I was eighteen and writing comic verse only when I felt cheerful, viz. not a whole lot. I was turning myself into an academic (because what else was there?), and trying not to notice that I kept falling in love with women. By the time I got to university at Cambridge, I had hit on a whizzo solution: the second person singular. I mention this in *The Fat Woman Measures Up* ("Good Old Body"):

those years of the many love poems
with no gender-betraying pronouns
no corporeal substance—and no punishment following

Looking back, I'm proud of my strategies. This example's rather grand, I think; it's the last verse of a poem about seeing my life as a cathedral, "a ruin still but on a massive scale." (How I squared all this with thinking of myself as a worm, which I also did, I shall never know.)

I am the breath of ever-flying storm winds
That whistle through the arches high above,
For though I see love unreturned is hollow,
I know myself and know that I shall follow
And, knowing you, I know that I shall love.

Trying to write seriously posed me several problems. I didn't entirely give up rhyme and strict scansion, since I tended to find free verse rather directionless. But I still found words so heady that I got carried along by them. The main problem was how to express *myself*, since this seemed to be required, without giving anything away. Needless to say, I tied myself in knots:

I'll weave my faith in plaited straw and poppies of the field
so concrete to make nothingness seem some belief concealed

not now the fine and subtle threads suspicion trails through love
but the coarse and plainer bonds that unreality will prove

Sometimes the end product is unpardonably twee:

when you look up puzzling
towards an almost sadness, nearly definite,
like the laced and tentative outmost of a wave
thoughtful in case it encroach upon the shore
the warmth of smile would bubble among the pebbles
scrabbling anxiously along like a very little crab

And some I still rather like. This is from a poem when I was twenty-one:

Then quiet will survey, I think, transparent realms where time is bred
Already past to rule no throne of space and hollow in the head,
A doctor nodding sadly to no mourners by the empty bed.

A major theme of the poems is tentative placating of someone who will only stay favourable if I stay tentative. Resignation is another general theme. Some of the poems aren't bad at all. I had received an excellent formal education and a lot of exposure to good theatre. So my formal sophistication was way ahead of the content. Once in a while it came together.

My tidy mind is troublesome, it governs all I do—
Moving away from a cupboard door
I first caught sight of you.

It seemed to me that things reflect into the conscious mind—
The (proven) tidy system proves
The giver not unkind

So pre-established harmony had seeped into my brain—
I never took my raincoat out
Except when it would rain.

To organise, anticipate the need that I could see
I often put the cup away
Before I had the tea

Caught before I realised that you could want to stay,
In my want of you I planned
And tidied you away.

About this time, there was one nice reversal of the knight/servant theme, which finished:

So I have knelt and so I kneel in my accustomed place
Where I have shown myself of old to ask for labour's grace.
Your proven servant now is turned to sprite, hobgoblin, elf:
You may not stay my angel, so my darling, prove yourself!

What had actually happened was that I had sat, one day, in a room alone and said to myself the word *homosexual*. Well, that did it. Falling in love and not saying anything was one thing; this had implications. As a consequence, I had stopped seeing my best friend, with whom I was quite in love. I was exceedingly miserable and hadn't been able to explain to Jane (or adequately to myself) what I was doing, and I had hurt both of us. And without admitting any of that, I had started in the poems to play more seriously with the idea that I was a participant and not a supplicant. At this time, I also wrote a lot of poems about dying. And a lot more wry ones about my habit of falling in love. I didn't need to add "with women"—who else would one fall in love with?

So when I met my First Lesbian (Alison Hennegan, my mainstay for the next decade), I was quite ready to align myself. But I couldn't. Because it was plain to me that if you said you were a lesbian, people would expect you to have sexual relationships, and I knew I couldn't. Because of being fat. Which meant no one would fancy me and anyway, I wasn't sure I would ever take my clothes off with someone else in the room.

This all put me in a position which was difficult to maintain. Besides, Girton College was for me, as Bromley High School had been, a pretty homoerotic experience. But you were only supposed to hint:

I listen with profundity
And eye the spent and dying flames.
We think together you and I
Of veiled, reflected, direct claims.
A hesitating movement changed
A moving sense; but I admire
With words the thought, with silent eyes
The sight, as to the dying fire
We speak and wonder who is playing
Which of many games.

Sometimes I just needed to blow off steam. From "Love in a tea cup":

You are my toast and my delight.

The stores of joy I rifle
To celebrate this highest tea—
My love is not a trifle

The milk of human kindness is
What you extend to me.
I kiss the cup but you are not,
Alas, my cup of tea.

From Germany, where I spent a year alternately trying to come out and trying not to, I sent Alison a poem filled with pig puns and quotations from *Hamlet, Prince of Denmark*, otherwise known as *Piglet, a Slice of Danish*. Footnote #7 reads:

> The Oedipig Complex in its streakiest form. That is to say, complex, the only good streaker being streakier in rashers and not, as previously thought, rasher when starkers. A stark complex.

I was twenty-four. I had by now backed myself into a corner. I was writing things and not letting myself see what I had written. I had always worked on the premise that Literature was like crossword puzzles and jigsaws: a self-enclosed, self-perpetuating system. And really, little enough of it had anything to do with my life. It echoed one's experiences, perhaps, or one echoed its, but really it was a game. I had never consciously used poems to reveal anything. Indeed, I thought I was pretty well concealed, and it hasn't been entirely a pleasant shock, writing this and seeing how obvious I was. No wonder no one (except perhaps me) was surprised when I came out.

But there we were. I came out, as a lesbian and a feminist in 1976, at the age of twenty-five. I did it as a matter of intellectual conviction, but without much actual thought. I then went into shock. I think now, I must have been waiting for the end of the world to arrive—wasn't that what I'd been protecting myself from? But nothing outside the normal range of coming-out experiences came my way. Still, I was stunned. I wrote hardly anything until 1978, except:

Justice is my darling
And I'm doing what I must:
I deal with much and many
And it's always only just.

Which still seems relevant. And for Jane, who I was belatedly grieving, I wrote:

> Your presence was specific
> To a stance or to a chair
> But now that you have gone I feel
> Your absence everywhere.

At the end of 1977, it hit me that I could write about my own experiences, directly and without subterfuge. But I didn't. I started writing again, however, rather shakily and without putting too much of my own feelings in. But more and more steadily.

By the time I fell in love and came to Toronto, in 1980, to live with Suniti Namjoshi, I had started to write about being fat. Being fat has been quite central to me. As I pointed out, it was the major stumbling block to my coming out when other forces had ceased to block me. It was Suniti who saw the poems as the start of a manuscript and who encouraged me to continue. It was Suniti who showed the manuscript to a publisher. I would not have done either of these things alone.

So now I know several things: you can write what happened, you can write what you feel, you can take it seriously and expect others to take it seriously too. And you don't die of it.

At every step of the way, something somehow became more thinkable. At every step of the way it has been women, first my mother, then my teachers, then friends and lovers, who kept me going.

SELECTED PUBLICATIONS

BOOKS

The Fat Woman Measures Up. Charlottetown, Canada: Ragweed Press, 1986; Devon, England: Jezebel Tapes and Books, 1987.

The Breaking Up Poems. Devon, England: Jezebel Tapes and Books, 1987; Charlottetown, Canada: gynergy books, 1988.

CO-AUTHORED BOOKS

With Ruth King. *Talking Gender: A Guide to Nonsexist Communication*. Toronto: Copp Clark Pitman, 1991.

ANTHOLOGIES

Poems. In *Ain't I a Woman! Poems of Black and White Women*, edited by Illona Linthwaite. London: Virago Press, 1987.

Poems. In *Gay and Lesbian Poetry in Our Time*, edited by Joan Larkin and Carl Morse. New York: St Martin's Press, 1988.

Poems. In *Mother Gave a Shout: Poems by Women and Girls*, edited by Morag Styles and Suzanna Steele. London: A & C Black, 1990; Volcano, Calif.: Volcano Press, 1991.

"Working from Photographs—Excerpts." In *Our Lives: Lesbian Personal Writings*, edited by Frances Rooney. Toronto: Second Story Press, 1991.

JOURNAL PUBLICATIONS

"First Draft" (poem). *Canadian Woman Studies* 5, no. 3, (Spring 1984); reprinted in 11, no. 3 (Spring 1991).

"For my christening," and "Nocturne" (poems). *Canadian Literature*, no. 116 (Spring 1988).

"Love, History, and How Logic Saved My Life" (talk given at 3rd International Feminist Book Fair, Montreal, 1988). *GO INFO*, July/August 1988.
French translation by Muriel Fortier: "Amour, histoire et comment la logique m'a sauvé la vie," and "Muriel's Bathtub" (poem). *Treize* 6, no. 4 (April 1990).

"When I was ten," "My mind," "Muriel's Bathtub," "You say you haven't," and "When you come" (limericks and poems). *Diva: A Quarterly Journal of South Asian Women* 1, no. 4 (March-May 1989).

ARTICLES AND INTERVIEWS

"The Very Visible Lesbian." *Gay News* (England), no. 235 (March 1982).

Maura Volante. Interview. "Christine Donald: Starting to Make Sense of Fat." *Kinesis*, (April 1987).

Irene Neufeld. Interview. "The Fat Woman." *Angles*, (April 1987).

Charmaine Beardsley. Interview. *Timmins Daily Press*, 14 August 1987.

SOUND RECORDINGS

The Fat Woman Measures Up (audio cassette). Devon, England: Jezebel Tapes and Books, 1987.

The Breaking Up Poems (audio cassette). Devon, England: Jezebel Tapes and Books, 1987.

The Common Woman

A Map of Seven Poems

JUDY GRAHN

I wrote the seven portraits of common women in twelve hours one night in the fall of 1969, published them on a mimeograph machine and distributed them by hand during the same year. I remember my own astonishment as the map of seven poems spread like wildfire, first among women I knew who immediately asked for copies to distribute, and then in wider and wider circles to across the sea, hand to hand. There was at this time no formal distribution network, no women's bookstores, nothing.

Shortly thereafter, my lover Wendy Cadden and I, along with a number of others, formed Lesbian/feminism[1] and all life flipped over and hasn't been the same since.

The poems became a focal point for welcoming women into feminism and political activism who had not been attracted to the Left. Before long, women's groups did more nearly resemble the variety of women portrayed in the poems, and still more variety followed. From my poet's point of view, the poems "worked" because the idea they imaged became embodied in the actions of women who had formerly been subsumed by male-dominated institutions, who then became interested in each other and themselves, meeting together, acting and working in common cause. The poems helped create a new social reality, and I consider them very useful for that reason.

My motivation for writing the Common Woman poems was my feeling of exclusion from American society, both as a Lesbian and as a working-class woman. I was invisible, my content unpublishable. I had been trying since I was twelve to have my poems published, and had succeeded only in *The Ladder*.[2] More specifically, I felt excluded because some women in the women's consciousness raising (C.R.) group I joined were terrified of the lesbian content of my life story. Depressed, I dropped out, and a few nights later I wrote the set of poems that would set lesbianism *and* working-class experience into a context, a commonality that included sexual identification and recognition that women are central, "hold things together," and have metaphysical as well as physical lives.

In particular, I constructed a set of women who, like lesbians, hadn't been represented in the C.R. group that couldn't handle my life. I was aware of setting "Carol in the park, chewing on straws" into a context in which she co-existed not as an exotic lesbian but as much a part of the fabric of women's experience as was Margaret, whose "husband called her a big baboon," or Detroit Annie, who dances off the dock "to prove her belief that people who cannot walk on water are phonies, or dead."

Years of experience with the Gay, Left and Civil Rights movements had sensitized me to the point that overturning stereotypes was an acutely-felt necessity in the presentation of these women. Consequently, when I got to the third portrait, Nadine, I dropped the idea of an animal *ka* (spirit double). Helen's poem identifies her as a crow, and Ella's as a snake. The creature who accompanies Nadine in her poem is the urban rat, an adversary, not a spirit of comparison. This is because the portraits were drawn as composites of women I knew at various times in my life. The group who gave me Nadine were a special population of Black women in Washington, D.C., who, in the early sixties, were recent emigrants from the rural south, where their families had been part of the tenant farm system since reconstruction had taken rights away from newly freed slaves following the Civil War. Hence, "she's a mud-chinked cabin in the slums, sitting on her doorstep counting rats and raising 15 children, half of them her own."

By the time I wrote her portrait in 1969, a militant Black Power movement had given me contact with sharp-tongued Black women who told me vehemently never to associate Black people with animals or "nature," as this was a racist stereotype to be fiercely opposed. So while I had no trouble thinking of red-haired Ella's power and powerlessness *as the same as a snake's power and powerlessness,* (for that is the way I think), with Nadine I settled on "nail" as her primary counterpoint metaphor.

Later, as the poems spread from hand to hand out into the world, I no longer thought of any of them as associated with any particular race, era, or area of the country.

While writing the seven poems, I used three notebooks to keep track of the interlocking patterns, so the commonality would be there throughout them all, in little recurrent poetic tricks of repetition.

I remembered sonnets and also Edwin Markham's poignant portraits of men he knew. I also remembered Anne Sexton's portrait of an unmarried pregnant girl, "Unknown Girl on a Maternity Ward," which invoked that horror of the middle class of the fifties and also how this sexual outcast was seen tenderly by another woman.

I thought of this whirlwind night partly as an exercise to improve my art, partly as a kind of Leftist prayer — a way of using poetry to lay down a map, not of terrain seen and experienced, but of terrain as it could become, if certain changes and understandings took place. I created my own version of a women's consciousness group, one that included such a variety of us as no one had yet seen in such groups. Written in the middle of the Vietnam war, when violent male imagery and colorful male rock stars riveted the national attention from one end of the country to the other, the poems helped focus women's attention away from men and onto each other and themselves, just as consciousness-raising and other forms of feminism were being discovered and taken into the public arena by disaffected women of the organized Left and Civil Rights movements.

Consciousness raising was the tool, entering the work force was the driving impetus, and women's poetry provided the initial rallying staff-and-drum, created the stories, rhythms and images needed to affirm and stir this massive movement. On the East Coast Marge Piercy and Rita Mae Brown, in particular, (and I suspect Robin Morgan also), provided vital poetic content that added to the foment. On the West Coast, the leadership was Alta, Pat Parker, Susan Griffin and me. We burst out of earlier movements and joined voices in a sudden commonality that rose to a great clamor.

By 1973, we feminist (and to a large extent Lesbian) poets had brought to public attention most of the issues that would preoccupy much of our generation for the next fifteen years. And we had snagged the attention of important writers such as Adrienne Rich, Audre Lorde and Diane DiPrima, older and far better known than we, and had turned their focus (or so we imagined) so that they, too, would deepen and extend the urgent messages of women-centered voices.

Ready or not, the Common Woman poems carried me out into the changing world and bumped me up against the class system. For though I loved them, and as far as I can tell millions of others did too — going to the trouble to memorize and paraphrase them when they couldn't get copies — snobs hated them, and people concerned with male-defined and class-defined literary standards (content control) were afraid of them, and disparaged them when they first appeared. The first English professor who saw them said they weren't poetry, but in later years college teachers told me there was a whole genre of poetic portraiture based in the Common Woman poems which women in and out of their classes were busy writing, and then I noticed that even some of my academic colleague poets had begun writing portraits of women in series, after the Common Woman poems.

For a dozen years, as I made my way across the country giving hundreds of readings, I could walk into almost any women's center and find Common Woman poems posted on the bulletin board or decorating someone's T-shirt, purse, or diary. Magazines, newsletters, bookstores, and coffeehouses named themselves after them, and "the common woman is as common as the best of bread and will rise," derived from the last poem, became a Movement slogan. This continues to be somewhat true as I write in 1991. As with other of my early poems, the Common Woman poems still appear as political statements scrawled on walls in the United States and other countries. A dozen times I have found them as graffiti on the walls of women's bathrooms, sometimes the slogan, sometimes an entire portrait.

More formally, the poems have been performed on stage and taught in hundreds of classes all across this continent and on others. A performance artist took them along with other women's poetry all across Australia. They've been set to music at least half a dozen times, especially by women in the countryside, singing them to each other. One early group of two white and two Black women formed the first multiracial women's music group I had witnessed in my generation. The woman who read the poems in this group was Black, so the line "plain white talk" evolved into "plain Black rap."

By 1978 various of the seven poems had appeared in anthologies and other publications, probably over a million times, and our independent women's press [The Women's Press Collective in San Francisco] managed to distribute 15,000 copies.

In the early eighties, I sent them to a literary magazine whose editor had

invited me to submit something. I'm so seldom accepted by magazines, especially after I'm invited to submit work,[3] that I decided to respond to him with
mischief, so I mailed off a typed version of all seven Common Woman
poems. He sent a polite note indicating that I showed promise and that he
would like to publish them *if* I would consider dropping the last two lines of
each one, as they greatly detracted from the poems! Our commonality at risk
again, or it would be if I were totally dependent on his judgment for
publication — that is to say, without free speech. Fortunately we have an
independent press movement that helps preserve a broader degree of representation of varied voices.

I have noticed that so-called "mainstream" (in my case this can mean
straight, middle-class, male and even materialist) anthologies often select
the thinnest, smallest slices of my work for reproduction. Most anthologists
apparently select from a poet's work exactly what they themselves can identify with. I certainly do. I notice that I want to know what men think of
women, so this is all-too-often the part of their work with which I identify.
Very often we choose to identify with the thinnest, smallest example — this
slice from the outside peel of the orange that perhaps never touches the big
juicy heart of it — because we feel overwhelmed by the big juicy heart of it.
And the justification for this thinness of selection will deliver up the fantasy
word "universality," in this case a cruel euphemism for "the editor's limitations." In my idea of "commonality," at least I understand that what overlaps
between circles is just a crescent of what exists within the integrity of each
poetic grouping and each poet.

In the absence of a publication network, much of my early work was
memorized by women who heard me read on the West Coast, and who carried
the poems from town to town in an oral telegraph that astonished me. The
poems acquired a rich life of their own during this time and nearly got away
from me, into the public domain. If Diana Press hadn't put out a hardback
collection of my work in 1978, I'm sure I would have lost control of it. This
happened in part because oral work, and underground (i.e., poetry and music produced by small presses and companies) is likely to be considered
"everyone's" while middle-class, written and published work is protected by
copyright.

Oral artists of all kinds are always in danger of being ripped off. This issue
has been brought to public attention by both Native American and Black performing artists and storytellers. My friend and co-poet Pat Parker (a brilliant
oral poet) was so leery of the problem that she refused copious invitations to

appear on KPFA radio in Berkeley, California. I thought this was a mistake on her part; I accepted the station's invitations, figuring I could always track down the unauthorized use of my work later and claim it. But in some cases I couldn't.

In the women's movement, we had no ethics about paying workers, including ourselves. Money was colonial (white) and male, and therefore to be scorned. Lesbians with money and advanced degrees are still forced by pain of ostracism and insult to hide them from other Lesbians in "the community" — a situation that leads to lying and no real sharing or analysis of what constitutes actual riches.

Meanwhile some enterprising (pro-socialist) women took the ending lines from the seventh poem of the Common Woman poems and made posters, selling them by the tens or maybe hundreds of thousands, for more than a decade. Several different groups across the country did this. I wrote to the best-selling group to ask for a royalty (which they refused) and credit (which they granted). I particularly wanted the book title, *Edward the Dyke and Other Poems* to appear on the back of the poster along with my name, because I didn't want women mouthing my words without understanding that a dyke had written them. To me, that was, and remains, the biggest rip-off of all: that society can benefit from Lesbians and despise lesbianism at the same time is one of the bitter fruits of the invisibilities of Lesbians.

I didn't get mad about the lack of money until later, when I had time to remember that I had toothaches for months on end and injuries from printing, and no health insurance during the years that movement groups made money from posters of my words. Since then I've learned to take better care of myself (keep my own money) and I'm not bitter about it now. I still don't have insurance but I'm proud that my poetry has some economic, as well as social, power.

I also appreciate being credited as much as anyone else does, and was absolutely thrilled when Ntozake Shange acknowledged that the seven women in *For Colored Girls Who Have Considered Suicide When the Rainbow is Enuf* were inspired by my seven common women. I also learned that an "out" lesbian in the Weather Underground read the Common Woman poems as a public statement as she was being incarcerated in the notorious prison at Lexington, Kentucky. A couple of years later someone I knew saw a poster with the "best of bread" slogan in the Lt. Governor's office in New York State, and was told by the secretary that the Weather Underground dyke had written the poems. I thought this miscrediting was funny; it's what makes oral work so interesting: the modern American Amazon mythology of the warrior poet. The miscrediting was not all that wildly inexplicable as our press had earlier taken on the distribution of poems written by Weather Underground women. As the wheel of your own generation turns, everyone on it belongs to you. This is commonality too.

At some other end of the social scale, a Stanford professor said publicly that the Common Woman poems had saved his marriage, giving him a way to understand women's issues at exactly the time he needed that knowledge most. In Houston, at a mass meeting of 5000 feminists in 1977, I was told that two women high in the administration of Jimmy Carter's government had quoted the "best of bread" slogan — without credit, true, but still. . . I was impressed. At the time one of the hottest burning issues of this mass group was whether or not to adopt a lesbian rights measure, and when they did my lover and I went outside to join in the victory yelling. I felt better, although her homophobic mother sat with us complaining about the measure the whole time. She feared that we would forget all about women on welfare in our selfish lust for acceptance. I was enraged with her arrogant, fearless articulation of a trite stereotype about Lesbians, and my fury carried me still farther along the way of revisioning and resurfacing what mythic parts Lesbians do play in human culture.

"Mythic Realism" is a term I coined privately late in the seventies after the movement no longer worked for me, to describe (to myself at least) what I was doing. I wanted to combine the two words mythic and realism precisely because they have been split apart by monotheistic structuralists.

The phrase "common man" has a strikingly different meaning than "common woman." His is an image of a laborer in the field, and of the collective industrial labor force. There is no sexuality in this image, derived as it is from humane feelings for the plight of European peasants, and a century later used by organizers of labor movements and communist ideology. There is no sexuality and (hence) no individuation and not a lot of depth of field in "common man."

"Common," all by itself, is such a loaded word, especially when it is applied to women. The Latin word "ordinary" simply doesn't have the emotional and social connotations which the Anglo Saxon "common" does.

In status or class usage, to call a woman "common" is to insult her morality — more than meaning dull, boring, everyday, as in "common housewife," the name also means *lacking taste*, having no special class or status, nothing singular; and further, more importantly, it means *belonging to just anybody*, especially sexually, of being a "common slut" or whore, of being *common* (sexual) property. This meaning is a reference to the former freedom of Celtic women to have many lovers, a freedom now treated derogatorily as in "any man could have her." For common refers to the old matriarchal custom of holdings belonging to an entire community, of common herds, common goods, land held in common. (This was through the female line.) Common Law is customary law, and common-law marriage is outside the instituted patriarchal legal system, and is older. The Commons are lands belonging to the public, and the House of Commons in English Parliament refers to representatives from "the people," rather than from the aristocratic class, with their House of Lords. A "common nail" is a penny nail used by carpenters. A commoner is a peasant, even in modern American minds, and in addition to all these meanings, the word also means ordinary and everyday.

The Common Woman poems, by virtue of their structure, redefined the word *common* from its earlier uses, and laid down the idea of overlapping commonalities among women that let each stay centered in her own life experience with their very real differences not lopped off to fit the narrow concept "universal." The seven women do not fit into a definition of class structure based on paid work. Some are paid, some not; some boss; some live in urban or rural ghettos of one kind or another.

For women, our sexual experiences influence our lives as materially as do our work lives: the difference between an abortion and an unwanted child is eighteen years of forced labor. The difference between a closeted and an out lesbian is public and family recognition of her adult, sexual status as a whole human being. The seven common women are not seen from the point of view of their sex partners; their supposed sexual desirability to "others" is not referenced, their own sexual lives are. Their bodies and life experiences are, therefore, their own: one at least is fat; one shaves her head defiantly; one balances old age and poverty with steadfast faith; one is a wild dancer; one has seven children; one shoots a gun in anger. They acknowledge individuation *within* commonality.

My seven poems of 1969 became something of an anthem for a social movement. More importantly, in 1991, they embody an embryonic ideal social structure based on overlapping commonalities that allow local integrity. This idea must be developed if we want societies based on multicultural symbiotic cooperation, including nonhuman societies of creatures, plants, insects and ecosystems.

In the Common Woman poems, the collective, overlapping "mythic meta-phor" is in the last two lines, "The common woman is as common as: the common crow, a rattlesnake, a nail, a thunderstorm, the reddest wine, (as solemn as) a monkey or a new moon, and the best of bread," repeated with variations throughout all seven poems. The repeated lines are an expression of my desire for a collectivity of womankind to re-establish woman-centered values in the world. While the poems are hardly a well-developed myth, they have pointed my work in a direction it will increasingly follow, away from the dogmatic materialism that denies myth, that equates tradition itself with op-pression and wants only to revolt and begin anew with what is currently vis-ible in the urban landscape of language and opportunity.

The popularity of the Common Woman poems helped catapult me into the making of a movement based on bonding with different kinds of women, and toward the founding of institutions that improved — in some ways — the qual-ity of our lives. And in other ways, their popularity revealed our inner destitution. The poems gave me a lot of networking, a lot of focus on working-class women, a lot to think about, and some images to think with. What others got from them, remains for them to say.

NOTES

1. The Stonewall riot formed the Gay movement several months before, in June 1969 — a move-ment so male-dominated that Lesbians left it sooner and later to join the separatist Les-bian activities we were initiating on the West Coast, which Rita Mae Brown and a small group of New Yorkers had been sparking off on the East Coast since 1968 and which Lesbians across the country soon joined.
2. *The Ladder* was a magazine published by Daughters of Bilitis in San Francisco. This orga-nization for Lesbians was founded by Del Martin and Phyllis Lyon in 1955, and pub-lished the only vehicle for Lesbians in the fifties and sixties.
3. I do want to remember that Marilyn Hacker, Alta, and Paul Mariah published "The Common Woman Poems" and "The Psychoanalysis of Edward the Dyke" before I came out with my first full-length book.

SELECTED PUBLICATIONS

BOOKS
The Work of a Common Woman: The Collected Poetry of Judy Grahn, 1964-1977. Introduction

by Adrienne Rich. Oakland, Calif.: Diana Press, 1978; New York: St. Martin's Press, 1980, 1981; Freedom, Calif.: The Crossing Press, 1984, 1985. Includes *The Common Woman Poems* (1969), *Edward the Dyke and Other Poems* (1971), *She Who* (1972), *A Woman is Talking to Death* (1973), and "Confrontations with the Devil in the Form of Love" (1977).

The Queen of Wands. Freedom, Calif.: The Crossing Press, 1982, 1985. Book-length poetry.

Another Mother Tongue: Gay Words, Gay Worlds. Boston: Beacon Press, 1984. Updated and reissued, 1990. Gay cultural and mythic history and theory.

The Highest Apple: Sappho and the Lesbian Poetic Tradition. San Francisco: Spinsters, Ink, 1985. Literary criticism and lesbian philosophy.

The Queen of Swords. Boston: Beacon Press, 1987, 1989. A full-length poetic drama. Includes a long previously published poem, "Descent to the Roses of the Family."

Mundane's World. Freedom, Calif.: The Crossing Press, 1988. Novel.

Really Reading Gertrude Stein. Freedom, Calif.: The Crossing Press, 1989. Three essays on Stein with selections of her work.

ANTHOLOGIES

"Boys at the Rodeo." In *True to Life Adventures Stories, Vol. 2*, edited by Judy Grahn. Freedom, Calif.: The Crossing Press, 1981.

"Menstruation: From Sacred to the Curse and Beyond." In *The Politics of Women's Spirituality*, edited by Charlene Spretnak, 265-279. New York: Doubleday, 1982.

Poems. In *The Norton Anthology of Literature by Women: The Tradition in English*, edited by Sandra M. Gilbert and Susan Gubar. New York: W.W. Norton, 1985.

Poems. In *Gay and Lesbian Poetry in Our Time*, edited by Joan Larkin and Carl Morse. New York: St. Martin's Press, 1988.

Poems. In *She Rises Like the Sun: Invocations of the Goddess by Contemporary American Women Poets*, edited by Janine Canan. Freedom, Calif.: The Crossing Press, 1989.

"Drawing in Nets." In *Conversant Essays, Contemporary Poets on Poetry*, edited by James McCorckle, 101-103. Detroit: Wayne State Univ. Press, 1990.

"Healing From Incest Through Art." In *She Who Was Lost Is Remembered: Healing from Incest through Creativity*, edited by Louise Wisechild. Seattle: Seal Press, 1991.

ARTICLES, REVIEWS AND INTERVIEWS

"Judy Grahn, From a Dialogue between Grahn and John Felstiner, Professor of English, Stanford University, 19 November 1980." In *Women Writers of the West Coast, Speaking of Their Lives and Careers*, edited by Marilyn Yalom. Santa Barbara, Calif.: Capra Press, 1983.

Judith Beckett. Interview. "Warrior Dyke." *Woman of Power*, (Winter/Spring 1986).

Sue-Ellen Case. "Judy Grahn's Gynopoetics: The Queen of Swords." *The Literary Imagination.* Georgia State University, (Fall 1988).

Margaret Spillane. Review. "Poet Judy Grahn: queen of words, *Queen of Swords*." *In these Times*, 13, no. 5 (7-13 December 1988).

Ursula K. LeGuin. "Up to the Earth." Review of *Mundane's World*. *Women's Review of Books*, 6, no. 5 (February 1989).

Catherine R. Stimpson. "Going to be Flourishing." Review of *Really Reading Gertrude Stein*. *Women's Review of Books*, 7, no. 8 (May 1990).

Sound Recordings

March to the Mother Sea: Healing Poems for Baby Girls Raped at Home (audio cassette). Oakland, Calif.: Lavender Rose Productions (Box 11164), 1990. Poetry written for multitrack tape.

II

Head Wind

Lesbian and Writer†

JANE RULE

I am a politically involved lesbian, and I am a writer. I do not see the two as mutually exclusive; neither do I see them as inextricably bound together. Yet one of those two conflicting views is held by most people who read my work. The editors of *Chatelaine*, for instance, would as soon their readers weren't reminded that the writer of the Harry and Anna stories, affectionately and humorously concerned with family life, is also the author of *Lesbian Images*. Most critics of my novels, on the other hand, use my sexuality to measure all my characters. Those who are lesbian are naturally the most persuasive. My male characters are considered weak. Even for those not so crudely tempted, I am judged as remarkably fair to all my characters when one considers that I am, after all, a lesbian. For critics who are themselves gay, I am held politically accountable for every less than perfect gay character and am warned that I will lose a large part of my audience if I insist on including heterosexual characters in my work. And in the academy, I am

---

†This essay was first published as "Making the Real Visible: Lesbian and Writer," *Fireweed*, no. 13 (July 1982): 101-4.

dismissed as a marginal writer not because some of my characters share my sexuality but because I am a lesbian, therefore somehow mysteriously disqualified from presenting a vision of central value.

Kind, straight friends have argued that, if I weren't so visibly a lesbian, my work wouldn't be so often distorted and dismissed. But short of denying my sexuality, there is little I can do. It is not I but the interviewer or reviewer who is more interested in the fact that I am a lesbian than in the fact that I am a writer. My only positive choice under the circumstance is to use the media to make educational points about my sexuality.

Many people in the gay movement do not understand why I don't use my work as I am often willing to use myself for propaganda. Though one heterosexual critic did call *Lesbian Images* a piece of propaganda because in it I make my own bias quite clear, even that book does not satisfy the real propagandists who would have me not waste time on politically incorrect lesbian writers like Radclyffe Hall, May Sarton, Maureen Duffy — in fact, nearly all the writers I studied in depth, but concentrate only on my most radical contemporaries, who are writing experimental erotica and separatist utopias.

I decided to be a writer not because I was a great reader as a child or had any natural gift for language but because I wanted to speak the truth as I saw it. To understand and share that understanding has been my preoccupation since I was in my teens. No political or moral ideal can supersede my commitment to portray people as they really are. What is is my domain. What ought to be is the business of politicians and preachers.

It is still a popular heterosexual belief that all homosexuals are at least sick and probably depraved, and they should, therefore, be, if not incarcerated in mental hospitals and jails, at least invisible. It is the conviction of gay militants that all homosexuals are victims and martyrs who must become heroically visible so that everyone will have to face the fact that education, industry, the law, medicine, and the government would all come to a grinding halt without the homosexuals who are the backbone of all our institutions. "Even Eleanor Roosevelt. . . " that argument can begin or end. The truth of experience lies elsewhere.

For offering a balanced view of society, I'm sure I know a disproportionate number of homosexuals, as I know a disproportionate number of artists, white people, Canadians. One of the truths about all of us is that we live in disproportionate groups. That is why novels tend to be full of Jews or blacks or soldiers or Englishmen or heterosexuals. Very few tend to be full of homosexuals because, until recently, homosexuals didn't live in social groups except in some places in Europe. My first two novels, *Desert of the Heart* and *This Is Not For You*, though they are about lesbian relationships, are not full of lesbians. I was writing about what was ardent, dangerous and secret, which is what lesbian experience still is for a great number of people. In my third novel, *Against the Season* which was the beginning of my preoccupation with groups of people rather than with one or two main characters, out of about a dozen characters two are lesbian. There are a gay male and a lesbian in my fourth novel, *The Young in One Another's Arms*, out of a cast of about ten. Three and a half of eight characters are homosexual in my latest novel,[1] *Contract with the World*. In all of my novels my gay characters move in an essentially heterosexual world as most gay people do. Though some of them are closeted in that world, some punished and defeated by it, they are all visible to the reader who is confronted with who they are and how they feel.

In a rare and beautiful comment about a character in *Contract with the World*, Leo Simpson says, "When Allen is arrested on some kind of homosexual charge, he has become so real that the laws of society immediately seem barbarous. Comfortable prejudices look like a tyranny of fear, which is of course part of what Rule's novel wants to say."

Yes, exactly, not heroic or saintly but *real*, and it is *part* of what I want to say. But in this book I am basically concerned with six or eight people, each of whom deals with barbarous law and comfortable prejudice, not always to do with homosexuality or even sexuality. What gathers the characters into one book is their involvement with art in a provincial city far from any cultural centre. To be an artist in this country is very difficult. To deal with the pain and doubt and wonder of such aspirations is my chief preoccupation in this book. My characters are neither necessarily greatly talented nor superior in vision simply because they are artists. They all have to face the fact that, except for the few greatest, artists are considered failures. A great many very gifted or not, can't stand such a climate. In this they share something of the strain it is to be homosexual in a homophobic culture.

I owe to my own art all the honesty and insight I have, not simply about homosexuals and artists, both of which I happen to be, but about the whole range of my experience as a member of a family, a community, a country. I don't write Harry and Anna stories to cater to *Chatelaine's* heterosexual readers though I like the cheques well enough when they come in. (No one could eat writing for *Christopher Street*, and I still give most of my short fiction away.) I write them out of affection for those men and women, like my own parents, who care for and love and enjoy their children and because I, too, have cared for and loved and enjoyed children. There are heterosexual men and women in all my work because there are heterosexual men and women in my life and world, to whom I owe much of my understanding.

A blind writer once said to me, "You're the only writer I know who includes characters who happen to be physically handicapped. In most fiction, if they are there at all, it's *because* they're handicapped." That for me is the real distinction between what I write and propaganda. I am trying to make the real visible. People "happen to be" a lot of things about which there are cultural phobias. I have never found either safety or comfort in a blind heart, as a way to work or live.

As a lesbian, I believe it is important to stand up and be counted, to insist on the dignity and joy loving another woman is for me. If that gets in the way of people's reading my books, I have finally to see that it is their problem and not mine. As a writer, I must be free to say what is in all the diversity I can command. I regret the distorting prejudices that surround me, whether they affect homosexuals or men or the physically handicapped, and I can't alone defeat them. They will not defeat me, either as a lesbian or a writer.

NOTES

1. Two novels, *Memory Board* and *After the Fire*, have been published since the writing of this essay.

SELECTED PUBLICATIONS

BOOKS
Desert of the Heart. London: Pandora Press, 1964; Vancouver: Talonbooks, 1977; Tallahassee, Fla.: Naiad Press, 1985.
This is Not for You. London: Pandora Press, 1970; Tallahassee, Fla.: Naiad Press, 1982.
Against the Season. London: Pandora Press, 1971; Tallahassee, Fla.: Naiad Press, 1984.
Theme for Diverse Instruments. Vancouver: Talonbooks, 1975; Tallahassee, Fla.: Naiad Press, 1990.
Lesbian Images. London: Pluto Press, 1975; Ithaca, N.Y.: The Crossing Press, 1982.
The Young in One Another's Arms. London: Pandora Press, 1978; Tallahassee, Fla.: Naiad

Press, 1984.

Contract with the World. London: Pandora Press, 1980; Tallahassee, Fla.: Naiad Press, 1982.

Outlander. Tallahassee, Fla.: Naiad Press, 1981.

Inland Passage. Toronto: Lester & Orpen Dennys; Tallahassee, Fla.: Naiad Press, 1985.

A Hot-Eyed Moderate. Tallahassee, Fla.: Naiad Press, 1985; Toronto: Lester & Orpen Dennys, 1986.

Memory Board. Tallahassee, Fla.: Naiad Press, 1987; London: Pandora Press, 1987; Toronto: Macmillan of Canada, 1988.

After the Fire. Toronto: Macmillan of Canada; Tallahassee, Fla.: Naiad Press; London: Pandora Press, 1989.

ARTICLES, REVIEWS AND INTERVIEWS

Judith Niemi. "Jane Rule and the Reviewers." *Margins* 8, no. 23 (1975): 34-37.

Helen Sonthoff. "Celebration: Jane Rule's Fiction." *Canadian Fiction Magazine*, no. 23, August 1976.

Geoff Hancock. Interview. *Canadian Fiction Magazine*, no. 23, August 1976.

Yvonne Klein. "An Interview with Lesbian Novelist, Jane Rule." *Front Page*, 21 February 1984.

Susan Crean. "Divining Jane Rule: a profile of progress." *B.C. BookWorld* 5, no. 2, Summer 1991, 11

FILMS

Desert Hearts. Samuel Goldwyn production, directed by Donna Deitch, 1985. Available as VHS video from Naiad Press.

Lesbian Writers
and Dyke Detectives

EVE ZAREMBA

I didn't set out to be a "lesbian writer." When the idea for my first book came to me while driving alone from Vancouver to Toronto, all I wanted was to produce a mystery novel well within the tradition of the genre, with a hard-nosed, street-smart professional private investigator. With just one small difference: the protagonist would be lesbian. That was back in 1975. There were no books with dyke detectives at that time. None. [1]

I was then, and still am unapologetically addicted to all manner of detective mysteries from hard-boiled to cozies. I wanted to write a mystery (or two or more) with a dyke Private Eye, just for the fun of it, to see if I could make it work. No overt political messages — lesbian, feminist or otherwise. Just stories about one middle-aged lesbian matter-of-factly going about her job as a P.I. That is message enough.

Knowing very little about the business I went ahead and wrote *A Reason to Kill*. It sold almost immediately to Paperjacks, a mainstream Canadian paperback house which published it in 1978 with a batch of nineteen other paperback originals for the so-called airport trade. There was nothing on the cover, back or front, to suggest the detective was a lesbian or that the subject had anything to do with homosexuality. I made $500.00 on the deal and got — to my knowledge — one small (bad) review in a Toronto newspaper and a spread in the *Body Politic*, at that time Canada's premier Gay Liberation magazine.

I went on to write three more mysteries with Helen Keremos, the dyke P.I. They have been published by Amanita Publications and Second Story Press in Toronto, with distribution also in the United States. Virago Press launched two of my titles in the U.K. in 1989 and 1990. A German publisher has bought German translation rights to *Beyond Hope* and *Work for a Million* for publication in 1991, and *Uneasy Lies* in 1992.

My career as a writer of mysteries, a lesbian writer of mysteries, a writer of lesbian mysteries, a lesbian writer of lesbian mysteries, a lesbian writer of mysteries for lesbians. . . I am not sure which designation is most accurate or how much it matters — let's just call it my writing career has been a learning experience in spades! A roller coaster of illusion and disillusionment. Full of painful booby traps and comic relief. It has taught me more than I cared to learn about literary culture in Canada and the publishing business here and elsewhere. It has affected my opinions about any number of political and social issues and has even influenced my view of myself.

Times have changed since 1975 — in the world at large, in the lesbian/feminist community, and very much so in the book trade. Recently I looked at some rejection letters from a number of U.S. agents (and one publisher) which I received in the early eighties when I was still trying to flog my manuscripts via regular channels. First of all, I was amazed at the courtesy, respect, encouragement and good advice. A stereotype undermined. Further, in reading them I realized how recent is the current popularity of mystery novels. From a letter dated February 16, 1982, a well-known New York agent wrote: " . . . we seriously considered taking you on as a client. . . However. . . I was not confident I could find a publisher for you (the places for mysteries are very few). . . " These days she couldn't claim that "places for mysteries are very few," even if all she wanted was to let me down gently.

Now mysteries are so popular even genre snobbery ain't what it used to be. In 1978 it was pretty up-front. Take the review of *A Reason to Kill* in the *Body Politic*. After the obligatory plot outline, reasonably accurate and positive, the reviewer made haste to disassociate herself from the book by explaining that she didn't normally waste her time reading mysteries. At the time I managed to be amused, although the put-down was gratuitous and to my mind, unseemly. Back then neither the reviewer nor the editor(s) saw it that way. Many still wouldn't.

Genre snobbery is by no means dead in the mainstream or alternative press. However, now that literary writers are jumping on the mystery bandwagon in ever increasing numbers, the genre is being taken more seriously — not necessarily to its benefit. Witness this bit of pomposity by Anthony Burgess in the August 1990 issue of *Atlantic:* "It is unfair — and unsophisticated — to demand of detective fiction the exhaustive moral imagination that one demands of that serious branch of letters to which we accord the honorific 'literature.' " The point is of course well taken; detective fiction as a category shouldn't be judged by inappropriate standards. But then neither should anything or anybody else. I consider myself lucky to work in a genre which makes no claims to the honorific "literature," where readers wouldn't put up for a moment with "exhaustive" imagination, moral or otherwise, and where any such pretentiousness would be laughed to scorn. I hope serious writers who enter the genre don't attempt to "transcend" it . . . and if they do I hope they fall flat on their cans!

With the current proliferation of mysteries from every variety of alternative press it is hard to remember that detective/crime novels were a feminist no-no just ten years ago. There was a lot of downright hostility towards those of us who started writing them. In addition to pure literary snobbery, part of the problem lay in the exploitation of violence with which the whole genre was — and still is — associated. The low status of the genre at that time, together with the absurd standard of political correctness which continues to be applied to lesbian/feminist writers, made it easy to accuse anyone who entered the field of condoning, if not glorifying, violence. I recall that soon after the publication of *A Reason to Kill*, I received a more-in-sorrow-than-in-anger letter from a respected lesbian prose writer whom I had asked for comment. She castigated me for stooping to writing detective fiction, and for the hard-boiled character of my detective, Helen Keremos.

I don't recall any reviews of *A Reason to Kill* in feminist/women's periodicals when it first appeared (1978). The nationality (Canadian), the nature of the publisher (mass market) and the fact that there was no precedent made it of little interest. It didn't help that *A Reason to Kill*, like the next two titles (*Work For a Million* and *Beyond Hope*), lacked explicit sex and wasn't romantic to any degree. Many lesbians didn't consider these books lesbian enough. Lack of lesbian sexual content kept *Work for a Million* and *Beyond Hope* from being accepted by a number of movement publishers in the U.S., notably Naiad and Persephone.

By the time mysteries became trendy my energies were focused elsewhere — I was running a used bookstore in Toronto. I still have 300 + pages of notes to remind me that I spent four years in the exciting although ultimately futile study of sociobiology. Finally in 1986, my lover Ottie Lockey and I decided to publish *Work for a Million* and *Beyond Hope* and to republish *A Reason to Kill* under our own imprint, Amanita Publications. This was to be the start of another small feminist press in Canada, with income from my mysteries funding other books. In any event, Amanita did publish two non-fiction titles: *In the Name of the Fathers, The Story Behind Child Custody*, by Susan Crean, and *Pornography and the Sex Crisis*, by Susan G. Cole. We produced five titles with the initial capital investment necessary for two or three — such is the power of cash flow! Of course producing books is not the problem; for small presses the problem is having them distributed and sold. Here we feminists/gays/progressives are lucky. We do have our own bookstores throughout the United States and Canada and, most crucially, we have *Feminist Bookstore News*. *FBN* is a trade paper out of San Francisco, without which feminist bookselling wouldn't be half what it is. When we start handing out medals for major contributions to the feminist/lesbian movement, one of the first must go to *FBN*'s editor, Carol Seajay. Amanita books sold almost exclusively through our bookstores, promoted and publicized via *FBN*. But that is another story.

Both in spite of and because of Amanita Publications' relative success, in 1989 Ottie and I decided to get out of the publishing business. It was taking most of my time and to keep it growing would have taken all of our spare cash, a common problem for small enterprises. Running Amanita no longer fitted our plans. We sold all five titles, inventory and rights. I went back to writing, producing another Keremos mystery. *Uneasy Lies* was published by Second Story Press in November 1990.

My best and worst reviews have been by lesbian/feminist reviewers. I don't necessarily mean the most positive and negative reviews, but rather the best and worst as reviews. When lesbian/feminist reviewers are good, they are very good; when they are bad, they are awful. With category fiction, acceptance of the genre and familiarity with its conventions are surely minimum qualifications for a reviewer — Burgess is right about that. I wish it were always so! I prefer a straight, mainstream mystery specialist, even male, to a lesbian/feminist who doesn't know the genre. Sure most mainstream reviewers give us short shrift; if you're lucky they replay a plot synopsis from the back cover. Sure some have trouble with lesbian content, some find it titillating, some ignore it. I remember one Canadian male reviewer condemned Helen's lesbianism as a gimmick, and another snickered about "girl meets girl." All that is to be expected. Still, experienced mystery reviewers at least understand what the writer is doing, or trying to do. The book has a chance of being judged in relation to this intention and to the efforts of others in the category. Jewels to be treasured, jewels beyond price, are lesbian/feminists who are both mystery freaks and experienced reviewers. Hi there, you know who you are, we love you!

Of all the good, bad and indifferent notices my books received, the most unnerving at the time was a hostile attack by a lesbian reviewer in the U.S. I am no stranger to negative reviews, but this piece was something special. The reviewer appeared not only to hate my book but me, personally. This wasn't literary license or mere exaggeration. With breathtaking hyperbole, she attacked what she perceived as the excessive violence in my work. Among other things, she compared me to Mickey Spillane. It's not easy to be categorized as a "Spillane." Spillane's hero, Mike Hammer, loves to shoot people (usually women) in the stomach and watch them die!

There is very little violence in my books, virtually none caused by Helen Keremos, and no brutal sex-and-violence of the kind which is so pervasive in general malestream fiction. I do meet with other, less extreme expressions of discomfort with Helen Keremos' tough-dyke persona. The trouble is that many of us still see women as victims and *only* victims. I don't think this is too facile an explanation. Why else do some lesbians/feminists view a female protagonist responding with confidence to physical aggression as somehow nonfeminist if not actually antifeminist? Many of these same women support "armed struggle," having no trouble understanding that there are situations where refusal to use force against force only benefits the status quo. Why the double standard?

In the recent spate of mysteries with women protagonists/ detectives who are more-or-less feminist (at least active subjects instead of girl Fridays or window dressing), there are very few lesbian professional private detectives doing their jobs in the world at large. Typically, dyke investigators are amateur detectives, set in plots heavy on romance and lesbian community dynamics. Judging by what gets published by Naiad Press and other lesbian presses, this is what lesbian readers expect from their writers.

Private investigators who are tough, female AND heterosexual get published very successfully by the mainstream press. To put it another way, the mainstream has learned to deal with female protagonists who are active, tough professional detectives — as long as they are straight. Prime examples are V. I. Warshawski by Sara Paretsky and Kinsey Millhone by Sue Grafton. Paretsky and Grafton are two of the most-read women mystery writers on this continent. They send their protagonists to bed with men at irregular intervals, thus saving them from appearing too dykey. While Warshawski's sensibility and politics are deeply feminist and Millhone's are not, both characters have more in common with their male counterparts than with any dyke I have found in current detective fiction.

To date ONLY feminist/lesbian small presses have published mysteries with lesbian detectives as heroes. Let me emphasize: NO lesbian detective — cop, P.I. or amateur — has appeared as chief protagonist under a mainstream imprint, whether in hardcover, trade or mass-market paperback.[2] (Paperjacks publishing *A Reason to Kill* in 1978 was an aberration. They didn't know what they were doing and anyway there was little if any lesbian content in it. The plot centered around Gay MEN, a very different thing.) Recently some mainstream publishers have started to pick off one or two of the most saleable lesbian writers nurtured by our own presses, so by the time this piece comes out a dyke detective might have made it to the big time (sic). But I don't believe we need worry much about losing our own; by definition, mainstream publishing will never be inundated with dykes.

I have been writing predominantly for lesbians/feminists; that is my audience, my market. I know this community, after all I am part of it. In spite of that I do NOT cater to its biases and prejudices, its likes and dislikes. Why isn't Helen Keremos more political, more likeable, more sexy, more what many lesbian/feminist readers want her to be?

How much is Helen Keremos like Eve Zaremba? I don't mean in a purely autobiographical sense, in which case the answer is obviously "not much at all." Nor do I wish to enter the debate about whether all fiction is "essentially" autobiographical. I have trouble with essentialist arguments on any subject, including that one. What I mean is, To what extent does Helen Keremos reflect Eve Zaremba?

She and I share at least one important demographic characteristic: age. Both Helen and I are pre-boomers; our working life goes back to the fifties. In all probability we are a full generation older than most of my readers. That makes a difference.

Helen Keremos doesn't fit younger expectations of what a lesbian/feminist hero should be. Passage of years has lowered her belief in the perfectibility of the world and of the people in it, including herself. The

seemingly wide-open possibilities of youth have been replaced by an acceptance of the limitations of age, time and human nature. Helen gets tired of
"isms" and other abstractions. She isn't an intellectual or a politico or highly
educated or even well read. She's just been around and picked up a thing or
two along the way. She can be dense, impatient and not at all nice. Life is too
short—literally—to suffer fools. She can be abrasive but seldom judgement-
al. Helen can be quite traditional. She is high on people who do their jobs
well, don't bitch, and get on with life.

The very notion of political correctness makes her suspicious. She's skep-
tical of any prescriptive ideology; high-sounding rhetoric puts her back up.
"It's a mind-fuck," she would have the guts to say, if asked. But then unlike
me, she is a Private Investigator, and P.I.'s are p.i.

Fundamentally, Helen is comfortable with her body and her life, a woman
who experiences her lesbianism as liberation. For her it's not an issue. She
wouldn't subscribe to the political claim that lesbians suffer double oppression, although she would understand the arguments if they were explained to
her. But nothing would make her deny her own subjective reality. Helen—
you and me both.

Helen isn't me and I'm not Helen. But there is a bit of each in the other. I
have lived with Helen Keremos in the first person for fifteen years, off and
on, through four books. Most of what I know about being a lesbian writer she
has taught me. But it may be time to wean us from each other. I plan to keep
her around for at least one more book, but from now on Helen Keremos will
shift into third person and share the spotlight with a couple of other characters. She'll take it in stride. Like the tough old dyke she is.

NOTES

1. In 1977 the classic *Angel Dance*, by M.F. Beal, was published by the now long defunct and
   still lamented Daughters Publishing Co., Inc. of New York. It has the distinction of being the first mystery with a hard-boiled dyke detective. *A Reason to Kill* came a close
   second. *Angel Dance* has recently been re-issued by Crossing Press.

2. Just to make a liar out of me, Sandra Scoppettone (a.k.a. Jack Early) has gone and written
   Everything You Have is Mine, about a dyke P.I. called Lauren Laurano, published in
   1991 by Little, Brown & Co. in hardcover. Brava Sandra. (My point stands).

SELECTED PUBLICATIONS

BOOKS

A Reason to Kill. Toronto: Paperjacks, 1978; Toronto: Amanita Publications, 1988.

We 'k For a Million. Toronto: Amanita Publications, 1987; London: Virago Press, 1990.
   German translation by Maria Mill. Frankfurt: Eichborn Verlag, 1991

Beyond Hope. Toronto: Amanita Publications, 1988; London: Virago Press, 1989.
   German translation by Maria Mill. Frankfurt: Eichborn Verlag, 1991.

Uneasy Lies. Toronto: Second Story Press, 1990.

EDITED BOOKS

Privilege of Sex, A Century of Canadian Women. Toronto: House of Anansi Press, 1972.

ANTHOLOGIES

"Shades of Lavender: Lesbian Sex and Sexuality." In *Still Ain't Satisfied! Canadian Feminism Today*, edited by Maureen FitzGerald, Connie Guberman and Margie Wolfe. Toronto: The Women's Press, 1982

ARTICLES

Bill Pronzini and Marcia Muller. In *1001 Midnights: The Aficionado's Guide to Mystery and Detective Fiction*. New York: Arbor House, 1986.

Falling Between the Cracks†

MARY MEIGS

"F"or whom are you writing?" This question has always surprised me, for it implies an intention directed outward, rather than the autonomous intention to write what one wants to say. It implies that a writer chooses a suitable group of readers, people of like mind, but unless one's books are addressed to a specific category of readers — children, scholars, nature-lovers, people who like to cook — the writer of a first book has no idea of who will be of like mind. It may be that autobiography is a genre of writing which is not aimed at anyone in particular. With my first book, *Lily Briscoe: A Self-Portrait*, (my coming out both as a writer and a lesbian) the audience cut across sexual, class, and gender differences and included heterosexual men and women, working-class women, lesbians, and gay men. Above all, I was surprised that parts of my experience as a white, privileged lesbian could be shared by people whose lives had been very different from mine, so my definition of the ideal reader for me became someone willing to enter my experience and listen to what I have to say. Of course, I immediately discovered

---

†This essay was first published in *Trois*, 5, nos. 1-2, (Autumn 1989): 145-151.

that there are readers (particularly critics) who feel it their duty to tell a writer how she should have written and how her experience is flawed. The writer should never make an appeal for understanding to any category of readers, for it is certain that this will be misunderstood. Without seeking readers, she will find them in unexpected places; she must patiently wait for the ideal reader to find *her*.

Inevitably after a first book, discrete audiences, pro and con, coalesce, and become more precise with every subsequent book. My work has been disliked by readers from the same groups who liked it, in particular those who feel threatened by it: closeted lesbians, daughters who have always lived in harmony with their mothers, privileged women who have had happily married lives, and all those who believe in the ideal of "privacy." The last shudder at close analysis of any human being *except in fiction*. Later I will discuss the peculiarly vulnerable position of the lesbian autobiographer, and how the decision to write autobiographical fiction might be an understandable form of passing. The range of reactions to my books stems directly from the fact that I chose to come out as a lesbian. Certain critics seem to be angrily holding up a germ-infected rag with a pair of tongs and warning readers away. They are offended by my very presence, even more by the fact that I presume to have ideas that question patriarchal institutions, and state them without apology. The writer of fiction can say exactly the same things, but she does not stand in full view as a tempting target.

"When gay people in a homophobic society come out," says Eve Kosofsky Sedgwick, "it is with the consciousness of a potential for serious injury that is likely to go in each direction" (51). She makes a parallel with Racine's *Esther*, based on the biblical story of Queen Esther, who came out as a Jew to her husband, King Ahasueras, and because she was loved by him, succeeded in saving her threatened people, but not herself. Later Sedgwick humorously scolds herself for her "sentimentality" in identifying with the noble queen. "At this moment," she says (meaning the moment when Esther is about to come out), "the particular operation of suspense around her would be recognizable to any gay person who has inched toward coming out to homophobic parents" (46). Or suspected homophobic siblings or friends, I should add. The entire future of a lesbian, or any gay person, lies in the few seconds of coming out, and the freedom one gains comes with a new experience of unforeseen penalties.

At the beginning of "Epistemology of the Closet," Sedgwick quotes Proust: "The lie, the perfect lie about people we know, about the relations we have had with them. . . the lie as to what we are, whom we love. . . — that lie is one of the few things in the world that can open windows for us on to what is new and unknown" (39). Yet even a great novelist's definition of fiction cannot protect him or her from being hounded by critics or interviewers who are determined to find the writer in the work. "Writing as a novelist who is routinely asked at every interview, 'Is your work autobiographical?' I know that looking to the writer's personality and history for one-to-one correlations with the writing is absurdly reductionist." This is Lisa Alther in "The Writer and Her Critics," a review of two books about Doris Lessing (11). "Such over-simplification relegates fiction to autobiography and/or neurosis, leaving little room for the predictive and prescriptive function of fiction, and granting insufficient credit to the power of imagination and craft" (Alther 11).

Well, the novelist may feel reduced and "relegated" to autobiography when she is plagued by the question, "Is your work autobiographical?" but she can always find legitimate refuge in Proust's "perfect lie." Even in a novel which can be called fictional autobiography, which sticks closely to the facts of the writer's life, the writer has enjoyed the freedom of the "perfect lie." "The lie," Proust continues, "can awaken in us sleeping senses for the contemplation of universes that otherwise we would never have known" (Sedgwick 39). The novelist, when asked if her work is autobiographical, can reply, "Of course I'm somewhere in it, but try to find me." The perfect lie has enabled her to be everywhere at once and to be nowhere in her own person. She knows that lurking in the question ("Is your work autobiographical?") is the accusation: if it is, it is less creative, it has been easier to write; it is suspect because it is supposedly subjective and the subjective view is assumed to be less truthful rather than more so. The reader of an autobiography accepts it much less readily as truth than she/he accepts fiction as truth, because many people believe (and I have heard several novelists say this) that fiction is "truer" than autobiography. Thus, the simple statement that an autobiography is fiction will, paradoxically, make it more believable. My autobiographical writing feels "truer" to *me* than any fiction I could write; for a novelist like Lisa Alther, a more complex truth than that of autobiography lies in the freedom fiction gives for "imagination and craft' (11). If the novelist is a lesbian who has chosen not to come out she benefits, as Proust did, from two perfect lies, one of fiction and the other of the closet. Her choice not to come out is understandable because it allows her a freer use of her creative energies. The perfect lie does not entirely protect her from the animus of interviewers and critics, but it allows her to elude direct charges against her, for she can refuse to fit definitions or to feel responsible for her characters (they are free spirits, after all).

The autobiographer who has come out is called upon to answer both for her own truth and for that of all the other people in the book. Sometimes they are seen as her victims, and the reader wishes to protect them from the writer's intrusiveness. "I feel as though I'm looking through a keyhole," said one of my readers about *The Medusa Head*, my second book, published in 1983. The keyhole image describes a particular kind of squeamishness which focuses on the lesbian autobiographer and spreads to her entire subject matter; she does not have the novelist's freedom to speculate on people's lives. Of course the lesbian autobiographer's own scruples have exercised a kind of censorship while she was writing the book; she is never as free as the novelist, and is responsible to her subjects whether they are alive or dead. But a homophobic reader will further narrow the lesbian autobiographer's freedom by presuming that her entire view of life is biased. If she attempts an interpretation of her subjects as she knew them, even if they give their own evidence in letters and diaries, she will be seen (because she is a lesbian) as an unreliable interpreter, particularly of heterosexual lives. A woman reviewer says of my recent book, *The Box Closet*, "In the end *The Box Closet* turns out to be a portrait of two people painted not as a faithful likeness but as a reflection of the author's view of her own subjects" (Barclay 9). She apparently believes that my book should have been composed *only* of letters and journals (she seems not to have noticed that the book contains portraits of more than two people), that I should have let them "tell their own story." I wonder how this critic arrived at her conclusions that my portraits are *not* faithful likenesses. Did she know my subjects? And how would she guarantee that a selection of letters, unless it was made by lottery, would not reflect a view of some kind? The choice of letters necessarily forms part of the work of interpretation and adds another dimension to the portrait. A book composed only of my family letters would have been criticized on the ground that it was not interesting, but, as we see from another review, even extensive cutting did not obviate this danger: "Meigs tries to present objective lifelike portraits of people very near and dear to her. . . but her family is not as interesting to the reader as it is to the writer" (McGrath 124).

This critic then goes on to say, in effect, that the only interest in my book lies "in the temptation it offers to the reader to trace the influences that helped to shape the character of the author and may have played a part in making her one of the respected voices of the gay community of today"

(124). I was struck by the mixture of kindliness and concealed sternness in this last sentence, which so firmly puts me in my place, and it confirms my view that a writer who has come out as a lesbian, no matter what the subject of a subsequent book or its percentage of lesbian content (about one percent in *The Box Closet*) is forever sealed in her lesbian identity like an insect in plexiglass.

Perhaps every lesbian has the secret hope that her book will dissolve homophobia, even in those straight people who, before they read the book, were unable to say the word *lesbian* without an overtone of disgust. Having read the book, they are now able to associate the word with a "respectable" woman of over sixty. But though amnesty is granted to this one lesbian writer, the homophobia is still intact and is ready to sound the alarm. The same readers who have granted me amnesty are as afraid as ever of having a lesbian daughter, or even an apparently straight daughter who might want to go to a women's college where there are said to be lesbian students or teachers. To me it is remarkable if a few college students have managed to slip through the net of homophobia in the school system. Eve Kosofsky Sedgwick speaks of the "unaccustomed perhaps impossible responsibilities that devolve on college faculty as a result of the homophobia uniformly enjoined on teachers throughout the primary and secondary levels of public school — where teachers are subject to being fired, not only for being visibly gay, but, whatever their sexuality, for providing any intimation that homosexual desires, identities, cultures, adults, children, or adolescents have a right to expression or existence" (10).

Many parents of both sexes see "contagious" lesbianism as a greater threat to their daughters than the danger of rape, alcoholism, drugs, or Communism. Their fear and ignorance are illustrated by the question a straight friend asked when I told her that a lesbian friend had been sexually abused by her cousin for ten years: "By a boy or a girl?" Lesbians are seen to be as dangerous for women as men are; we are also working from within, like the Communists; if we are allowed any power, we "take over."

To us lesbians, it is natural to enjoy the little power we have in an overwhelmingly heterosexual world. But the lesbian who comes out in a book finds that along with the euphoria of sisterhood comes the gradual knowledge that she has been sealed in. She discovers that she has done straight people a favor by coming out; now, whether they are mildly or violently homophobic, they know what to expect. If they once found it difficult to say the word *lesbian*, they are now unable *not* to say it. "You wanted to be known as lesbian, didn't you?" The prejudicial stereotype in these readers' minds will from now on colour everything I write. In every subsequent book I will be assumed to be writing from a lesbian viewpoint, primarily for lesbian readers. *"The Medusa Head* merits a 'For Lesbians Only' sticker" wrote Alan Twigg about my second book (6). For just as books by feminists are considered both by many men and by certain women to be propaganda, so books by avowed lesbians are seen as not worthy of attention or belief because they are based on false premises (that women can really love other women, and, above all, that they do not need men).

Belittling words about lesbian relationships have the power to hurt even established writers, now dead, who never come out of the closet. The caution of writers like Willa Cather, Virginia Woolf, or Elizabeth Bishop protected them during their lifetimes from the contamination of loaded words. They were also protected from open speculation about whether a relationship with another woman was sexual or not, since sexual activity between women is considered a proof of lesbianism, unless it is seen as an aberration in an otherwise heterosexual life. Proof of it releases the homophobic poison which has been held in suspension. A lesbian in the closet is preternaturally aware of herself as a substance which can release this poison, which may contaminate her relationships and affect future judgements of her work. She is also aware of unspoken thoughts, of facial expressions, covert put-downs, and of the slightest sign of uneasiness or fear—fear by association. Still closeted, she feels this fear herself. She hopes that coming out will banish this fear, and indeed, after coming out, she feels the exhilaration of her victory. But she discovers to her surprise that each coming out to straight people, now expected of her because she has become a spokeswoman for her lesbian sisters, is almost as difficult as the first. The first seemed like an affirmation; in those that follow she confronts straight people who are bored with the subject and may perceive it as irrelevant and gratuitous.

It is perhaps because I belong to an older generation of lesbians, for whom coming out was (and still is, for many of us) unthinkable, that I still quake when I have to make yet another public avowal. Let us call it *post-euphoria*, the state in which the joy has seeped out of avowal, and the nagging question, "Is it really necessary?" has taken its place. This past summer, I was the only lesbian member of the cast of *The Bus*, a semidocumentary film made by the National Film Board of Canada,† about seven women, all over

---

† released in May 1990 as *The Company of Strangers*.

sixty-five. In one scene I was supposed to talk to Constance (aged eighty-eight), who in real life had read my first book, about coming out as a lesbian. But she did not want to give me the cue that would lead to my coming out on camera. "I don't see why we have to talk about all those things," she said. Constance had voiced a common view of straight people who hope that lesbian subject matter will disappear from the work of a lesbian writer. Yet they cannot forget that the lesbian is lurking behind everything she writes, and they comb each book for the reassurance that she is still there and can be judged accordingly. I am not talking here about readers who like my work, those who were responsible for the joyful aspect of coming out, but about those who reject it for the prejudicial reason that I am a "lesbian writer." The lesbian writer who comes out is squeezed between those who want less (or no) lesbian content in subsequent books, and those (other lesbians) who want more. In the interval between the appearance of my first book (1981) and my third (1987), the idea of the audience a lesbian writer is supposed to seek has become narrowed and politicized, and an implicit accusation hangs in the air, "You aren't writing for me (or for us)."

Even as powerful a novelist as Jane Rule, who writes, one might say, for any intelligent reader, is harried from both sides. Lesbians may say, "There isn't enough about *us*," yet I have heard, after the publication of *Memory Board* in 1987, the question addressed to her by a man in her audience at McGill University, "Do you call yourself a lesbian writer?" This question, which is legitimate when posed by a lesbian, was in this case intended to be a trap similar to, "Do you still beat your wife?" Everybody knows that Rule had the courage to come out many years ago and is, strictly speaking, a lesbian writer. I would argue that by coming out she renounced the protection of the second perfect lie in her novels, and, in spite of her stature as a novelist, is still the victim of homophobia. "Jane Rule . . . is known as a lesbian writer — a label she encourages rather than resists," writes John Godard in the Montreal *Gazette*. He adds, "She officially launched *Memory Board* at l'Androgyne Bookstore in Montreal . . . where her books can be found under 'Lesbian Literature,' and where she drew an almost exclusively female crowd" (12). Rule, perceiving the trap, replied, in effect, that she does not write exclusively about (or for) lesbians but about life as she sees it. She *resists the label*, rather than encouraging it, for the intention of the labeler is to cast suspicion on her vision of the world.

Lesbian writers who are proud of the label in its positive meaning know immediately if it is being used negatively, to express homophobia. After the publication of *Sexual Politics* in 1970, when Kate Millett was still in the closet, reporters anxious to pin the label on her closed in like sharks that have smelt blood. Perhaps people are more polite now, but they can sometimes barely conceal their interest in the lesbian as prey that must be run down and kept apart from heterosexual writers, and even from writers who have stayed in the closet. The writer (a lesbian) can be thankful for the continuing freedom which the "perfect lie" has given her. In its largest meaning, it is the discreet silence which protects all lesbians still in the closet from their parents and employers, and, if they are writers, from the hostility of straight readers. It is, in the story of Alice and the Fawn in *Through the Looking-Glass*, the "wood where things have no name" (Carroll 64). As they emerge from the wood, the Fawn, who has been walking close to Alice, sees that she is a "human child" and runs away in terror. It is a perfect parable of coming out; the person who is named ceases to be herself and immediately embodies the fear-inspiring name, and she can never return to the sheltering wood. The writer who stays in the wood has the freedom to say everything except, "*I* am a lesbian." She can say, "My heroine is a lesbian," or, "in my book there are women who love women"; she can suggest that this is natural, that it can be beautiful, that these women are happy in their love, and she will still not be labeled a "lesbian writer."

The writer-lesbian, or indeed any lesbian who has come out of the closet, must learn to live with the role of scapegoat; she must develop special gills for breathing homophobic air, special muscles for a robust sense of humour. The lesbian writer suffers less from the charge contained in the word *lesbian* than the teacher or editor who wants the word to work positively in her students or readers and who runs the risk of being seen as subversive. Lisa Weil, the editor of *Trivia*, in a talk she gave in Montreal in March 1988, discussed the difficulties of giving a course at Hamilton College, which was listed in the course catalog as "Lesbian Literature." "Students, mostly lesbians," said Weil, "began coming into my office saying that they really wanted to take the course — but they couldn't have 'that word' on their transcripts... With parents paying for their education, it was hard enough for some of them to get away with 'Women's Studies.' " Weil discovered that "no one had ever offered such a course. And for this very reason... it was too threatening... and teachers didn't want it on their résumés any more than students did... So, at the last minute, I changed the title of the course, which is now officially called 'Female Voices: Reclaiming the Monster' " (2). In the same way, the title of a course in lesbian literature to be given by

Yvonne M. Klein at Concordia University in Montreal, was changed by the administration to "Women's Sexuality," with the result that the first lecture attracted a horde of curious male students, who dropped out when they discovered the real subject of the course.

Under cover of her new course name, Lisa Weil was able to keep the focus entirely on lesbian writers of poetry, fiction, and nonfiction. Her reading list, particularly of contemporary writers (Broumas, Gidlow, Grahn, Lorde, Marchessault, Morgan, Rich, and Rule, among others) gives one a sense of the richness of lesbian writing. Weil succeeded in getting her students to think about what the words *lesbian writing* meant to them and to air both their positive and negative reactions. She interested them in the possibility of reclaiming the "Monster," a conventionally negative and threatening image of the lesbian, as a source of lesbian power. "I chose a group of books and poems," she said in her Montreal talk, "that exhibited. . . a distinctively lesbian quality, in the way that Bertha Harris uses *lesbian* — that is, *monstrous*, in some significant way, unassimilable, awesome, dangerous, outrageous, different, distinguished" (4).

Weil belongs in spirit with the Quebec feminists who have been developing a theory of language supple enough to express the whole being of each writer. In *La Théorie, un dimanche*, six of these writers who have experimented with "unassimilable, dangerous, or outrageous" language (that is, outside the patriarchal mainstream) discuss their theories of language. "A feminist consciousness is essential to the creation of a subject," says Louise Cotnoir, "because it permits the re-creation of a self-image which corresponds integrally with what I know I am" (155). "So where. . . and *how*," asks Gail Scott, "might my subject, denied her full existence in any patriarchal paradigm. . . *be* a subject-in-the-feminine?. . . If she. . . cannot be expressed in any established form, she needs to find another place where the words she speaks will fit her gestures" (Scott 20-21). And she continues, "The subject's resistance to drawing rigid boundaries around herself. . . *makes her incomprehensible to the male modernist*. . . and embarrassing" (22-23). All these writers are "unassimilable," that is, they refuse to conform to patriarchal expectations, and are viewed with the "embarrassment" that monsters provoke. Scott's heroine (her subject-in-the-feminine) also refuses to conform to feminist or lesbian expectations: she refuses to be "correct." She is "suspicious of transcendence," including that of feminist utopias, "a suspicion that has led me to place myself (in writing)," she says, "between certain expectations of my feminist community and my desire to be excessive" (25-26). She wants, like Persephone, to descend into the Underworld: "the areas of repression in the mind, the darkest corners, that if worked through, lead to fascinating places" (26). In my own view, Persephone, who was kidnapped by the patriarchy (Pluto) and forced into the bondage of marriage, is not a model for the freedom to be excessive, but Scott likes to think of her in her triple aspect: "Diana in the leaves, Luna, shining brightly, Persephone in the Underworld" (22). The Luna aspect means brightness in darkness, like the humour which is so much a part of Quebec life, "the laughter that in the same breath assures transgression" (20).

Humour is often overlooked by readers, perhaps because they perceive that its true purpose is to mock covertly their most cherished beliefs. A tragicomic novel is seen by some readers to be unremitting tragedy, and the lesbian writer who has intended to be funny at times (I am one of these) can actually provoke anger. Yet humour is part of the language of defiance that enables feminists to live in a repressive climate. For Gail Scott it is a carnival mask, which is "a comment on her current grasp of meaning" (30). A mask, like the perfect lie, enables the wearer to see without being seen; in the same way, the play of laughter conceals a serious intent. Mary Daly and Jane Caputi have "conjured" a whole new language of mockery in their *Wickedary (Webster's First New Intergalactic Wickedary of the English Language)*. In the last fifteen years, lesbian laughter has broken out in a language revolution. "In search of woman-identity: dictionaries were blown wide open, words uprooted, neologisms coined, punctuation upset or willfully ignored, codes, genders and syntax fissured, personal pronouns mixed around" (Cotnoir, "Quebec Women's Writing," 13). Cotnoir continues, "This subversive revolt takes the form of texts where fiction and theory overlap" (14). The "space-in-between theory and fiction" (15) is the space of the "imaginaire," a word coined by the lesbian/feminist translator, Susanne de Lotbinière-Harwood, to convey "the sense of an inner landscape, a territory of possibilities" (16). Lesbian writers have found freedom by enlarging *spaces-in-between*, including the space between the cracks. I have found my own freedom in the territory where theory and autobiography overlap, in defiance of patriarchal rules that a piece of writing be one thing or the other. And I've come to think that defiance is the only answer a lesbian writer can make to the exigencies of *all* expectations, and that each of us must learn to free-fall in our almost unlimited space of possibilities.

WORKS CITED

Lisa Alther, "The Writer and Her Critics," *Women's Review of Books* (Oct. 1988): 11.

Pat Barclay, "Memoir," *Books in Canada* (Oct. 1988): 9.

Lewis Carroll, *Alice Through the Looking-Glass* (New York: Macmillan, 1906).

Louise Cotnoir, "Quebec Women's Writing," Translated by Susanne de Lotbinière-Harwood. *Trivia* 13, no. 3 (1988): 13-16.

———. *La Théorie, un dimanche* (Montreal: Les Editions du Remue-ménage, 1988).

Mary Daly and Jane Caputi, *Webster's First New Intergalactic Wickedary of the English Language* (Boston: Beacon Press, 1987).

John Godard, "Books," *The* [Montreal] *Gazette*, 14 Nov. 1987.

Joan McGrath, "Collected Essays," *Colliers* 4 (July 1988): 124.

Mary Meigs. See books in *Publications List*.

Gail Scott, "A Feminist at the Carnival," *Trivia* 13, no. 3 (1988): 17-30.

Eve Kosofsky Sedgwick, "The Closet, the Canon, and Allan Bloom," *Gay Studies Newsletter* (Nov. 1988): 1, 8-10.

———. "Epistemology of the Closet," *Raritan* 7 (1988): 39-51.

Alan Twigg, "Books," *The Magazine*, 15 Jan. 1984, 6.

Lisa Weil, "Reclaiming the Monster: Lesbians in Academe," Public lecture. Montreal, 13 March 1988.

SELECTED PUBLICATIONS

BOOKS

Lily Briscoe: A Self-Portrait. Vancouver: Talonbooks, 1981.
> French translation by Michelle Thériault: *Lily Briscoe, un Auto-portrait*. Montreal: L'Arbre HMH, 1984.

The Medusa Head. Vancouver: Talonbooks, 1983.
> French translation by Pierre Desruisseaux: *La Tête de Méduse*. Montreal: VLB Éditeur, 1987.

The Box Closet. Vancouver: Talonbooks, 1987.

In The Company of Strangers. Vancouver: Talonbooks, 1991.

ANTHOLOGIES

"My Evolution as a Lesbian Feminist Writer." In *Language in Her Eye*, edited by Libby Scheier, Sarah Sheard and Eleanor Wachtel, 194-196. Toronto: Coach House Press, 1990.

"Reflections." In *Living the Changes*, edited by Joan Turner, 169-177. Winnipeg: Univ. of Manitoba Press, 1990.

JOURNAL PUBLICATIONS

"Illustrations for Two Novels by Marie-Claire Blais." *Exile* 4, no. 2 (1977): 47-52.

"From *Lily Briscoe: A Self-Portrait* with Five Drawings for a Novel by Marie-Claire Blais, *Les Nuits de l'Underground*." *Exile* 6, nos. 1-2 (1979): 39-64.

"Portfolio" (with photographs of work). *Fireweed* 13 (n.d.): 8-11.

"Illustrations for Jane Eyre." *Exile* 10, no. 1 (1985): 78-83.

"The Island." *Room of One's Own* 9, no. 4 (1985): 18-31.

"Memories of Age." *Trivia* (Fall 1988): 57-65.

"Interval." *Brick*, no. 40 (Winter 1991).

ARTICLES, REVIEWS AND INTERVIEWS

William French. Review of *Lily Briscoe: A Self-Portrait*. *Globe and Mail*, 5 December 1981.

David Watmough. Review of *Lily Briscoe: A Self-Portrait*. *Canadian Literature*, Winter 1982.

Michael Lynch. Review of *Lily Briscoe: A Self-Portrait*. *Body Politic*, March 1982.

David McFadden. Review of *The Medusa Head*. *Quill and Quire*, February 1984.

André Renaud. Review of *Lily Briscoe: un Auto-portrait*. *Lettres Québecoises*, April 1985.

Elena Cliche. Review of *Lily Briscoe: un Auto-portrait*. *Spirale*, April, 1985.

Susanna Egan. "From the Inside Out: *Lily Briscoe: A Self-Portrait*. An Autobiography by Mary Meigs." *Prose Studies*, special issue on "Autobiography and Questions of Gender," Spring 1991; London: Frank Cass Publishers, 1991.

The Double "L"

Latina and Lesbian: A Testimony

LUZ MARÍA UMPIERRE

Immanence

for Gail

I am crossing
the MAD river in Ohio,
looking for Julia
who is carrying me away
in this desire.

I am crossing
the river, MAD,
afflicted by the rabies
for those who'll call me
sinful, insane and senseless,
a prostitute, a whore,
a lesbian, a dyke
because I'll fall,
I'll drop,
I'll catapult

my Self
into this frantic
excitement for your
    SEX
my Margarita,
my yellow margarita,
my glorious daisy.

I am traversing
this river MAD,
crossing myself
against the evil eye,
hectic, in movement,
my narrow body
covered with pictures
of women I adore or I desire,
armies of Amazons
that I invoke
in this transubstantiation
or arousal
that will bring my Julia forth.
Julia
who'll lose her mind
over your glorious vulva,
my Margarita,
my yellow margarita,
my luminous daisy.

I am traversing
this body full of water,
    MAD,
cursing all Hopkinses,
incestuous writers,
who fucked your head and mine
in spring and summer
with images of death and sin
when all we wanted
was to touch the yellow leaves,
the fall under our skirts.

I am transferring my Self,
changing my clothes,

spitting three times,
clicking my heels,
repeating all enchantments:
    Come, Julia, come,
come unrestrained,
wild woman,
hilarious Julia,
come Julia come forth
to march the streets
at winter time,
to walk my body,
to proclaim
over the radio waves
the coming of the lustful
kingdom,
in sexual lubrication
and arousal
over my Margarita,
my yellow margarita,
my brilliant daisy.

I am crossing
the MAD river in Ohio,
leaving possessions and positions,
shedding my clothes,
forgetting, oh, my name,
putting life on the line,
to bring my Julia forth,
lesbian woman,
who'll masturbate and rule
over my body, Earth,
parting the waters
of my clitoral Queendom,
woman in lust,
who'll lose her mind
and gain her Self
in want,
in wish,
in pure desire and lust
for the rosie colored lips
covered with hair

of Margarita,
my yellow margarita.

(pause)
I am Julia,
I have crossed the river
    MAD,
I have come forth,
new lady lazarus
to unfold my margarita,
my carnal daisy
that buds between
my spread out legs.

I touch my petals:
"I love me,
I love me not,
I love me,
I love me not,
I love me!"

from *The Margarita Poems*

"Poetry," says Audre Lorde, "is not a luxury." Poetry is the only viable way I have of showing the effects that exile has had on me as a triple Minority: Puerto Rican, woman and Lesbian. My poetry is an accusation which I wish to make of those who, on a daily basis, attempt to steal my identity both as a Lesbian and a Latina.

I don't write with the purpose of leaving behind volumes of precious and futile words. The word "volume" is often used to denigrate the work of a warrior woman in an attempt to diminish her importance, her strength, her valor. I write poetry carefully; I choose my words with precision because they are the best artillery I have on this battlefield where I find myself alone as a warrior Latina Lesbian. I know that the best defense I have is my pen and my intellect. My poetry is an attempt to leave a testimony which will serve as a beacon and a flamethrower for other women and for those who find themselves in similar battles because they are different. My words are my bombs, my rifles, my guns; but they are also my daughters, my most endearing selves, my loves.

My words are perceived as "dangerous" by the whites and by those members of my Latina group who find themselves living a life of conformity and playing the game of the "American dream"; a game in which there is no part for me and other Latina Lesbians like me. I have been criticized publicly by Latino men who say that my openly Lesbian Latina poetry is alienating and that I do not represent and cannot represent Latino people in this country. My answer to these attacks is a loud "carcajada" because I know that my poetry is an attempt to create a free Amazonian island; an island in exile. And my poetry intends to serve as a marker and hope for Latina Lesbians towards the future. My poetry has taken in the sap of two Puerto Ricans: Julia de Burgos and Victor Fragoso and mixed it with the wisdom of other Latina women, Black women and Lesbians. Therefore, my poetry is bilingual. My poetry makes use of the two weapons of the colonizers — English and Spanish. But after using these weapons my poetry breaks them because I learned early on that "The master's tools will never destroy the master's house." (Lorde). My poetry is free; my poetry is "I" as a loving warrior woman; my poetry is a homeland for the future.

Most of the time I write out of a profound need to communicate with a wide range of audiences. I must express my feelings and vicissitudes as a Latina Lesbian, working and living in these United States. I used to have little confidence in my writing until I met a professor at Bryn Mawr College who gave me the courage to write. His name is John Deredita. He allowed me to submit poems following a given style of writing instead of or in addition to term papers. My courage to write has also sprung from other Latina Lesbians, Cherríe Moraga, for example; from the power of Black Lesbians like Audre Lorde; the spirit of Victor Fragoso.

I started writing when I was thirteen years old as an imperative to put into words the fact that I had been a victim of sexual molestation since age seven. I was frightened my parents would see what I was writing. I had kept silent about the molestation out of fear that my father, who had a gun in the house, would kill the person involved. Although in my mind this person indeed deserved to be shot, the terror of getting my father thrown in jail prevented that. When I was fourteen my writings were found by one of my cousins and I was so panicked over this fact, that I burnt all the writings. It wasn't until I was at Bryn Mawr that I took on writing again.

One of the most interesting things for me to see has been the effects of my writings as a Latina Lesbian on different people. A white woman critic, who is very well known in this country in the field of Latin American Literature, seems to have felt personally attacked by my poems. She has difficulty with my writings about racism and about how white women have been oppressive to Minority women. She has written me insulting letters saying that I am not a "feminist" — the letters are the living proof of what I expose in my poems. The majority of the time, however, I get positive feedback from my readings. One of the most positive responses I've had to my poems came from a group of young men who were in jail in New Jersey and who asked me to do a poetry workshop for them. My poems on oppression, on being a Latina Lesbian, on the lack of communication between my father and me were met by them with a special interest and empathy. Some of these youngsters have continued to be in touch with me and have sent me their writings.

The attacks that I have been a victim of as a Latina Lesbian from Latino straight poets and academicians has thus been balanced by the interest and empathy of marginal men and Gay Latinos. I am not a man hater, contrary to the opinions of white straight women and men. Some people hear a strong Latina Lesbian voice in my poems and they believe that because my words are strong and felt and womanly, that I hate men. I have several poems dedicated to or written for men. The sexual molestation that I was a victim of as a child did not turn me into a man hater.

I have had many influences on my poetry. I believe that there are three stages in my writing and the influences vary from stage to stage. In the first stage, which I would label as an effort to deal with racism in the United States, I was influenced by Vanguardista poets of South America, especially Vicente Huidobro. I wanted to write poems at that time that made a political statement using a format that had never been perceived as political. My visual poems *En el pais de las maravillas* come out of this need.

A second stage in my writing involved my fears of coming out as a Lesbian. Some of my poems in . . . *Y otras desgracias/ And Other Misfortunes* . . . deal with that fear but also with the lure of suicide. Dealing with both issues in that collection initially helped to develop my openly Lesbian collection *The Margarita Poems*. But *The Margarita Poems* are also about the creation of that new free land in exile of which I spoke in the beginning of this testimony. "The Mar/Garita Poem," which ends that collection, was written in 1985 during a time when there were so many forces raging against me that I became severely ill and thought that I would not survive. "The Mar/Garita Poem" was written as a legacy. My victimization at Rutgers University — because of my open views on Lesbian and Gay issues and my defense of Minority women — was crucial in my elaboration of *The Margarita*

Poems. I wrote to survive, and thanks to that power to write and the love of many friends throughout the nation, I did.

Since this presentation is a testimony of survival as a Latina Lesbian, I take this opportunity to speak of the impact that my students at Rutgers University had on my survival from 1984 to 1989. Outside of their open protests at Rutgers due to the fact that I was banned from teaching in 1988, they took a very personal interest in my survival. They would call me on a daily basis for months to tell me which new form of protest they had devised to complain about my being banned. Many of them wrote poems to me, some of which were published in the university's student newspapers; others wrote editorials; still others got their parents and state legislators, including Jim Florio, to write to the university on my behalf. Although I was left alone in that battlefield by my colleagues at Rutgers out of fear of reprisals, I was never abandoned by my students. To them I dedicate this testimony.

And since this *is* a testimony of survival I must also tell you how a prominent Puerto Rican woman writer lent herself to be used against me by Rutgers University by agreeing to teach my graduate seminar while I was being banned. This poet, who calls herself an "independentista" and who allegedly believes in women's rights, needs to be exposed here as a tool for patriarchal oppression and for homophobia. I have spoken and written elsewhere on the political elite in Puerto Rico as a limiting group and as an "in" organization that fosters homophobia and lack of unity among Puerto Ricans. The actions of this woman writer *are* my best example of this political elitism that needs to be abolished for unity to rise among Puerto Ricans.

I am now in a third stage in my writing and in this one I have chosen to grapple with the subject of death. To this end I have started a new collection of poems for men and women whose death has made an impact on me. I am taking on this subject matter not out of wanting to deal with my own mortality, although that may certainly be there, but because the women and men who I am writing about — including Julia de Burgos, my mother, Sylvia Plath, Victor Fragoso and Elliot Gilbert — have had a great impact on my survival as a Latina Lesbian.

Why do I keep writing? I write because writing is the only tool I have to maintain my sanity in a world and country that have grown increasingly insane and insensitive to difference and to the vital importance of difference. I write to communicate with special audiences: Latinas, students, Lesbians, my mother, myself. In writing I find a developing identity. In writing I can define our story.

WRITER'S NOTE

The following articles address my discrimination case:

"She Won't Leave." *Womanews*, (June 1987): 3, 13.

"Latina Lesbian vs. Rutgers." *Gay Community News*, 14, no.46 (14-20 June 1987): 1.

"Lesbian Professor Charges Bias at N.J. University." *The Advocate*, 487 (8 December 1987): 5, 17.

"Latina Lesbian Professor banned by Rutgers. *Gay Community News*, 15, no. 38 (10-16 April 1988): 1.

SELECTED PUBLICATIONS

BOOKS

Una puertorriqueña en Penna. San Juan, Puerto Rico: Masters, 1979. Out of print.

En el país de las maravillas. Prologue by Eliana Rivero. Bloomington, Indiana: Third Woman Press, 1982; Berkeley: New Earth Publications, 1990.

Nuevas aproximaciones críticas a la literatura puertorriqueña contemporánea. Puerto Rico: Editorial Cultural, 1983. O.P.

Ideología y novela en Puerto Rico. Spain: Playor, 1983.

... Y otras desgracias/And Other Misfortunes... Prologue by Nancy Mandlove. Bloomington, Indiana: Third Woman Press, 1985. O.P.

The Margarita Poems. Prologues by Julia Alvarez, Roger Platizky and Carlos Rodríquez. Bloomington, Indiana: Third Woman Press, 1987.

Essays. Forthcoming. Berkeley: Univ. of California, Third Woman Press.

ANTHOLOGIES

"Metapoetic Code in Julia de Burgos' *El mar y tú*." In *In Retrospect: Essays on Latin American Literature*, edited by Elizabeth and Timothy Rogers. S. Carolina: Spanish Literature Publications, 1987.

"The Breaking of Form in Lorraine Sutton's *SAYcred LAYdy*." In *Conversant Essays: Contemporary Poets on Poetry*, edited by James McCorkle. Detroit: Wayne State Univ. Press, 1990.

JOURNAL PUBLICATIONS

"De la protesta a la creación: una nueva visión de la mujer puertorriqueña en la poesía." *Plural* (Puerto Rico), 1984; *Imagine* 2, no. 1 (1985).

"Lesbian Tantalizing in Carmen Lugo Filippi's 'Milagros, Calle Mercurio.' " Nominated for Crompton Noll Award, Modern Languages Association, 1988. Excerpts appeared in *Gay Studies Newsletter* (Toronto). Forthcoming in *Lesbian Studies*, 1991 and *Texto Crítico* (México), 1991.

"Dos textos homosexuales de la novísima literatura puertorriqueña." *Revista Hispanica Pos-naniensia* (Poland) Forthcoming, 1991.

"Out of the Margin, Into the Stream: The Inclusion of Women, Minorities and Gays and Lesbians in the Curriculum." *West Virginia Philological Papers*. Forthcoming, 1992.

ARTICLES, REVIEWS AND INTERVIEWS

Elda Maria Phillips. "Luz María Umpierre-Herrera—Bilingual Poet in Wonderland." *Verbena*, (Washington, D.C.) Fall/Winter 1984.

Interview."Encuentro con Luz María Umpierre." *Línea Plural* (Univ. of Illinois), Spring 1988: 22-25.

Lourdes Torres. "A Passionate Muse." Review of *The Margarita Poems*. *Conditions* 15 (1988): 157-160.

Ana Terri Ortiz. Review. "The generous poetry of Luz María Umpierre and Chrystos." *Gay Community News*, 4-10 September 1988, 7 & 14.

Asunción Horno-Delgado. "Señores, don't leibol mi, please!! ya soy Luz María Umpierre." In *Breaking Boundaries: Latina Writings and Critical Readings*, edited by Asunción Horno-Delgado et al. (Amherst, Mass.: Univ. of Mass. Press, 1989).

Roger Platizky. Review of *...Y otras desgracias/And Other Misfortunes...* *Frontiers* (Colorado) 10, no. 3 (1989): 85-87.

Carlos Rodríquez. Review of *The Margarita Poems*. *Linden Lane Magazine* 9, nos. 1-2 (January-March 1990): 23.

Changing the Focus

DAPHNE MARLATT

Why is anger the first word that comes to mind when you try to talk about your writing now? What does anger have to do with writing?

It can get in the way sometimes, the depth of anger at having my values or my sense of reality — what i feel are the real conditions i write out of — ignored, denied, passed over as unimportant in their specificity. It renders me speechless.

What do you mean by speechless? You're still writing.

It has to do with the difference and hence the inarticulateness of my experience — more recently as a lesbian, earlier as an immigrant — when faced with a dominant system of thought. A kind of vertigo sets in, a sense of having the carpet pulled out from under, of falling without a trace (no, there still is writing) into the reality-version the dominant system represents.

Well, you've described how it feels but can you give me an example of the kind of thing that occasions this anger?

Here's an incident that's very much on my mind. Recently a poet whose work i admire, a feminist i have regarded as a writing companion, published a review she'd written of my novel, *Ana Historic*.[1] I was taken aback when she suggested that the ending of my novel is prescriptive because it ends with the erotic pleasure of a beginning lesbian relationship. This was not the first time i'd heard a heterosexual feminist critic charge a lesbian writer with prescriptiveness. We began a correspondence about it in which i pointed out that the ending is a solution for Annie, the narrator, not a solution for everyone, and that i thought the difference between herself as a heterosexual reader and myself as a lesbian writer needed to be accounted for. She wrote back that she didn't understand why she would need to account for it: "Are those boundaries that defined? That pure? Isn't your labelling somewhat presumptuous? Are we going to place women within a conceptual frame of universal sexual opposition the way we did with men and women?"†

But doesn't she have a point there? Isn't this black and white of binary opposition exactly what we're struggling to move away from?

Yes, there's a crucial need for the dialogic and the non-exclusive, as she says. But that doesn't mean erasing difference. I don't feel we can have a real dialogue without her recognition of my difference as a lesbian. To assume there is no significant difference in the ways we read the world is to assume a false unity. But, and again but, recognizing difference doesn't have to equate with reinforcing opposition. I'm not interested in having lesbian women opposed to straight women, though i *am* interested in our differences as well as in what we share. In fact my novel is about the shift that can happen in a woman who has thought of herself as heterosexual but who discovers that she has entered another space, a marginal space in our culture, where her passionate relationships are with other women. That is where the erotic begins to occur for her and her relationships with men fade into the background. They're there, but they're no longer crucial to her story. There's something

---

†Lola Lemire Tostevin, letter to the author, August 14, 1990. With thanks to Lola for permission to quote. It seems to me that our difference is not so much a personal conflict as it is a symptom of a much larger area of silence and fear between many heterosexual and lesbian women. Misreadings of each other will continue to fracture the feminist movement unless we can begin to speak into the silence, probing our differences as well as what we have in common.

else that's more crucial for her, a realization of the power of another woman as a — we don't really have a word for this relationship — guide, path-breaker rather than competitor, a witness for women's lives — and the reciprocity of this. It's as if Annie has used up the usefulness of identifying with men — this hasn't got her very far in discovering her own presence, especially in the presence of other women. She discovers how crucial it is for her to allow herself to be stirred by women. There's a shift here to re-valuing female intellect, attraction, spirit, empathy, all of which she realizes she has a stake in, even a new understanding of shared uncertainties, doubts, fears. But she goes further, toward desiring a woman close-up, wanting to know her on all levels, even the most intimate. She feels a tremendous curiosity and sense of loyalty to the woman she is drawn to and to other women who share this openness towards what's possible between them. To look at a range of female presence in relation to women rather than in relation to men is not to displace "phallocentrism" with "vulvalogocentrism," as my friend's review suggested, but to change the focus from a male-positive one to a female-positive one.

But how can you expect her, as a heterosexual woman, to read your novel as a lesbian would?

I can't expect her to read the pull of a woman-to-woman erotic in the way a lesbian would. But i can expect her as a feminist to be aware of the power of women guides in our lives — to be interested in this as an aspect of what has been called women's culture. The fear of woman-centredness is a homophobic fear, and it angers me that a feminist can use feminist theory to justify it.

But is it homophobic to be wary of the monologic? Isn't that what she's saying about woman-centredness? That "vulvalogocentrism," to use her word, might be as one-sided as "phallocentrism" in the end?

Given the long history of women's oppression in patriarchal cultures, especially the suppression of women loving women, and the fact that, despite our struggles and subversions, we are still involved in patriarchal cultures on this continent, i don't see how the female term can simply reverse the male term. That's oppositional thinking right there. It's interesting that she gives the "logos" to the vulva and not to the phallos, considering that language is

the area of struggle for us both as women writers. How do you think differently in a language structured by male domination where one term in any comparison has to come out "on top?" White is to black as God is to man (sic) as
man is to woman as het is to lezzie, ad nauseum. Those are a few of the obvious ones, but trying to work our way loose from old habits of thought is a
sticky proposition, especially when we're talking about difference. For instance, it often seems to be difficult for heterosexual women to imagine a lesbian culture, a culture focussed on women rather than, as they see it, a culture without men. Even those with a more feminist awareness still tell their
stories in resistance to men, in distinction from men, yet still want the powerful ear of that necessary other. Such women often unconsciously equate lesbians with sameness, one-sidedness, one/uni, making woman the universal.
So many heterosexual women friends have asked me if i miss the company of
men (as if i were entirely without it!), miss a certain male strength of rational
intellect, a certain saving clarity (saved from women's "sea of emotion"),
etc. Which only goes to show how deep the gendered expectations are. It's
when you look away from men to women that you see the incredible variety of
women, even of the so-called "masculine" attribute in some women, who
aren't "failed" women as heterosexism decrees, but an attractive and diverse
range of marvellously capable women. And in all these differences there is
still something we recognize when *we* say "lesbian."

Aren't you talking identity politics here?

Yes, which i know is considered essentialist in theoretical circles. But a
sense of identity is very important to us exactly because it's so often objected
to, erased or denied in the feminist movement as a whole, and maligned or
oppressed in the mainstream. How can we work for change if we can't name
ourselves collectively? At the same time, we aren't a unified collectivity but
only a loose coalition of women with very different cultural, racial, and class
backgrounds, and very different bodies. When i think about who "i" is, i
don't necessarily think lesbian right away. The context i'm speaking or writing in calls forth how "i" designates herself. This used to puzzle me a great
deal when i was an adolescent. I filled pages of my diary with the question,
"who am i and why am i different with different people?" Coming from an ex-
patriate family with a fairly devout Christian background, i saw this as a
moral issue, as hypocrisy, or not standing up for my family, for my "real beliefs," whatever those were, not understanding then how context constructs

who any of us is. Identity politics is a strategy for any oppressed group, a strategy of selective identity to bring us together rather than keep us dispersed in our silence, our anger, and confusion. Action, political action, calls for a sense of "we." And when it moves into action in writing, a sense of "we" as audience becomes crucial in determining the voice, its sense of intimacy with the reader. This kind of voice creates a space for recog-nitions to jump the gap between reader and writer. It leads to a certain kind of humour, a certain kind of pathos and anger and beauty we recognize as "ours."

But your novel is about a woman who hasn't begun to identify herself as a lesbian yet, or at least she only begins to near the end. Isn't this book more about her gradual re-definition and doesn't this suggest the evolution of a single unified identity?

The problem with writing a novel is that you're always stuck with a narrative line, a line of development, even a minimal one. Or maybe it's just that i haven't learned how to avoid it and still keep the novel moving. Forward motion, "development" in all senses, seems to be such an obsession in North American culture. But there is something fascinating about the movement backwards and forwards in psychic time, back and forth in the senses one has of oneself — only it's more like trying to fit the pieces together rather than leaving behind an outdated version of oneself. The pieces never "add up" to a single version because none of them are outdated — that's just it, they all coexist in whoever "i" is. I could say, looking back, that my writing has always been from a woman's perspective, but a change occurred in its focus, which used to be largely on what men thought and how i stood in relation to that. Then when i began to be aroused by women — aroused on all levels, the intellectual, the erotic, the imaginative, the spiritual, the domestic, all at once — the focus shifted entirely. I've been intrigued by the cultural and political implications of that shift. That's what i was exploring in *Ana Historic*, in the figure of a woman who comes to embrace her love for women at a later age, having experienced marriage and children along the way. When this happens there's such an incredible feeling of familiarity and surprise. As if you've finally embraced something you knew dimly, somewhere, was always a possibility but which you resisted for so long that when it becomes actual it seems to take you, with its sudden eruption in your life — and it is an eruption — by surprise. You ask yourself, what led to this? Why should it feel so familiar? And the movement back and forth begins. I found myself looking back at my own sexual conditioning and my history of intimacy with women, starting with my mother — trying to fit the disparate pieces together. In all the versions of myself, i'd shifted a significant one, a deeply politicizing one, as the fallout in my own life taught me. When family and friends reject you, that tells you less about them than about the power of heterosexist versions of reality. You begin to feel a solidarity with other marginalized peoples. To be a lesbian is to become aware of your difference, no matter how you come to it or whether you've felt you've always been one.

But aren't you still wanting to prescribe a certain kind of reading of your work?

Let's face it, the work goes out into the world and has to speak for itself there. Every reader brings her own sets of conditioning, her own reading identities to a text. So to some extent the argument with the critic is a futile one. Still, you want people to read your work on its own terms. To want this is not so much to prescribe others' readings as to call them to take account of what may be a different cultural context for them. If a reader isn't open to letting another context inform her, then she's not doing much more than travelling through a foreign country expecting to eat at McDonald's.

You began by talking about anger, but in rather negative terms. Do you have anything else to say about it?

Yes, anger is a necessary fuel. The passion in anger drives a lot of feminist and lesbian writing. Given a little distance (as in writing), it can push you to articulate what has been inarticulate. And it seems to me there is certainly something "essential" in this, as in necessary — something you avoid at your own peril. Yet, i'm also aware of the duplicity of writing. On the one hand, there is the seductiveness of language, which holds the potential for saying anything, for constructing anything as "real." And on the other hand, there is what we experience as authenticity (as the author-ity of subjectivity) of the i that writes, full of conflicting and multiple identities as it is. For me it's a lower case i, it isn't monolithic, or massive and solid — it has very permeable boundaries, is on a footing of exchange, sometimes even con-fusion, with lower-case you. And still this i has a sense of her own ground — ethics, politics, history — her own specificity which won't be denied.

NOTES

1. Lola Lemire Tostevin, "Daphne Marlatt: Writing in the Space That is Her Mother's Face." *line* 13 (Spring 1989).

SELECTED PUBLICATIONS

BOOKS

Frames of a Story. Toronto: Ryerson Press, 1968. Out of print.

leaf leaf/s. Los Angeles: Black Sparrow Press, 1969. O.P.

Vancouver Poems. Toronto: Coach House Press, 1972. O.P.

Steveston. Vancouver: Talonbooks, 1974; Edmonton: Longspoon Press, 1984. O.P.

Our Lives. Carrboro, N. Carolina: Truck Press, 1975; Lantzville, Canada: Oolichan Press, 1980. O.P.

Zocalo. Toronto: Coach House Press, 1977. O.P.

What Matters: Writing 1968-70. Toronto: Coach House Press, 1980. O.P.

Net Work: Selected Writing. Vancouver: Talonbooks, 1980.

How Hug a Stone. Winnipeg: Turnstone Press, 1983. O.P.

Touch to My Tongue. Edmonton: Longspoon Press, 1984. O.P.

Ana Historic. Toronto: Coach House Press, 1988.

Salvage. Red Deer, Canada: Red Deer College Press, 1991.

CO-AUTHORED BOOKS

With Nicole Brossard. *Mauve* (bilingual chapbook). Montreal: Nouvelle barre du jour and Writing Presses, 1985. O.P.

With Nicole Brossard. *Character/Jeu de lettres*. Montreal: Nouvelle barre du jour and Writing Presses, 1986. O.P.

With Betsy Warland. *Double Negative*. Charlottetown, Canada: gynergy books, 1988.

EDITED BOOKS

Steveston Recollected: A Japanese-Canadian History. Victoria, Canada: Provincial Archives of B.C., 1975. O.P.

CO-EDITED BOOKS

With Carole Itter. *Opening Doors: Vancouver's East End*. Victoria, Canada: Provincial Archives of B.C., *Sound Heritage* 8, nos. 1-2, 1979. O.P.

With Ann Dybikowski, Victoria Freeman, Barbara Pulling and Betsy Warland. *in the feminine: Women and Words/les femmes et les mots Conference Proceedings 1983*. Edmonton: Longspoon Press, 1985.

With Sky Lee, Lee Maracle and Betsy Warland. *Telling It: Women and Language Across Cultures*. Vancouver: Press Gang Publishers, 1990.

INTERVIEWS

Ellea Wright. "Text and Tissue: Body Language." With Betsy Warland. *Broadside* 6, no. 3 (1984-85): 4-5.

Janice Williamson. "Speaking In and Of Each Other." With Betsy Warland. *Fuse* 8, no. 5 (1985): 25-29.

Eleanor Wachtel. "An Interview with Daphne Marlatt." *Capilano Review* 41 (1986): 4-13.

George Bowering. "On *Ana Historic*." *line* 13 (1989): 96-105.

Janice Williamson. "Sounding a Difference: An Interview with Daphne Marlatt." *line* 13 (1989): 47-56. Also in *Sounding the Difference: Interviews with Canadian Women Writers*, edited by Janice Williamson. Toronto: Univ. of Toronto Press, 1991.

Brenda Carr. "Between Continuity and Difference." In *Beyond Tish*, edited by Douglas Barbour, 99-107. Edmonton and Vancouver: NeWest Press and *West Coast Line*, 1991.

Letter of entente

Lettre d'entente

Translated by Marlene Wildeman

ANNE-MARIE ALONZO

Montreal, the 23rd of August, 19... ,

Galia, dear one,
Today is the anniversary date. She — the one with eyes like sloops — is,
it's now two years ago, gone. i am still here! Still torn apart,
shocked by this wound
as if with a knife.
Split open by this blade.
Subtly put to death.
Do passions die before we do?
Do women really love each other differently?
And the evil which slices us to pieces like this,
where does it come from?

Date. Split-up. Her.
Always.
Don't say her name anymore.
Trying to shut up the her in me, not saying her name anymore.

Scratch out the name, make it
something else, foreign, inert.

Indifferent.

Her absent.
Mortally present.

And you!

A night in Autumn — you — like a cry of alarm.
Parachuted in;
A shout, a voice, a song in fact.

You say: if i don't talk to you, i'll die.
You don't breathe when you say it.
You wait.
Maybe you are dying to wait.
Maybe you are just dying.

You say: poets do not disapprove.

You are sure i am listening to you/hearing you and i am listening,
you're right.

It's a night in October. i am stretched out, almost asleep.
It is around midnight. You telephone, you make the call,
you laugh, you don't know me.

You say: what are you doing, were you sleeping?
You laugh when you say that.
You rouse me, take liberties, make fun of me.
You say: how come you're already asleep?

Why do you phone me, you don't know me.

You say again: . . . poets. . . i don't want to be judged. . .

That night, i would not sleep.

I lay there, tensed, open, i want,
I wait, i go in quest of, i know, i listen, Galia,
I listen, as if with you came salvation, or something resembling it.

That very night, i know that i love you.

That very night, though you call but twice, i love you and
I want you.
But who are you, how is it you come to me, and
What is it you want of me? Love is dead.
There is nothing left to live for and nothing to die for either.

You have been drinking.
Not much, you say.

Your pain is elsewhere. You sigh, you talk,
you read from a page your letter of love,
you have never seen me, you know me better than you know yourself.
And me, you.

Alone together, we wander from your life to mine and back.

Alone together, we look to each other for what will
save us, destroy us, save us or, is it just a dream then
for those who don't dream anymore.

Alone together, Galia, lodged desperately in what is called "love."

We don't know each other, i tell you. Yet
I'm the one you call in October. Me, none other.
Me, woman and/or poet, me before any other.

For this, on this day in October — one year later — i am crying.

You say: talk to me.
Then you are quiet.

You read this page, a letter.
You say: it's a gift.
You don't say from whom.
You say: let's say . . .

You say: you love me.
You say it, sure of yourself.

You know that since that night, since but a few hours, since the
first breath of voice, i love you wholly and completely.

I love you without desire though.

You say: i hate men.
As you would say: i love them.

You say: i love women.
As you would say the opposite.

You want love, Galia, i am not indifferent to that.
You want love at any price.
You want me. You don't want *of* me.

You want a woman's heart, a man's body.

You don't know what you want anymore. You are looking around.
You are in search of something. You are crying.
Sometimes you say: i want a husband.

You are dangerous love.

We are linked, welded, screwed together, only death will part us,
know it.
I slip away though, at times, i drift away.

At times, Galia, your gaze arouses me, at times you die in me.
A welcome death.
You die Galia and your death kills me.

Struck down, nothing will come of me, not a thing.
Who am i for you?
What name do you give me, do you sometimes call me by name?
Do you silently name me love?

Your voice comes courting, Galia, i am reeling,
you are firm in desire, you want me
yours alone. You play at dance and seduction,
you waltz with your heart and i pitch wildly, roll and fall,
at your touch i become shadow.

I give up.
I love you and with desire too.

I feel as if i've been spared. A laughing child, that's you.
You let me be everything for you and
I let you come to life over me, Galia,
for i want you full of life to survive this hope.

You plunge me into despair. Cry-baby, you hesitate.
You let me be everything for you
and i let you die over me, Galia, for i know that you are dying of hope.

At times — late, so i can rock you — i sing laments, chant litanies.

At times i speak Italian to calm you.

And then this rage pulls me from you. I refuse
to listen to you, watch you drive me crazy.
You make my head spin, you disturb me, annoy me.
I do not want then to see or hear you,
nor do i care to know whether you are unhappy or
well or anything at all.

Get out!

May this letter, Galia, make you disappear forever.

Get going, run, vanish but get out of here before i get so
attached to you that i neither
live nor die, spare me.

I no longer have either the strength or the structure
to sustain you. I am weak, small, and alone.
You, you see me otherwise, you see me as you,
such as you would like me to be.
You cheat, fabricate between us what has no right to be there,
what will not be.
You cheat, *amore*.
You lie.
You think we are mad.

You, you.
Kill it!

You wish i were a man so you could seduce me,
you want someone who is not me, yet it is me you plead with.
You say: love me, without words.

It is me you are talking to, Galia.
Me you betray in betraying yourself.

And so then we are going out to eat,
you smile when you see me, your eyes
take me in.
Is there no end to this torture.
I love you.
You no.
          Same to you.
You love me.
And me.
We turn in circles, we speak Chinese just to hear ourselves talk, i
love you, is that not enough, and what do i see in you, i am
past the age for crushes, i am no longer prepared

to see but not touch, touch but not take, take
but not love.

Help me!

Would you kindly tell me who and what you are.

Do you know, or must i guess,
walking on fragile ground not knowing
whether your spirit will smother mine,
whether your body will come to mine,
you want me love, not lover.

How is it i am the only one who sees this?

Women, i swear it, love differently. You cannot love me if
it is a man you are looking for — invisible — in me.
Galia, you do not love me, you want me
as a friend, you need me and i you.

Leave the body dashed   in peace.

Let's make a truce. Look at me, i am not this husband
you want so much,
i am a woman who loves a woman who wants to open her heart to
a man's body.
Look Galia, i love you but without desire.
I love you forever and for all the centuries to come.
I love you, listen to me, with all the love ever known,
love you in new languages and foreign languages,
love you the way you would say:
ti voglio bene; I mean it.

I want you well. . . is that how it's translated?

Is that how it's understood, for my love
you are of the finest silk chosen,
may you be happily joyfully received.

Come, let me embrace you,
my lips open to breathe you in, i cover and envelop
you.
I am yours Galia, you know it.

FOR THE RECORD / Journal de bord

write. write. find a way to change the tone. find a way to say.
add. feel. know. to most of all acknowledge.
this writing is it lesbian? must i absolutely proclaim express
explain
the writing of lesbian reality?
i am not INTO theory.
i don't do (hypo)theses.
i don't prove.
i write to make the reader feel   sense   quiver   tremble.
sometimes i succeed.
and sometimes not.

so there is this text. *Letter of entente*. a fiction.
a heterosexual woman a lesbian woman.
two women to begin with. who love each other.
for love. who love each other, that's all.
and then there is the problem of not finding oneself again. of not
understanding one another. then love is platonic.
the other, Galia, loves a woman's heart and a man's body.
whence the impasse.
and the pain.

i ask the question therefore. where in writing do we touch on
the tragedy of women who are (dis)similar
in their loving, in their sexualities?
can two women with different sexualities have
an affectionate emotional i mean loving relationship
that lasts.
without frustration without pain without bitterness?

just how much can a lesbian woman love another woman without
blossoming into the sexuality inherent in the(ir) process?

Letter of entente is therefore totally fictive.

Fiction tells the story — by letter — of the loving and painful encounter — for
they are different the two women — of all those among us who have loving relationships with heterosexual women who quite candidly and affectionately
embark upon affairs of the heart which tear the body apart without ever
touching it.

SELECTED PUBLICATIONS

BOOKS

Geste. Paris: Des Femmes, 1979.

Veille. Paris: Des Femmes, 1982.

Blanc de thé. Montreal: Les Zéditions élastiques, 1983. Out of print.

Droite et de profil. Montreal: Lèvres urbaines 7, 1984. O.P.

Une lettre rouge orange et ocre. Montreal: La Pleine Lune, 1984.

    German translation by Traude Buhrmann. *Ein Brief Rot Orange Und Ocker*. Forth-
    coming.

Bleus de mine. Saint Lambert, Que.: Le Noroît, 1985.

    English translation by William Donoghue: *Lead Blues*. Montreal: Guernica, 1990.

French conversation. Laval, Que.: Trois, 1986. O.P.

Écoute, Sultane. Montreal: L'Hexagone, 1987.

Seul le désir. Montreal: NBJ, 1987. O.P.

Esmai. Montreal: NBJ, 1987. O.P.

Le Livre des ruptures. Montreal: L'Hexagone, 1988.

L'Immobile. Montreal: l'Hexagone, 1990.

La Vitesse du regard. Laval, Que.: Trois, 1990.

CO-AUTHORED BOOKS

With Denise Desautels and Raymonde April. *Nous en reparlerons sans doute*. Laval, Que.:
    Trois, 1986.

With Dôre Michelut, Charles Douglas, Lee Maracle, Paul Savoie and Ayanna Black. *Linked
    Alive*. Laval, Que: Trois, 1990.

    French translation by Pierrette Laberge-Ferth. *Liens*. Laval, Que.: Trois, 1990.

FORTHCOMING BOOKS

Galia, qu'elle nommait amour. Montreal: L'Hexagone.

Margie Gillie La danse des marches. Montreal: L'Hexagone.

Tout au loin la lumière. Montreal: L'Hexagone.

. . . et la nuit. (poésie).

Mémoires d'une autre: Biographie de Ludmilla Chiriaeff.

Lettres à Cassandre. (with Denise Desautels).

ARTICLES AND REVIEWS

Gloria Escomel. "La Geste." *La Nouvelle Barre du Jour* (Montreal), no. 90/91 (May 1980): 204.

Mona Latif-Ghattas. "A la recherche du geste — image dans la mise en scène de *Veille* d'Anne-Marie Alonzo." *Pratiques Théâtrales*, (Montreal), no. 13 (Fall 1981): 27-32.

Ginette Michaud. "*Veille*/Anne-Marie Alonzo." *Jeu (cahiers de théâtre)* 4, no. 21 (Winter 1981): 189-93.

Alain Laframboise. "Vigile" (essay on *Veille* and *Geste*). *La Nouvelle Barre du Jour* (Montreal), no. 109 (January 1982).

Richard Boutin. "A quelle adresse?" Review of *Geste* and *Veille*. *La Nouvelle Barre du Jour*, no. 129 (September 1983).

Claude Beausoleil. "La parole comme un geste." Review of *Geste, Veille* and *Droite et de profil*. In *Les Livres parlent*. Trois-Rivières, Que.: Ecrits des Forges, 1984.

Louise Dupré. "Poetry Returns to Love." Review of *Ecoute, Sultane* and *Seul le desir*. *Ellipse* (Sherbrooke, Que.), no. 39: 4-23.

Original French version: "Quand la nouvelle poésie devient amoureuse." *Trois* (Laval) 4, no. 2: 19-24.

SOUND RECORDINGS

With Denise Desautels. *Lettres à Cassandre* (audio cassette).Laval, Que: A.M.A. Productions, 1990.

Fuck You and the Horse You Rode In On

ANNE CAMERON

I was doing a series of Canada Council sponsored readings in Haida Gwaii and a young woman came up to tell me she had enjoyed "most" of my feminist western novel *The Journey*. But not all of it. She objected to the ending, when Anne and Sarah realize they truly love each other... and do something about it. She was, she said, sick and tired of reading stories about strong women who turn out to be lesbians. Sick and tired, she insisted, because there are so few stories about truly strong women, and when you finally find one, the writer turns around at the end and makes those women lesbians, and not "just ordinary women." What's more, she added very defiantly, my husband agrees with me.

I resisted the impulse to say I was glad he agreed with her because they do tend to get shirty if they don't agree. Instead I suggested it was hardly fair of her to go at me for writing about lesbians; better to put her energy into trying to change the BS put out by all those other writers who depict non-lesbian women as a bunch of wimps. I suggested to her that a writer cannot in all fairness be expected to present everyone's vision of the world in each story and that I felt no obligation to even try. As we talked her face registered the realization. "But you have children!" she blurted.

"Yes," I laughed, not at her but at the mind-set her conditioned response exposed. We're supposed to be some sterile form of inverted weirdness, not the same at all as ordinary women, normal women . . . and I haven't managed to figure out, yet, whether my children and grandchildren "prove" I am "not really" a lesbian, or whether my dyke identity is considered a temporary side-path on my road of life and I am expected to wake up tomorrow and get back on the highway. In which case, I suspect, I will be forgiven this lapse of good taste because, after all, isn't a writer supposed to experience life as fully as possible, then process everything for the jamtarts who didn't dare step permanently out of line?

I suspect I have also given them something else to get their shirts in a knot about, something almost as bad as lesbian identity, but much easier to discuss and tsk tsk tsk about in disapproval: my chosen vocabulary. One reviewer recently felt herself absolutely obliged to mention my "pithy prose" and as an example, dredged up "cow cack." She was stretching points and trying to find a way to equate my work to that of Lucy Maud Montgomery. Rather than dare take a look at Lucy Maud's private opinion of marital relations, she hit on the fact we both lived in small towns on or near the sea, and wrote about the places where we had chosen to live. Lucy Maud, she suggested, would never have written "cow cack." And usually I wouldn't either. I would, most of the time, be more apt to just come out and say or write "bullshit."

I received a letter from a nice lady chiding me for cursing and suggesting this only gave my detractors, such as Real Women, ammunition to use against me. I admit, I do it on purpose. And when, occasionally, someone calls me on it I suggest they would be much better off to use their time and energy to protest the mentality which not only uses but condones such disgusting obscenities as the terms "peaceful weapon" or "survivable nuclear war." Until those foul terms are challenged, don't give me any static about "bullshit" or "fuck!"

Mostly, nobody seems prepared to mention in a review that I am a dyke who has not tried to hide the fact. I knew, at the same time as I realized who I really was intended to be, that I could not write and live in the closet. For me writing is a deliberate giving over of Self, and I find it physically impossible to write something I know to be a lie. I also knew my work would wind up being marginalized and basically ignored by what passes itself off as the literary establishment in this country. Look in Mel Hurtig's many-volumed The Canadian Encyclopedia of who's who and who thinks who's who and you won't find my name or any list of my publications. It would lead a tender soul to suspect Mel doesn't like me and yet he has never met me. Male writers with one or two publications are listed, non-lesbian writers with fewer books sold are mentioned but. . . not the mother-grandmother-dyke-who-curses.

Earth Witch, I am told, has sold more copies than any other book of Canadian poetry, and *The Annie Poems* promises to continue to sell well. *Dreamspeaker* has won awards as both a work of fiction and as a film. Every year we hear the hoopla about the B.C. Book Awards and so far the Awards have managed to overlook my work.

Now, it might well be that my work is shit; a lot of shit gets published. Why would I dare think of my work as not being as crappy as some of that other stuff? In which case a lot of readers are spending hard-earned money to buy shit. But, as my schizophrenic and alcoholic uncle used to say "I know what I know." And I know there is a very influential group of self-appointed nice people out there who work overtime at trying to ignore me, my work and what I have to say. And that's fine; I've decided to take a decidedly Vancouver Island view of the entire non-issue and ignore them before they get the chance to ignore me.

There's a huge freedom in that. It means they can have their Twinkie awards and I don't have to put any energy into it. They can write their reviews or not write them and the net result, for me, will be the same. A reviewer from Victoria, for example, exposed her lack of research by writing recently that *Dreamspeaker* was the story of a native youth alienated from his culture. Bullshit. Peter is clearly described as being blond-haired, fair-skinned, with green eyes. How can anyone have any respect for the opinion of a reviewer who makes that kind of stupid mistake? If she didn't read any of the other books she felt free to criticize any more thoroughly than she read that book, how valid is any criticism she feels free to make?

Every now and again a reviewer or critic writes of the humour inherent in the situations in which my admittedly off-beat characters find themselves. Well, here you have more proof that I can't possibly be a REAL dyke; everyone knows we are a humourless bunch — why none of us has been seen laughing at a woman-driver joke in years. And if people laugh when they read my work doesn't that prove it isn't lesbian writing?

When I was first approached about this collection I was puzzled, spent several days talking with friends, some of whom are and some of whom aren't lesbian. I realized again that I am not an analytic or academic person and I respond most often from the heart and gut, not from the head. I never did expect to be considered another Dickens or Thackeray; I did not plan to become another Margaret Laurence; and while I cut my teeth on Lucy Maud, I do not think my work will survive as well as hers continues to survive. I am often asked if my work is "autobiographical" and of course it is. Of course it isn't. Of course it might be. Of course it might not be.

And what does it matter? Whether it is or isn't won't cut ice with the arsletarts who sit on awards juries of one sort or another and decide who is and is not a "minor" writer; what is and is not important; who does and does not accurately reflect some segment or other of Canadian thought. Directly or indirectly those followers of the big patristic I-Am have been conditioned, educated, and even funded by those pillars of society who are also the bulwarks of the patriarchy, and I am the one not only born beyond the pale, but who has never been willing to move up the social ladder to join them. So I am doubly ignored. My environmental work criticizes and curses the major corporations; my political work is aimed at destroying the oppression of the least protected; and my personal life is little more than an upraised finger in the face of the penis-worshippers. So the more their interests are vested in the Philistines who would poison our home planet, the more they have to either trivialize or ignore me and my work. It's a couth version of "ignore it and maybe it'll go away."

Well, I won't. And that is where being a dyke does definitely influence my work and life. Those who ignore us and try to trivialize our work, negate our influence, and poison our own family and friends against us are the inheritors of the same disgusting shit which for centuries tortured us for the greater glory of their Prince of Peace. They are the legatees of what was left after twelve million of us were turned to ashes at the witch fires. Women no different than myself were slaughtered by men and women no different than the ones who today continue to try to pretend either we don't exist or that we are only some kind of exotic freak show.

A non-lesbian writer might be able to convince herself there were reasons to make herself and her work more "acceptable" to the mainstream, but a dyke writer knows in the marrow of her bones their applause only hides their own hidden agenda.

It is the mainstream who profits most if there is no disclosure of what is really going on in a society in which arguably 80% of our children are sexually assaulted and possibly 8 to 10% of them attempt or achieve suicide. They support and are in turn supported by a racist, sexist and classist academia which is little more than a sausage factory, taking in fresh, young raw meat full of promise and grinding it down until what comes out the other end are clones of the system. Those who destroy our forests, poison our water, sell alcohol to kill our spirits and allow famine to claim the lives of the helpless while destroying what they will insist on calling "surplus" food, pick up the tab, sit on the boards of directors, own the newspapers in which horse-puckies get passed off as literary criticism, and pay the salaries of those who discount lesbian reality as being peripheral.

And when I sit down to write I know that. I know it and know they can only have an influence over me if I allow them. There is a giving over, but not to them. I open myself to spirits, but not to theirs. And over my windowsill they come, the charred dykes of the BeforeTime, telling their stories, and easing my own fear and pain. They urge me, these our dyke foremothers, to disclose, to listen to what women all around me are struggling to say, to give credence to and take heed of what is truly real. They give me energy, they give me love, they give me courage, they tell me that the ones who ignore the rape of babies have become too suave and too slick to dare build public bonfires today, and so have to creep around like ferrets, finding other ways to try to erase what they cannot allow themselves to look at and see.

By our very existence we prove they failed. By our very existence we demonstrate that not all the hatred in the world can wipe us from the face of the earth. We are the living proof that we were, we still are, and we always will be unimpressed with the patriarchy. We are the ones who, by just breathing in and out and putting our words on paper defy those who would control and ultimately destroy this beautiful home. All we have to do is keep suckin'er in and blowin'er out and we help defeat them. And they can ignore us, negate us, mock us, or censor us, but they cannot silence us.

Some days they do get to me; I'd be a liar if I suggested otherwise. On those days, when I am feeling bummed out or tired, those scarred and charred old dykes come over the windowsill and cavort, naked, on my desktop. They tell terrible jokes, sing bawdy songs and back-room melodies, and chant loudly "fuck 'em all and the horses they rode in on."

SELECTED PUBLICATIONS

BOOKS

Dreamspeaker (fiction). As Cam Hubert. Toronto: Clarke-Irwin, 1978; New York and Toronto: Avon Books, 1978; Toronto: General Publishing, 1989.

Daughters of Copper Woman (fiction). Vancouver: Press Gang Publishers, 1981.
    U.K. edition. London: The Women's Press Ltd., 1984.

Earth Witch (poetry). Madiera Park, Canada: Harbour Publishing, 1982.

The Journey (fiction). New York: Avon Books, 1982; San Francisco: Spinsters, Ink, 1986; Madiera Park: Harbour Publishing, 1983.

Dzelarhons (fiction). Harbour Publishing, 1986.

Child of Her People (fiction). San Francisco: Spinsters/Aunt Lute, 1987; Madiera Park: Harbour Publishing, 1988.

The Annie Poems (poetry). Harbour Publishing, 1988.

Stubby Amberchuck and the Holy Grail (fiction). Harbour Publishing, 1988.

Women, Kids and Huckleberry Wine (fiction). Harbour Publishing, 1989.

Tales of the Cairds (fiction). Harbour Publishing, 1989.

South of an Unnamed Creek (fiction). Harbour Publishing, 1989.

Brights Crossing (fiction). Harbour Publishing, 1990.

Escape to Beulah (fiction). Harbour Publishing, 1990.

Kick the Can (fiction). Harbour Publishing, 1991.

. . . *A Whole Brass Band* (fiction). Forthcoming. Harbour Publishing, 1991.

CHILDREN'S BOOKS

How Raven Freed the Moon, illustrated by Tara Miller. Harbour Publishing, 1985.

How the Loon Lost Her Voice, illustrated by Tara Miller. Harbour Publishing, 1985.

Raven Returns the Water, illustrated by Nelle Olsen. Harbour Publishing, 1987.

Orca's Song, illustrated by Nelle Olsen. Harbour Publishing, 1987.

Lazy Boy, illustrated by Nelle Olsen. Harbour Publishing, 1988.

Spider Woman, illustrated by Nelle Olsen. Harbour Publishing, 1988.

Raven and Snipe, illustrated by Gaye Hammond. Harbour Publishing, 1991.

Raven Goes Berrypicking, illustrated by Gaye Hammond. Harbour Publishing, 1991.

DRAMA, TELEVISION AND FILM SCRIPTS

Windigo. Stage adaptation of a documentary poem, 1972. Winner, 1973 British Columbia Centennial Drama Competition.

We're All Here Except Mike Casey's Horse. New Play Centre, Vancouver, 1974.

Dreamspeaker. Canadian Broadcasting Corporation feature-length drama special, 1979. Ralph Thomas, producer. Claude Jutra, director.

Emily of New Moon. CBC television drama, "Magic Lies" series, 1978. Beverly Roberts, producer. Stephen Katz, director.

A Matter of Choice. CBC television drama, "For the Record" series, 1979. Anne Frank, producer. Frances Mankiewicz, director.

The Tin Flute. Five-part television adaptation of Gabrielle Roy's novel, 1980.

Ticket to Heaven. Feature film, co-written with Ralph Thomas, 1981. Ron Cohen, producer. Ralph Thomas, director.

Halfbreed. Feature-length drama adaptation of Maria Campbell's novel, for Four Nine Film Productions and the CBC, 1984. Maxine Samuels, producer.

History of the Métis. Drama for the National Film Board's "Daughters of the Country" series, 1985. Barbara Eino, producer.

Cantata: The Story of Sylvia Stark. A two-act play produced by the Montreal Playwrights Workshop and the Black Actors Workshop, 1989.

III

Site Reading

The Ex-patriot and Her Name

ELANA DYKEWOMON

But in being faceless unmentionable nameless lesbians... in being unable to find catch words in newspapers or the books we read in our dormitories, for that, for what that meant, women loving women — in that we could have no fads. That was where some of us began our resistance, learned to change... who we thought we were doomed to be into who we are. Tough, strong, proud: free women.[1]

N ames define reality. As soon as I heard the word "lesbian" I knew I was one. As soon as I grasped that people could call themselves writers, I started calling myself a poet. In 1975 I changed my name from Nachman to Dykewomon, and started publishing for womyn only.[2]

These are difficult realities. I struggle with the sense of isolation my choices contain while living a full (crowded) life in a field of extraordinary and loving dykes. I admire, learn from, talk to, engage with many other lesbian writers at the same time that I feel typed as the "lunatic fringe" for wanting lesbians to cast their lot (material as well as emotional) with other lesbians. The tension between my present realities — the misunderstood,

cranky, exiled writer vs. the active, happy cultural worker enfolded in her
community — gnaws at me.

> We were standing there sharpening the axes that would bring down our father's
> trees. We were pulling our mothers from their houses, we were talking to each
> other, we were devising witch dances where all the women of all the races and all
> the classes were going to dance in the cleared spaces hidden in the New England
> trees, we were going to teach each other all the steps and movements of the supple
> belly and the ways to use our breasts and many were coming together, and the
> axes were taken from us. How?[3]

It's the sensation of ineffectiveness that's the most frustrating. Like the
generations before us, when we were in our twenties we thought we were going to change the world. Unlike the generations before us, we also thought we
were going to change the word — that changing the word would be our instrument for changing the world. We were going to change the word "woman."
From woman to women, from women to womyn (wimmin), from womyn to
lesbian, from lesbian to dyke to amazon, from outsider to compañera, from
competitor to sister. We worked hard, we had some success (perhaps we
never agreed to go far enough, to disappear words like "marriage" and
suspend the use of the word "love."†

I believe the individual lives of many womyn and lesbians have been
changed by what I and other lesbians (of all political persuasions) have
done, but it's hard to see where the aggregate effect of that work exists in the
world. And our new words, where they still survive, when they can't be co-
opted, have often been diminished to "side-issues" or to cute/eccentric personal preferences.

————

I was locked up in 1962 at the age of thirteen — a queer, fat, suicidal

---

† "Why 'love' when lesbians are trying to reclaim it for ourselves?" my friend SJ asks me.
"Think how we might feel about each other if we didn't always have to call it by the same word
that's in every song on the radio, and couldn't say 'I love red sneakers' or 'I just love a good cry.'
We might find other directions for our thoughts, new ways to act towards each other," I say.
"Alright," she says, "but womyn aren't going to know what you mean."

child. I looked around the wards. I could only think of one way to transcend a life that offered either marriage or chronic institutionalization: to be a writer. Writers, I thought, might not have to be "women," are not necessarily "sane."[4]

But by the time I was in my twenties, I was grieved by my doubt that a Jewish lesbian could ever be taken seriously by the *New York Times Book Review*. I must have been twenty-five or twenty-six when my novel, *Riverfinger Women*, was published by Daughters, Inc., one of the first feminist/lesbian publishing houses. Daughters took out a full page ad in the *New York Times Book Review*, in which only the description of *Riverfinger Women* contained the word "lesbian," despite *Rubyfruit Jungle*'s appearance in the same ad. I decided if I could make it into the *Times* that way, it was too easy. So I changed my name to Dykewomon.

Why I really changed my name to Dykewomon: it was the mid-'70s, everyone was changing their names, I liked my first name fine, but my last name connected me too directly to the long male Hasidic tradition, to a huge extended patriarchal first-generation U.S. Jewish family from which I wanted out.†

And I was afraid of something. I was knee-deep in the hustle writers play, waist-deep in ego. Under the pseudonym s.p. wonder, my poems were getting published in various alternative and college magazines. I knew a small group of avant-garde writers and gay guys in the arts who knew others, who had connections in New York. A couple of straight men in a small Berkshire, Mass. press wanted to publish a book of my poems. I was living on Rainbow Grease Farm with straight people who loved me, who lent me their landrover to go to Northampton where I found the women's movement and later, when I was living with lesbians, co-founded Lesbian Gardens (a lesbian-only loft space that was a political and cultural focal point in the mid-'70s).

Somewhere in the midst of the anti-war, civil rights, women's and lesbian movements, I started to question the value of identifying as "the outsider." Of course these movements provided a cultural space where, for the first time in my life, I didn't *have* to be an outsider. I began to feel that "being a writer" was removed from daily life, from the ordinary and essential life of womyn, in a hollow and destructive way. You either had to choose a set of values tied to

---

† If I had it to do over again, I would choose a name more easily identified as Jewish.

male institutions — academia and capitalist publishing — or you had to choose community. If you wanted to get reviewed in the *New York Times* you had to write *for* the *New York Times*. No two ways about it — you'd have to cozy up to their perspectives, their understanding of vital writing (almost always translated as virile writing).

> I lay in bed next to a woman who was going away from me, to live in Israel. I said. The only thing left for me is to become famous. She was revolted. She turned from me in bed. Certainly when everyone turns from you in bed there is only one thing left to do. That is to become famous.[5]

The pursuit of that recognition struck me first as the pursuit of privilege and second, as the pursuit of male approval. So I changed my name, hoping to keep myself honest. I changed my name so I would be in a constant state of self-examination about my motives in writing; so I would have to write as a member of the community in which I placed my heart and cunt, as a participant with a specific talent.

I have an analysis of capitalism (how it crushes us), of what happens when writers enter a male market economy, of sexual and racial politics — who gets to speak and for whom and when and why. I have an analysis of ego as motivation, and I long for my motivations to be somehow divorced from my ego. After all, I have a state-made ego, that north american sense of individual entitlement: I could win the lottery, I could be rich and famous, I could have a best-seller. I long to never wish again for a best-seller; I hope to be able to write for another twenty or forty years but I have little hope of being able to support myself as a writer.

Writing may be a question of what you name yourself, but publishing is a social contract. Wanting to publish for womyn or lesbians only, for instance, is a violation of our common beliefs about the social contract between writer and audience. The most commonly held belief is that the printed word no longer "belongs" to the writer, but to the "public," to "the ages." The writer who believes that controlling context is as important and political as content is considered by many as foolishly utopian at best, more often, as a self-important scold.

Wanting to publish for womyn-only and read for lesbians-only, my intentions are threefold:

• to give, open-heartedly as I can, the gift of attention. Writing and reading aloud are the most intimate things I do in life, after making love. I want that intimacy to carry over, I want to always write with my whole body, my full mind; I want to live in a lesbian context where we expect that from each other. Wanting to have that context means wanting to create it, to live in the creative process of encouraging lesbians to attend to each other.

• to insist that we have communications we need to protect, that we may be endangered individually and collectively when men read what we write; and that we undermine our strength when we disguise our messages so we will be safe if men do read them.

• to encourage lesbian network building, to encourage lesbians to understand that we need each other for economic as well as cultural survival, that we need to buy from and trade with each other to create a lesbian economic power base.

Those intentions haven't changed. I want to keep making those choices, yet it often feels like saying: I choose to walk the streets of a lesbian village on the moon—they're choices without a real location. If, for instance, you studied to be a carpenter in order to build homes and communal structures in lesbian villages, only to find there are no lesbian villages being built, you must still work, and find ways to make your work meaningful to you.

I struggle with this—I make compromises. I stop insisting that the books I'm published in be for women only. I allow, with discomfort, that my work be included in anthologies published by some small heterosexually-owned presses (like Crossing or Beacon). I edit *Sinister Wisdom* knowing that some men read it (although I did delete the guy whose address was the state department). I don't always require that readings I do be advertised as "for lesbians only," though I continue to insist on reading to womyn-only audiences.

> We were delighted to speak of passion and hatred. We went on forever, looking into it, trying to lay new plans, finding ways we could use our passion and hatred as strengths, tools, shields, spears, and not get garroted with them, as we have in the past. As passion dims, resolve must stay.[6]

Certainly I want my work to move and reach as many lesbians as it can. The great lesbian network of the '70s never really exercised its potential economic power. Most lesbians don't seem willing to buy books or journals marked "for womyn only" (where *Riverfinger Women* sold over 13,000 copies in three years, it took eight years to sell 3,000 copies of *They Will Know Me By My Teeth*, marked "womyn-only," to the same audience). Women's bookstores usually don't want to deal with womyn-only books. Most other writers think writing "for women only" cuts you off not only from the possibility of livelihood† but from your intended audience and "the real world."

I live every day in "the real world" — I've made my living as a secretary, administrative assistant, printer, typesetter. When I am able to work for lesbians it's a wonderful thing — not a privilege or a luxury, but a rare essential — that which gives my life substance and meaning.

Right now I work four days a week, eight months a year as a typesetter, and between fifteen and forty hours a week on *Sinister Wisdom*. I have friends and a lover, I try to keep writing. It would be a lot easier to keep writing and editing if 1,000 (only 1,000) more lesbians subscribed to *Sinister Wisdom*. Not just because I could quit being a typesetter, but because it would create more resources, more hope. I want to see lesbians continue the conversations we start at music festivals and conferences, more lesbians engaged in creating lesbian space.

> think of all the implications
> remember to be a comparative shopper
> we dont have enough money for guns
> we dont have enough money for printing presses
> no cash for parks, for children
> dont go to the movies
> give us your money
> dont publish with macmillan
> give us your money
>
> What can we ask from each other[7]

Lesbian and womyn's space has always been difficult to get, harder to

---

†I can only think of five or six lesbians alive who have (maybe) lived for as much as a year from having their own out-lesbian work (not anthologies) published. But livelihood as a writer includes being able to get a job teaching, getting speaking engagements, writing book reviews and other magazine pieces, getting grants and acceptances at writers' colonies. All of these things depend, to some degree, at some point, on being able to please a man, to turn your attention to men and to include men in your social and political framework. To want to work only for womyn (here I don't mean publishing only for/with womyn, but simply wanting all your creative attention and effort to be directed towards womyn — let alone lesbians) means you are effec-

maintain, always subject to intense questioning. The "humanist" trend of the '80s continues to enforce heterosexual values even in queer nation, where the unwritten rule is boys and girls have to play together as if we are all equals now, and the subordinate must not question the values of the dominant; must not, in fact, let on they realize that dominant groups still exist. For instance, early in 1990, *Out/Look* magazine staged a lesbian and gay writers conference in San Francisco and invited me to speak on a panel. I declined when I found out there would be no lesbian/womon-only space *allowed* at the conference ("You can caucus in a restaurant if you want," one organizer said). It's incredibly frustrating to be back at square one; to have to say again: womyn have different experiences in life than men; lesbians have different experiences than gay men; we have different concerns and whole other languages that come from our differences, and we need our own spaces to (at least) consolidate our own political power and develop/explore our sense of identity.

We need our own senses of identity. We lesbians, we do. We need our own racial/cultural affinity groups in which to develop trust, culture, identity, language, economic and psychological survival strategy. Latina/Chicana, African, Native, Asian, Jewish, ethnic, working class, fat, old, young, disabled dykes need our own groups. Then we need larger groups — lesbian conferences, lesbian buildings, health care, monetary systems, agriculture, publishing — in which to work together, learn from each other, have a base from which we can do anything that strikes us as important in life. Without our own bases, we will always get co-opted. Capitalism seduces us from the Right, humanism seduces us from the Left. It makes sense to me that we should want to control the context of our work/communities as well as their content. To start with "your own" and

---

tively stopped from making a living in any of these ways. The interesting thing is that this desire,to want to put all your most intimate, thoughtful and loving energy into womyn, has been so suspect among lesbians. As if admitting to that desire constituted a threat to understanding the dynamics of race and class; as if one (or fifty) lesbians having that desire threatened the whole fabric of coalition politics. There must be millions of men (including "radical" and "sensitive" men) who go through life doing everything they do for the benefit of themselves and other men, and if a woman should benefit it's incidental. But that a lesbian should want to make a living working for and with lesbians somehow threatens the whole structure of society from the Right to the radical Left; and consequently, rarely happens.

move outwards is to have a wide vision grounded in self-respect.†

In the real world, I've made choices I can live with, that I'm glad to keep making. Writing for womyn and lesbians is a clear, political and pleasurable choice. What's hard in my choice is (only) what was hard twenty years ago: the world is so geared towards men we often don't notice what we lack in terms of attention. But lesbians keep talking to each other, keep changing each other's lives and minds. Sometimes I look at the immensity of the forces ranged against us and am amazed at our persistence. We keep coming back to each other with new words and fresh juice.

I complain, but the more I think about what I'm doing in life, as a lesbian and a writer, the happier I feel. I want to share this happiness. I'm lucky to be in this struggle, listening to what other lesbians say and write, re-evaluating my own motives and analyses. I am full of experience and reflection, of questions and answers, of work to do.

Sometimes when I'm alone at night, I look at my bookshelves, the piles of my and other lesbians' manuscripts that live in my rooms, and I have the sensation of being rocked in the hammock of lesbian words. The difficulties, the pleasures, the endless arguments and conversation, the voices of womyn who have died and young dykes just starting, becomes a humming that infuses me with wonder and satisfaction. And there's always the possibility that our words are working out there:

> i thought i saw for a second a letter from the other alphabet. . . the one i secretly dream i am participating in making. . . one flaming new letter. . . all of us who make the new letters from the language of our lives, from the honesty, howl and longing that rise up from us — we will recognize these letters instantly — begin to be able to communicate with them — in a language which, when it is drawn, changes the mind, and when it is spoken, changes the world.[8]

---

†I realize lesbians are often faced with difficult decisions in defining who, exactly, is "their own," and I don't mean to minimize the potential pain in our choices. I do think that the more choices we have and validate for each other, the more connection between us is possible.

NOTES

See Publications List for complete sources.

1. *Riverfinger Women*, 15-16.
2. In the late '60s I started getting published in college journals and the straight alternative press. Since 1974 I have published in the feminist and lesbian press (see Publications List). Since 1987, I've been the editor of *Sinister Wisdom*, a journal for the lesbian imagination in the arts and politics, founded in 1976.
3. "They Will Know Me By My Teeth," *They Will Know Me By My Teeth*, 48.
4. For both theoretical and personal reflections on this experience, see "Surviving Psychiatric Assault & Creating Emotional Well-Being in Our Communities," *Sinister Wisdom* #36 (Winter 1988/89).
5. "Certain Scarcities," *They Will Know Me By My Teeth*, 13.
6. "They Will Know Me By My Teeth," op. cit., 46.
7. "What Can I Ask," *They Will Know Me By My Teeth*, 63.
8. "Journal Entry," *For Lesbians Only: A Separatist Anthology*, 548.

SELECTED PUBLICATIONS

BOOKS

Riverfinger Women (novel). As Elana Nachman. Plainfield, Vermont: Daughters, Inc., 1974; re-issue forthcoming, with a new Afterword. Tallahassee, Fla.: Naiad Press, 1992.
    German translation by Irmtraut Rüber and Karin Wilms: *Frauen aus dem Fluss*. West Berlin: Amazonen Frauenverlag, 1977.

They Will Know Me By My Teeth (short stories and poetry). Northampton, Mass.: Megaera Press, 1976. Available only from the author at P.O. Box 3252, Berkeley, CA 94703, USA.

Fragments from Lesbos (poetry). Langlois, Oreg.: Diaspora Distribution, 1981. Out of print.

EDITED JOURNAL

Sinister Wisdom: A Journal for the Lesbian Imagination in the Arts and Politics. Berkeley, Calif.: 1987-present (issues 33-44 +).

ANTHOLOGIES

"The Fourth Daughter's 400 Questions" (essay) and "Fifteen Minutes from the KKK" (poem). In *Nice Jewish Girls: A Lesbian Anthology*, edited by Evelyn Torton Beck. Boston: Beacon Press, 1982, 1989.

"learning to breathe" (poem) and "Traveling Fat" (essay). In *Shadow on a Tightrope: Writings by Women on Fat Oppression*, edited by Lisa Schoenfielder and Barb Wieser. San Francisco: Aunt Lute Books, 1983, 1990.

"Manna from Heaven" (short story). In *The Tribe of Dina: A Jewish Women's Anthology*, edited by Melanie Kaye/Kantrowitz and Irena Klepfisz. Montpelier, Vermont: Sinister Wisdom Books, 1986; Boston: Beacon Press, 1989.

"Journal Entry." In *For Lesbians Only: A Separatist Anthology*, edited by Sarah Lucia Hoagland and Julia Penelope. London: Onlywomen Press, 1988.

"I had a dream" and "Even My Eyes Become Mouths." In *Naming the Waves: Contemporary Lesbian Poetry*, edited by Christian McEwen. London: Virago Press, 1988; Freedom, Calif.: The Crossing Press, 1990.

"My Grandmother's Plates." In *Speaking for Ourselves: Short Stories by Jewish Lesbians*, edited by Irene Zahava. Freedom, Calif.: The Crossing Press, 1990.

JOURNAL PUBLICATIONS

"The Mezzuzah Maker" (short story). *Common Lives/Lesbian Lives* 8 (1983): 93-98.

"the real fat womon poems." *Sinister Wisdom*, no. 33 (1987): 85-93.

"On Passing." *Sinister Wisdom*, no. 35 (Summer/Fall 1988).

"Surviving Psychiatric Assault & Creating Emotional Well-Being in Our Communities." *Sinister Wisdom*, no. 36 (Winter 1988/89).

"Lesbian Theory and Social Organization: The Knots of Process" (paper delivered at National Women's Studies Conference, 1988). *Sinister Wisdom*, no. 37 (1989): 29-34.

INTERVIEWS

Louise Turcotte. "Entrevue avec Elana Dykewomon." *Amazones d'hier: Lesbiennes d'aujourd'hui* (French/English), no. 21 (1990): 36-54.

Suzette Triton et al. "Elana Dykewomon, L'Espoir radical." *Lesbia* (Paris), no. 88 (November 1990): 28-31.

SOUND RECORDINGS

Poetry reading. On *Dyke Proud: A Lesbian Poetry Reading from the 3rd International Feminist Book Fair in Montreal* (audio cassette). Montreal: Annor Productions, 1988.

Taking Risks

Becoming a Writer as a Lesbian†

JUDITH McDANIEL

It is ironic. Sanctuary is about living dangerously. Sanctuary is about taking risks beyond the ordinary. Risks of class security or race security. Risks of the heart. Physical risks. I have never in my life felt as secure in myself as during those twenty-nine hours of captivity on the Rio San Juan. I knew well I might be killed. But I also knew more clearly than I had ever known before that I was in the right place. I was in the right place in that jungle and I was in the right place in myself. Taking the risk allowed me to be the person I had always wanted to be.

from *Sanctuary: A Journey*

I wrote that paragraph after my return from a trip to Nicaragua in 1985 — a trip during which my Witness for Peace delegation had been fired on by U.S.-backed Contras, held in the jungle of Costa Rica for twenty-nine hours,

---

†This text was originally published in *The American Voice*, 17 (Winter 1989).

and then released to a chorus of disbelief from the U.S. State Department officials who suggested we had kidnapped ourselves. I gave talks all over the country on my return to counter that lie, including one for the Gay Women's Alternative in New York City titled, "What's a Nice Lesbian Like You Doing Down Here in the Jungle?" It was a question I had indeed asked myself as I prepared for the trip, while I was a captive being marched at gunpoint through knee-deep jungle mud, and as I tried to understand the full range of implications the trip, capture, and release had for me both personally and politically.

Taking risks, however they are defined, was not something new to me in Nicaragua. In fact, I believe I became a serious writer when the risks I was taking in my life — risks like being "out" as a lesbian in my academic teaching job — began to have real consequences in my life and art; and when the risks I was taking in my art — like writing about a lesbian relationship as though it were the norm — began to have real consequences in my life.

Taking risks, it has been suggested to me, is a literary cliché, the stuff of undergraduate poetry workshops. Or, I've been told, taking risks is what those early feminists did in the sixties and seventies, and our job now is not to take risks, but to consolidate our access into the system. But I am convinced that we need to continue the discussion of risks, perhaps reminding ourselves now and then that the original meaning of risk was "danger and loss." The risks I refer to are the risks that lead to a profound change in our landscape, both the emotional landscape of our lives and the physically present landscape.

I began writing poetry seriously in 1975, the same year I affirmed, both publicly and privately, my lesbian identity. I *didn't* change the pronouns in my poetry, didn't try to pretend the "you" in my love poems was other than my woman lover. Being out as a lesbian gave me the assertive energy I needed to do the writing that had been hiding in me since childhood. Nothing in me wanted to deny my lesbian reality. Quite the contrary. In my first few poems, that was all I wanted to say: Hooray, I love a woman, I am loved by a woman, I feel wonderful about my life.

And for the first few years I wrote poetry, I felt generally supported. I was, after all, a novice and didn't expect notices about my work in the usual straight literary journals. I read my poems a couple of times, attended by faithful, but honest friends who gave me feedback I needed. A new lesbian journal, *Sinister Wisdom*, published two of my first poems in 1976. Other poems and publications came slowly; I was primarily a college professor, teaching other people's literature, and it was nearly seven years before I had enough poems I was pleased with to consider publishing a chapbook.

Even then, I thought myself fortunate. A local arts group was starting a publishing venture and offered to publish my first chapbook, *November Woman*. They received a small grant from the Arts Council and began the process. Just before we went to press, they asked me to come for an editorial conference. One poem, they felt, didn't fit, wasn't as good as the others, was off tone.

"Acadia" was, of course, the only explicitly lesbian and sexual poem in this collection, a poem that today seems to me almost obscure in its lesbian references. The sea and the landscape are the obvious metaphors, standing in for more specific sexual imagery:

> we create our life in the suck and pull
> of rhythms timeless, perfectly timed, reflected
> in the lap and eddy of the tidepool.

Not a reference that would send the average reader scurrying for cover I thought. Nor even the more overt lovemaking at the end of the poem:

> When I call your name, I have not named you
> and we lie in the heat of an august sun
> obscured at dusk by the round
> silhouette of the hills. Your breasts
> rise softly, roundly, are not the hills
> in whose shadows we lie. I lie
> shadowed, your breasts outlined
> by facing light, imaged in the shape
> of the hills behind you. . .

from *November Woman*

I withdrew my manuscript from consideration. After several difficult conversations — and circumstances that made it impossible for them to publish any other book with the funds they had received — they agreed to publish my book in a reduced print run on less expensive paper. They wanted to use up the grant money, but had no intention of trying to sell the book locally and so did not want any of their money tied to this venture.

This experience was difficult for me, but not devastating. I went on writing, continued to find an audience for my work, and received the feedback — both positive and negative — that would help me to become a better writer.

Today, with some distance, I can compare my experience to that of another lesbian writer who wrote a poem in the same genre as "Acadia." The poet is Barbara Deming and this love poem was written in 1935:

> she held the flower cold up against her cheek
> bones in the dark the petals flattened cold up
> against her cheekbones this flower your
> fingers you had danced with this flower in your
> mouth your tongue had been pink like a cat's
> tongue and slender touching the petals you had
> danced with this flower in your mouth held in
> your teeth your teeth biting the petals the
> petals cold up against her cheekbones she held
> the flower cold up against her cheekbones in
> the dark.

This poem is, I think, quite wonderful. It is written as though in one spontaneous breath, written without self-consciousness. It uses enjambment and syllabic stress to create the breathy rhythm and contains no punctuation, asking the reader to provide the emphasis and pause usually given by punctuation.

Many people have known Barbara Deming from her book *Prison Notes*, an account of her struggles during the Civil Rights movement, a struggle that found her in jail in Albany, Georgia. Some may have known her from *Revolution and Equilibrium*, which recounts the anti-war struggle during the Vietnam years, including her trip to Hanoi during the height of the U.S. bombing of that city. Others first knew her when they read *We Cannot Live Without Our Lives*, an early book about feminism that was published in 1974 and dedicated "to my lesbian sisters." And women who were at the Seneca Women's Peace Encampment in upstate New York in the summer of 1983 may remember Barbara Deming as she walked from the Seneca Falls Women's Hall of Fame toward the Women's Peace Encampment at the Seneca Army Depot, was stopped with many other women on a bridge in Waterloo, was arrested with fifty-four women and thus became one of the "Jane Does" of the Peace Encampment. But few, I think, remember her as a poet.

I am now the literary executor of Barbara Deming's estate, and I found that poem among manuscripts containing many other poems and letters. When she wrote it in 1935, Barbara was seventeen years old and having her first love affair, her first sexual experience with a woman. She fell in love with her neighbor, Norma Millay, sister of Edna St. Vincent Millay, a woman twice Barbara's age. In a letter written to her mother in 1974, responding to her mother's criticism of Barbara's dedication of her new book "to my lesbian sisters," Barbara writes: "I have always been grateful to you for the fact that when you first told me about homosexuality you spoke of it very simply and did not condemn it to me as anything ugly. Because of this, when I fell in love with Norma I felt no hatred of myself. My first experience of love was free of that poison. I've always been grateful to Norma, too — for *she* taught me no shame. But I learned it all too soon."

That must be true — that she learned it all too soon — for in the upper-right-hand corner of that poem written in 1935, and on dozens of other love poems like it, is penciled in Barbara's handwriting the word "omit." Omit. Omit this poem from being sent out to journals for publication, omit this poem from the collection she was putting together, and from all collections after this.

I have been reading the poems Barbara published during her lifetime and the poems she didn't publish, and if I didn't know something about oppression and the way it inhibits the risks we can take, I think I might simply conclude that Barbara Deming failed to become a "great" poet because she never developed the faculty of self-evaluation where her poetry was concerned. But today I believe that Barbara Deming had no forum in which to truly test her poetic powers, no magazines or journals to which she could even submit a lesbian poem, no identified audience to whom she could read a lesbian poem, and therefore no feedback about which poems "worked" and which did not.

I was more fortunate than Barbara when the people from the local arts council challenged the quality of my poem. I had read "Acadia" in front of an audience of several hundred women earlier that year at a National Women's Studies Conference event. I knew from the reaction of women in that audience, women about whose opinion I cared, that "Acadia" was not the problem with my book of poems. So even if I had not been able to judge the poem for myself, exercising that elusive faculty of self-evaluation, I had information that would help me decide whether or not to omit that poem from my book. It was a risk, there were consequences, but I knew it was not a risk that would annihilate me, and I knew that not to take the risk would carry far more serious consequences to my work. Those are the consequences Barbara Deming experienced. If we do not choose to take some risks, or if we are forbidden to take them, then we are denied the chance to test ourselves in the world, and I believe that denial leaves us less skilled generally, leaves us in a child-like or adolescent state rather than letting us experience ourselves as adults.

For writers who are lesbians, the difficulty we face in seeking out, receiving, and evaluating feedback and criticism about our work is that frequently that criticism is not about our work, even when the work is the ostensible subject of discussion. When I was denied tenure at a small liberal arts college a number of years ago, my lesbianism and the lesbian content of some of my work were never mentioned. Instead, I was said to be a poor teacher, a weak scholar, and an unimpressive poet. Would I have been "safe" in my job if I had hidden my sexual orientation? I'll never know.

The effect of taking a risk, being punished for taking the risk, but having the risk itself unacknowledged, is chilling. It makes it nearly impossible for us to evaluate the risks we are taking, decide for ourselves whether the consequences make the risk worthwhile for us. It may have the effect of making us unwilling to risk, afraid of taking risks.

"I want to write down everything I know about being afraid," writes Audre Lorde, "but I'd probably never have enough time to write anything else. Afraid is a country where they issue us passports at birth and hope we never seek citizenship in any other country." Lorde is writing in *A Burst of Light* about her experience of living for the previous three years with liver cancer, but the image holds true every time we risk traveling past the boundaries set for us by a misogynist or racist or homophobic society. Every time we choose a risk, we are traveling outside of the limitations — real or perceived — of our lives. When we choose a risk, we are choosing to face down a fear, or at least to walk with it past the boundaries of our previous experience.

Sometimes art is that risk and sometimes art makes it possible for us to face the fears that are inhibiting our journey. I began this essay with the assertion that I became a serious artist when the risks I was taking began to have "real" consequences in my life. One of those consequences, obviously, was being denied tenure, losing the career and definition of myself that I thought would always be mine. To stay sane, to face my fear of what I was losing, I began to write down what I was feeling. I couldn't yet put the words down about my own feelings and my own experience, and so I created a fictional college professor, a young woman named Anna who was a poet, a good poet, and I gave her a teaching position at a college like one I had been at many years before, and then I fired her. And this professor, who was not me, could have all of the feelings I was afraid of until I was able to have them myself. I wrote every day for three months, usually about three pages a day, and before I finally left my job, I had a draft of my novel *Winter Passage*, and I had a grasp on myself.

I had a very similar experience in writing my second book of poems about recovery from alcoholism, *Metamorphosis: Reflections on Recovery*. I do not advocate art as therapy or presume that every self-expression that may be therapeutic is therefore art, but I have found that poetry and fiction are excellent places to begin to walk past the boundaries of our lives. The explosions and flying shrapnel of our emotional lives are not usually fatal in art.

And the risk we experience when we tell our stories truly is the risk of change: the risk that we will be changed by the telling and the risk our audience similarly experiences, that they will be changed by the hearing. In some traditions, this kind of truth-telling is called witnessing.

I had to think about this process when I began to work with the Sanctuary Movement in 1984, began to meet refugees from El Salvador and Guatemala who believed that their work was to tell the story of what was happening in their countries. As I was hearing and being changed by the stories of refugees from Central America, I realized that this process had happened to me before:

> Those of us who are feminists, who have lived the experience of feminist process, know the power of witnessing. That was what we did when we heard one another's stories of oppression or connection with the kind of attention that is nearly passion. We always knew the truth of a story, knew when the speaker had found the core of what she was seeking to express. I know my life is not the same today as it would have been if a feminist poet had not stood in front of a group of academic women and challenged them to hear their own hearts by exposing hers. My decision to live openly as a lesbian in the moment I claimed that identity was only possible because I had met other women who were living openly lesbian lives.
>
> Witness, I learned again in my life, is a circle. I heard [a Central American] tell his story and my consciousness was changed by hearing him. I decided to go to Nicaragua. When I returned I told my own story. If other lives are changed by the hearing, and others feel moved to act differently, there will be new witnesses to that experience.

from *Sanctuary: A Journey*

And with *Sanctuary: A Journey*, I began to understand risk in a new way. I began to understand the artistic risk of political writing and I began to understand that while physical risks and emotional risks are not the same, they are sometimes joined. What I understood in a new way in Nicaragua was that my political life, my artistic life, my emotional life, and my spiritual life could not be separated and that they all grew from the same source. When I began *Sanctuary: A Journey*, the first poem I worked on was the long poem about beginning the journey, called "Leaving Home." In the last section of that poem, I wanted to say something about the journey. I was writing about home, trying to understand some of the things home can be and what it cannot be. In the poem, I remember:

> there are words you must never use
> in a poem I have told students
>
> soul   love   and yet I have found
> no image to bear the weight of knowing
>
> that home is the place of the heart.

It was that word "love" that followed me during the writing of this book, and each since — the word love and the recognition that loving is the first risk we take. Loving is the risk we have to be willing to take in order to encounter any of those things that allegedly come to us in maturity: the ability to make art, to engage in political dialogue, to grow in personal and spiritual complexity and joy. And because those of us who are lesbian or gay have been taught silence about who we are and how we love, risking love openly, daring to tell our stories openly, and witnessing our own lives, become crucial and central features of our growth and survival as individuals, as writers, and as a people.

SELECTED PUBLICATIONS

BOOKS

November Woman. Glens Falls, N.Y.: The Loft Press, 1983.

Winter Passage. San Francisco: Spinsters, Ink, 1984.

Sanctuary: A Journey. Ithaca, N.Y.: Firebrand Books, 1987.

Metamorphosis: Reflections on Recovery. Ithaca, N.Y.: Firebrand Books, 1989.

Just Say Yes. Ithaca, N.Y.: Firebrand Books, 1991.

CO-EDITED BOOKS

With Linda Hogan and Carol Bruchac. *The Stories We Hold Secret: Tales of Women's Spiritual Development.* Greenfield, N.Y.: Greenfield Press, 1986.

DRAMA

Home Tales. Script for a performance piece produced by Paula Sepinuck, Swarthmore College and Painted Bride Theater, May/June 1991.

Moving Parts†

BETSY WARLAND

The struggle for the self-determined body is absolutely crucial to all women. For lesbians, who are twice defined by our feminine gendered bodies, this struggle is doubly crucial. As our bodies propel us away, inciting a desire which is greater than fear—we take a leap into the unknown, which is the unnamed. With our desire we rename everything: slowly; passionately. And with the gathering of our words we own ourselves: become self-responsible. This takes years. This takes a lifetime.

In the process of becoming a self-named lesbian, every woman must find her way through a myriad of fears. As she does, she becomes less afraid. As she does, **she** becomes the focus of fear within the heterosexual world. Although inevitably mediated (to varying degrees) by patriarchal socialization and economics, she-the-lesbian, has nevertheless, gotten out of hand! For hetero-he, she is no longer manageable. For hetero-she, she is no longer a companion in resentment.

Given this, do lesbian-defined perspectives and imagery speak to or

---

†Excerpted from *Proper Deafinitions*, Press Gang Publishers, 1990.

include non-lesbian women?

Considering that language and the canon (as we know them) are central in the maintenance and perpetuation of the values of male-dominant, white culture, where does the lesbian writer, and the lesbian body, stand in relationship to the generic reader?

And, where does the reader stand in relationship to the lesbian writer and the lesbian body?

My first book, *A Gathering Instinct*, was published in 1981. Among other topics, this text records the shift from the final years of my marriage to my first lesbian relationship.

   this circular force

    i must tell you
    i have held the sun in my arms
    i must tell you
     i have held the sun in my arms
      have become its burning reflection
           its hot shadow
      have become its definitive horizon
      have become the lids of this burning eye
                opening like a flower
                closing like a mouth
     opening wildly like a flower
     closing knowingly as a mouth

    i must tell you
    i have held the sun in my arms
     have made love to this circular force
         more times than i can remember
     have risen more powerfully than the sun
         more powerfully than the sun itself
        it has shrunk in my shadow
              shivering

    i must tell you
    i have held the sun in my arms

Within this poem the lesbian body remains obscured, non-gendered and hidden behind the illusory veil of universality. As the lesbian writer, I associate woman with nature and the mystical. The erotic female writing body is searching for a language which is not forged by the heterosexual, male experience. Typically, I opted for the vocabulary of nature, which has been woman's only rightful turf of representation.

The lesbian writer's position is secret. The poem is written in isolation from the relationship: in solitude, as is often the male poet's tradition. It is from this position of apartness that objectification of the woman lover in the lyric poem can spring. The poem (and the relationship) is also isolated from the peopled world.

Although the generic reader may identify with the sentiments of the poem, she or he, in fact, is not trusted by the writer. The reader can either transpose the facade of universality onto "I" and "sun" (which encourages this unspecified gendered kind of imperialism), or the reader must attempt to read between the lines: sleuth whose bodies these are.

As a young lesbian writer, I chose this tangentiality for self-protective reasons. At that time, I knew of no poet who was publishing her books as a self-identified lesbian writer in English Canada. The only models were writers such as Adrienne Rich, who published *Twenty-One Love Poems* (1976) well into her writing career, or writers like Pat Parker—*Pit Stop* (1974), Judy Grahn—*edward the dyke* (1971), and Alta—*BURN THIS and Memorize Yourself* (1971), whose books circulated essentially within the North American lesbian underground. Olga Broumas's *Beginning With O* (1977)—winner of the Yale Series of Younger Poets competition—was the first book (to my knowledge), by a beginning lesbian writer, to be published in the American poetry malestream. In his introduction to *Beginning With O*, Stanley Kunitz writes that because of her ". . . explicit sexuality and Sapphic orientation, Broumas's poems may be considered outrageous in some quarters. . . " Somehow I knew that the Canadian Broadcasting Corporation Literary Competition wasn't about to promote feminist lesbian lyrics in Canada! Nor is it still.

My second book, *open is broken*, was published in 1984. By this time I had fallen deeply in love with another feminist, who was also a writer—Daphne Marlatt. Throughout the first year of our relationship we wrote a series of poems to one another. Although during their writing it had not occurred to us that these poems would be published, our manuscripts were subsequently solicited by a publisher (Longspoon Press). It was then that we began to realize the importance of creating a literary space for books like *open is broken* and *Touch to My Tongue*. In the interim years since *A Gathering Instinct*, I had read, and been deeply provoked by Audre Lorde's *Uses of the Erotic: The Erotic as Power* (1978); Hélène Cixous's essay "The Laugh of the Medusa" (which I read in translation in 1981 in *New French Feminisms*), and by an eloquent talk given by Mary Daly on the subject of presence and absence. Still, bringing our love poems "out" into the public was a terrifying thought. But publishing and reading from our books together not only made it possible, but empowering.

III (from the "open is broken" suite)

the leaves witness you unsheathing me
my bud my bud quivering in your
mouth you leaf me (leaf: "peel off")
in front of a window full of green eyes we climb
the green ladder: "clitoris, incline, climax"
on the tip of your tongue you flick
me leaf: "lift" up
to tip tree top
point of all i am to the sky
"roof of the world"
leaves
sink slow into darkening
with my resin on your swollen lips
leave us in our
betrothal: "truth, tree"

In *open is broken* the lesbian body becomes site specific: her body cannot be easily appropriated. Through the use of explicit erotic imagery, the act of lesbian self-naming begins the process of deconstruction of woman as object. Woman's relationship to nature is no longer a passive/receptive or symbolic state but rather an intensely interactive, interconnected state where boundaries blur. The lesbian body, through the the use of word play and etymology, reclaims the existing sexual vocabulary of intimacy. As the body breaks out and opens itself, so too the language opens up — revealing not only the patriarchal codes embedded within our most intimate words, but also revealing how these codes can be broken open: how the language can be inclusive — not exclusive.

My position as the lesbian writer of this text has changed dramatically. Homophobia is confronted directly (in another poem in the book), and as the writer, I affirm my sexuality, which is no longer a source of deception but a source of creativity and power. Here, the lesbian writer chooses to publicly name the terms of her reference: chooses not to remain mute — having them misnamed by the uneasy reviewer or critic. With our books together, objectification is further disrupted by the equal, active presence of both lovers, both lesbian writers. Our two books seem to have been the first of their kind to be published in North America. Suniti Namjoshi and Gillian Hanscombe published a joint collection of their love poems, *Flesh and Paper*, in 1986.

The reader's position has also shifted dramatically. Confronted explicitly by the presence of the lesbian body and the lesbian writer, the reader is admitted openly into the text. The code that the reader is now active in breaking (along with the lesbian writer), is the code of patriarchal language — not the code of an underground deviant language from which most readers automatically disassociate themselves. Subtexts surface and familiar surfaces are turned inside-out.

serpent (w)rite was published in 1987. This book represents my most intensive work in decoding and analyzing language as the bedrock of The Great White Fathers' value system. Dale Spender's *Man Made Language* (1980) was a crucial source of confirmation about the necessity of this language-deconstruction project, as was Nicole Brossard's deconstruction of woman in *These Our Mothers* (published in translation in 1983). Eve and Adam, original molds for gender indoctrination, are also deconstructed as is the experience of being lost (our post-Garden condition). As the writer, I submerge myself in the experience of being lost: through relentless deconstruction of clichés and decodifying of language; through the interruption by other voices excerpted from a wide variety of material I was reading during the writing; and through the resolution to not go back over and read any of the writing until the text came to its resting point. Consequently, the writing wanders in circles (as one does when one is physically lost), sometimes with recognition of earlier passings but more often with no conscious recognition of the textual landmarks — and so another perspective is laid down in the groove. There are no page numbers, and only in the latter editorial stage did I set the text into eight "turns" which function as indicators of the text's inherent movement (which also evokes women's cyclical orgasmic movement).

from "turn eight"

we are open circle
word without end
a well-come
break down in communication
breg-, suffrage + *down, from the hill*

over the hill
we are split subject
split, slit, *slot,*
hollow between the breasts
no longer divided against our/selves
we are the subject of two mouths
which now *face, form*
words of our own
prefix and suffix in dialogue
no longer waiting to be heard
no longer eating our hearts out

my word!
eating pussy
             cat got my tongue

we make love in the company of four

two Eves four mouths
refuse, refundere, to pour back
the scent/se of opposition
dis-cover
             language, lingua, tongue
has many sides
dialects,
a variety of languages that with other varieties constitutes a single language of
which no single variety is standard

Although the lesbian body continues to be site-specific in *serpent (w)rite,*
it is no longer foregrounded. Out of 128 pages, there are only eight erotic lesbian passages. In essence, the lesbian body now becomes the ground from

which the writing in *serpent (w)rite* is generated. Having established the terms of the speaking voice in *open is broken* as lesbian, I am centred and prepared to speak of the world as I know it beyond the lesbian littoral.

In breaking the greatest taboo of naming myself in *open is broken*, I am now free to address topics (such as war and new technologies) which my status of woman has previously disqualified me from. The search for an integral language is no longer side-tracked by Mother Nature metaphor. It is now situated solidly in the deconstruction and redefining of the very language itself. The lesbian writer's lover relationship, however, still functions essentially in resistance to, and as a retreat from, the world.

In *serpent (w)rite* the reader and the writer are both thrown out of the garden: both are lost; both must be acutely present, for the role of non-participatory observer is no longer viable. Through the use of numerous quotes from disparate sources, as well as meditative white spacing throughout the book, the reader is compelled to enter the text and play an active role in its interpretation. With the emerging concept of dialects, the text is open to any reader whose life and perspective have been marginalized and oppressed.

Double Negative, published in 1988, was written in collaboration with Daphne Marlatt. The first section of the book, "Double Negative," is a lyric collaborative poem which we wrote during a three-day train ride across the continent of Australia. We were motivated to write this text out of our curiosity to discover how our process of collaborative writing had evolved since we had written the poems in *Touch To My Tongue* and *open is broken*. We were also inspired by the beauty of the Australian desert we were passing through and we felt challenged to re-vision the traditional phallic symbolism of the train. The second section of the book, "Crossing Loop," is comprised of a discussion we had, after we returned to Canada, about the constraints we experienced by staying on the literal and narrative track. In the third section, "Real 2," we broke the lyric and narrative frame by alternately taking a phrase from one another's poetic entries and running away with it — going off track into our own idiosyncratic associative prose reflections.

Perhaps one of the most remarkable things about *Double Negative* thus far is that it has received practically no reviews. Collaborative writing seems to be a radical and unnerving approach for the North American critical mind which champions individualism. It is likely that reviewers' analytical processes have been disturbed by the fact that our individual authorships are not clearly marked in the text. In *Flesh and Paper*, although Namjoshi's and Hanscombe's individual poetry entries are not specified, the reader can identify their individual voices in relation to their differences of race, culture and country.

from "Real 2"

"he says we got to stay on track"

well trained he is we are the only difference being it's his job he profits from it stopped for twenty minutes desert beckoning through conditioned glass he doesn't make the rules — just enforces them dissociative division of labour no one directly responsible for anything fill out a form someone will get back to you form letter replying to form (form is form) she looks out the window what she longs for is the absence of the symbolic to lose track of disappear into this emptiness (his key ring tight around her neck) why this vigilance it's not survival of the fittest (he no dingo she no emu) hand to mouth not their relationship no their hunt is on another plain food for thought word to word fight for defining whose symbolic dominates whose (Adam complex) she wants to migrate she wants to mutate she wants to have no natural predators be nothing looking at nothing thrive in her own absence be out of focus out of range of The Gaze hide out from The Law under assumed names but there's no way out even the desert cannot escape imagin-a-nation of the imaginations of 113 billion who have lived and recorded their mindscapes (real to reel) she reads the "Percentage of those whose memory survives in books and manuscripts, on monuments, or in public records: 6" she calculates possibly 1 per cent represents her gender's memory wonders how woman has even survived the wedge-tailed eagle circles above and the train begins to roll as her hand moves across the page spiral movement (imagin-a-nation) here she can rest here she can play encounter her anima(l) self pre-sign pre-time touching you i touch kangaroo words forming then shifting desert dunes her desire to untrain herself undermine every prop(er) deafinition she throws the switch on train as phallus ("bound for glory") train as salvation leaves it behind at the crossing loop feels words falling from her like the 50 million skin scales we shed each day breathing stars, moon saltbush scrub your hand moves across my body (imagin-a-nation) and we settle into this endless motion once again settle into the beginninglessness the endlessness of this page this desert this train this shared desire wholly here with a passion that humbles us what is woman (in her own symbolic)?

In *Double Negative* the lesbian body (although still site-specific) enlarges its symbolism to embrace any woman who is impassioned with her own quest for self-naming and self-determination. Society's negativism toward lesbians is understood to be symptomatic of the larger patriarchal attitude which sees woman as negative space. In this text not only does the lesbian body locate itself intensely in the present, but it interacts publicly with "the world," because escape from the patriarchal grid of symbols and values is neither practical nor possible. For even in the desert, which is considered **the** earthly symbol of negative space, the oppressions of race, sex and class are relentlessly carried out; nuclear testing, war games, and archeological thievery thrive.

The lesbian writers' position is now one of writing in the **presence of** and **with** each other as contrasted to writing in the **absence of** and **to** each other. As the private interaction between us (writers/lovers) is documented and embraced, so too is the inherent collaborative process at work in all writing. This acknowledgement calls into question the notion of one authoritative voice (version) crying out in the wilderness. By her existence the lesbian challenges one of the basic concepts of property: she belongs to no man. So too, we-the-lesbian-writers in *Double Negative* defy a basic patriarchal principle of the written word: individual ownership. The collective and collaborative essence of oral communication (the language of the mother and the language of love), is infused into the written word, and the fluvial movement engenders a new in**her**textuality.

The lesbian writers also dismantle another literary formal fence — the division between writer and reader. We-the-writers also become we-the-readers of our own text: we discuss (and document in "Crossing Loop") our reactions (as writers **and** readers) to the first section, and then, we integrate what has resonated with us as readers into a new contexture ("Real 2"). The reader is not isolate and passive but partnered. But — there's the rub! Because love poetry (particularly erotic love poetry) has been essentially the tradition of male poets, the reader's familiar "entrance" to the poem has been "through the eye of the beholder:" the subject; the viewer. With the presence of both lovers, who are speaking, seeing/writing and receiving, the reader's former position is rendered obsolete. The gaze is up for grabs! It is no longer a fixed position of author/ity and control. Because our writers'/lovers' roles are in a continual state of flux and redefinition, the reader's role is also unhinged. No longer standing at the door of voyeurism, the reader must now dive into the unpredictable currents of the text and assume all the varied writers'/lovers' roles. The reader must pass through the initial fear of intrusiveness into the pleasure of inclusiveness. No safe text here. At the outset, often the non-lesbian reader is disoriented by being in the swim of lesbian sense-ability and vision, or the lesbian **and** non-lesbian reader is disoriented by the flow of the language and form. Here is the irony, for in its defamiliarizations, *Double Negative* is the most faithful and therefore the most open text I have written—for fixed roles can only be dispensed with when we are able to move into a state of shared power and trust.

The lesbian writer is passionate: she has risked, and will risk a great deal to love. She knows she is not alone. She believes that when you never manage to get around to reading or reviewing or teaching her books, you erase essential parts of yourself.

Reading, perhaps more than writing, is an act of faith. Faith in the future. Lesbian writers, along with other marginalized writers, are the voices of the future (which is the present) simply because our voices have been so absent in the past. We are the sources of the knowledge which has been repressed, and it is these very repressions which have put the world at such risk.

WORKS CITED

Alta. *BURN THIS and Memorize Yourself* (Washington, New Jersey: Times Change Press, 1971).

Nicole Brossard. *These Our Mothers* (Toronto: Coach House Press, Quebec Translations, 1983).

Olga Broumas. *Beginning With O* (New Haven, Connect.: Yale University Press, 1977).

Judy Grahn. *edward the dyke* (Oakland, Calif.: The Women's Press Collective, 1971).

Audre Lorde. *Uses of the Erotic: The Erotic as Power* (Brooklyn, N.Y.: Out & Out Books, 1978).

Elaine Marks and Isabelle de Courtivron. *New French Feminisms* (New York: Schocken Books, 1981).

Daphne Marlatt. *Touch to My Tongue* (Edmonton: Longspoon Press, 1984).

Daphne Marlatt and Betsy Warland. *Double Negative* (Charlottetown, Canada: gynergy books, 1988).

Suniti Namjoshi and Gillian Hanscombe. *Flesh and Paper* (Charlottetown, Canada: Ragweed Press, 1986).

Pat Parker. *Pit Stop* (Oakland, Calif.: The Women's Press Collective, 1974).

Adrienne Rich. *Twenty-One Love Poems* (Emeryville, Calif.: Effie's Press, 1976).

Dale Spender. *Man Made Language* (London: Routledge & Kegan Paul, 1980).

Betsy Warland. See books in *Publications List*.

SELECTED PUBLICATIONS

BOOKS
A Gathering Instinct. Toronto: Williams-Wallace, 1981.
open is broken. Edmonton: Longspoon Press, 1984.
serpent (w)rite. Toronto: Coach House Press, 1987.
Proper Deafinitions. Vancouver: Press Gang Publishers, 1990.

CO-AUTHORED BOOKS
With Daphne Marlatt. *Double Negative*. Charlottetown, Canada: gynergy books, 1988.

EDITED BOOKS
InVersions: Writing by Dykes, Queers and Lesbians. Vancouver: Press Gang Publishers, 1991.

CO-EDITED BOOKS AND JOURNALS
With Ann Dybikowski, Victoria Freeman, Daphne Marlatt, and Barbara Pulling. *in the feminine: Women and Words/les femmes et les mots Conference Proceedings 1983*. Edmonton: Longspoon Press, 1985.
With Sandy (Frances) Duncan, Erica Hendry, and Angela Hryniuk. *(f.)Lip* (a newsletter of feminist innovative writing). 1986-89.
With Sky Lee, Lee Maracle, and Daphne Marlatt. *Telling It: Women and Language Across Cultures*. Vancouver: Press Gang Publishers, 1990.

ANTHOLOGIES
With Daphne Marlatt. "Reading and Writing Between the Lines." In *Resurgent: New Writing by Women*, edited by Camille Norton and Lou Robinson. Champaign, Ill.: University of Illinois Press, 1991.

JOURNAL PUBLICATIONS
With Daphne Marlatt. "Subject to Change: a Collaboration." *Trivia*, 18 (1991).

ARTICLES, REVIEWS AND INTERVIEWS
Ellea Wright. Interview. "Text and Tissue: Body Language." With Daphne Marlatt. *Broadside* 6, no. 3. (1984-85): 4-5.
Janice Williamson. Interview. "Speaking In and Of Each Other." With Daphne Marlatt. *Fuse*, 8, no. 5. (1985): 25-29.
Di Brandt. "Interview: Betsy Warland, author of *serpent (w)rite* talking with Di Brandt, October 1987." *Contemporary Verse 2*, 11, no. 4. (Fall 1988): 42-47.

Tara Kainer. "Breaking the Shackles of Language: an interview with poet Betsy Warland." *Between The Lines*, 16-29 November 1990: 13.

Janice Williamson. Interview. In *Sounding the Difference: Interviews with Canadian Women Writers*, edited by Janice Williamson. Toronto: Univ. of Toronto Press, 1991.

Susan Standford Friedman. "When a 'Long' Poem Is a 'Big' Poem: Self-Authorizing Strategies in Women's Twentieth Century 'Long Poems.' " *LIT*, 2, (1990): 9-25.

Lynn Crosbie. Review. "Betsy Warland, *serpent (w)rite*." *Journal of Canadian Poetry*, 4, (1987): 113-16.

A Writer On a Dig in Limbo

L'archéologue des limbes
Translated by Marlene Wildeman

GLORIA ESCOMEL

There is a fascination I have for writing which, while it is being created creates me otherwise and yet myself, someone unknown whom I discover, to the extent that I unearth what writing alone lets me explore: "terra incognita," for it is deep within, revealed to me by this scratching away at it.

The archeologist of limbo — what I would like to be — creates what she believes lies in her hand as the earth falls away from it, her gaze crystallizes nothingness, her words make something of nothing, of what is absent. To do this she must have an absolute desire for newness, a logical suspicion of what is manifestly tainted, a weariness of what we've already seen, read, known. I imagine her; the image imposes itself on me, seduces me, but just when I have begun to let myself be fascinated by the new fantasy, I recognize it: it's the same old god figure fashioning his creation out of nothingness, faded somewhat by this notion of archeology which assumes foreknowledge of an object in existence since some time in the past waiting to be discovered. A bifid image that reflects my own powerlessness. Creating something from nothing is impossible.

The image of a limbo archeologist appeals to me though, not only because it is impossible but also paradoxical. It *charms* me. I can't resist it, because it means female creativity to me. Rejecting what we already know — the male model — and with it a number of works that once seduced her, the archeologist of limbo exhumes material she would like to believe has never pre-existed.

What I exhume bears the marks of multiple sedimentation: strata of successive influence, cultural or otherwise, requiring careful examination. With respect to myself, these images are all quite interesting since they reveal knowledge I didn't know I had. There is, however, knowledge I would rather not have, knowledge which comes from influence I reject, seductive though it may be. Influence and seduction elude control. They have to be screened by analysis, like dreams, which give off diffuse and hieroglyphic messages. They have to be screened by my values, for images are permeated with preconceived values, secular judgements I have had no hand in and that a patriarchal culture has imbibed and which I must now distill, transform, lest they become, in turn, permeated with these same notions for others, and the circle allowed to perpetuate itself, only to be broken eventually in order that a spiral evolve from it.

I try to control my writing and the imaginary, so that they do not make me say what I do not believe. There are delusions and hatreds I do not wish to pass on, and writing vomits them up, just as the earth vomits up its skeletons and its ardent lava. For writing creates worlds, people, ideals. It has its origins in a me who is not pure enough, not distilled enough in her initial impulsive movement, carrying along in her currents tumbleweed and traps that others could fall into, and I would have had a hand in it.

I am responsible for my own shadow and my dreams, for my delusions and my passions, my quests, my exploratory ventures. If these carry monsters within them it is up to me to take them apart before I show them, demonstrate how they work, show that they are only marionettes — they have strings, they are manipulated, they are harmless. And if my fantasies prove dangerous, I must exorcise them, definitely.

From the time I understood that as a woman who writes I would have to dis-alienate myself, and familiarize myself with new essences, I have known that this metamorphosis would not take place overnight. The tasks that other women writers set for themselves — set for us — are not all available to me. I cannot create a new language, understood everywhere: I have neither the genius to do it, nor the time. Other words are needed, other grammatical constructions; they need to be codified. Enormous energy is required to have them accepted, to make them public, comprehensible, universal. Is what we need a female esperanto, bearing in mind that the women of our planet speak more than six thousand languages? Or "femin-ized" national languages, distinct from the existing masculine ones? Here again, a lifetime would not be enough.

In the face of so much wanting to tell, I must hold onto my language, but I can put forward my values, my images, my imaginary, my symbols, my myths. For there is too much to analyse, make comprehensible, protest against, expose, and there is so much hope to nurture, so much solidarity to create or reinforce that the archeologist of limbo must be more than a linguist, a creator, a poet, a musician, a mythologist; she must also be a sociologist, an ideologist, a pamphleteer, a lawyer, a journalist: a lifetime is not enough from this point of view either.

Face to face with too much and wanting so much to write, she must also ensure that other women follow suit. Biblical myths assure us that the word is creative, the verb sacred: it is this verb we must take hold of, but with our gaze turned toward overlooked realities, those of women, knowing that the little that has been said, considered, revealed so far is always too much for those who panic at the thought that their men's world is going to be upset, and may even, in turn, be usurped by the one we are trying to bring about, and that the women characters they have created will not bear up next to the ones we are presenting them with; worse still, the masculine character they have so solidly erected may well be completely overturned by the image we're sending back.

I don't believe in brutal iconoclasm: defensive reactions are always so violent that they are inevitably destructive. In other words, I don't believe that we can rectify the vision of the world, and establish the values we would like everyone to have, by completely destroying what presently exists and walking away from it. On the other hand, I believe in the power of suggestion and I believe in mirages; I believe in the power of wind erosion and that of water polishing the hardest rocks, sculpting them into new contours. It is the job of the archeologist of limbo to exhume new worlds which appeal to us by their perfection and their harmony, and to make available what seems to be merely a mirage, in order that it slowly takes the place of dreadful reality, by osmosis. I believe in the power of dreams, ideals, equity, fantasy, and the imagination. I believe that women's writing must impose on reality this initial idea of vision, in order that from it a dream forms, in order that the idea becomes a sketch becomes a drawing which comes to life.

The archeologist is inclined toward limbo, she un-baptizes it and draws it toward life. Where there was but troubled nothingness, the power of mirage has created another world so fascinating that the old temples and ancient cities shudder and collapse into dust without a word, without a single casualty, and all that they ever were blows about in the wind. This is the magic I want for us.

SELECTED PUBLICATIONS

BOOKS

Exorcisme du rêve. Paris: St-Germain-des-Près, 1972.

Ferveurs. Paris: St-Germain-des-Près, 1972.

Fruit de la passion. Laval, Que.: Trois, 1988.

Tu en parleras . . . et après? Laval, Que.: Trois, 1989.

ANTHOLOGIES

"Analyze du discours médiatique: L'Image homosexuelle refletée dans les medias." In *Homosexualités et tolérance sociale*, 153-159. Moncton, Canada: Éditions d'Acadie, 1988.

"The Vicious Circle of Violence." In *The Montreal Massacre*, edited by Louise Malette and Marie Chalouh. Translated by Marlene Wildeman. Charlottetown, Canada: gynergy books, 1991. (French original: *Polytechnique, 6 décembre*. Montreal: Les Éditions du Remue-ménage, 1990).

JOURNAL PUBLICATIONS

"Les Animaux morts" and "Cathédrales d'argile." *Correspondances* (Paris), February 1962.

"Les Dentelles du temps" and "Errants." *Traces* (Paris), May 1963.

"La Fugitive." *Les Pharaons* (Paris), Winter 1972.

"A moi les vents du nord" and "Je suis cet arbre." *L'ACILECE, L'Université littéraire* (Paris), February 1975.

"Le Piano." *Requiem*, February 1977.

"La peur" and "Le réel." *Journal des poètes* (Brussels), July 1977.

"La Photographie." *Evasion*, February 1978.

"Le Paysage." *Evasion*, May 1978.

"Le personnage." *Les Cahiers Bleus*, issue "Spécial fantastique" (Troyes, France), 1984.

"La part du rêve" and "Le Temps sans mémoire." *Les Cahiers Bleus*, issue "Lettres du Québec" (Troyes, France), Summer/Fall 1986.

"Magma lucide." *Coup de soleil* (Paris), February 1988.

ARTICLES AND REVIEWS

Odile Tremblay. "Créatures de rêve." Review of *Fruit de la passion*. *Le Devoir*, 18 February 1989.

Jeanette Laillou Savona. "La passion rompue." Review of *Fruit de la passion*. *Spirale*, March 1989.

Lise Harou. "Itinéraire de reconnaissance: Gloria Escomel et Georgette Gaucher Rosenberger." *Ecrits du Canada français* 66 (Spring 1989): 157-77.

Benoît Pelletier. Review of *Tu en parleras... et après?" Nuit Blanche* (December 1989).

Green Night of Labyrinth Park

La Nuit verte du parc Labyrinthe
Translated by Lou Nelson

NICOLE BROSSARD

It is a story. I did not see the night. I entered the night one solstice day in
Barcelona. Exiting the Montbeau Metro, I walked side by side with the voice
of Nonna Panina to the gates of Labyrinth Park. In the incalculable green of
the night, already hearing the music and first sounds of celebration, I slowly
climbed the steps that lead to the terrace overlooking the labyrinth. There,
among the voices and eyes that have loved as many books as I have, I walked
between Traude Bührmann and Liana Borghi, between Mireia Bofill Abello
and Susanne de Lotbinière-Harwood. For a long time in the eyes of Lea Mor-
rien I watched the waters of the Rhine follow their course to Mexico in the
hair of Adriana Batista. I did not see the night, only the blue shawl slipping
from Simone Carbonel's shoulders. Then other women appeared. I saw but
the white of their T-shirts, their nipples pressing against the names of Virginia Woolf, Frida Kahlo, Gertrude Stein, and **Mujeres sublimes.** Farther
off, other women declined verb tenses with mysterious signifiers in the curve
of their lips. I did not see the night but Sonia looking for the end of the world
in Catalan, Sonia who closed her eyes saying that the night, this night, was
the most beautiful the West had known for centuries. It was then, in the
només per dones night, that I turned my eyes to the labyrinth, scintillating

in all its mystery in the **for women only**† night that amplified all senses.

The night was green, I could not place limits on desire and words. The night was as perfect as a celebrated lesbian with the ability to bypass the word country without nostalgia. I was about to go down into the labyrinth when a woman behind me said: "The sea creates fissures in political life." Another: "In Ireland, the noise is unbearable at night when a woman doesn't want a child." And another: "The taste of strawberries is an indelible taste in the mouth of Quebec mothers." I moved slowly toward the labyrinth, steeped in the fragrance of cypress and orange blossoms.

Gradually the sound of voices fades away. I am alone. I want to be alone like poets are when questions follow on one another in archipelagos of meaning. The night is green, I will seek its centre. Even if poetry makes me look at the world, the pain, and winter sometimes when snowflakes fall on your forehead, I wish only to be hurt by beauty, too much beauty. The night is green. I will find the exit. I will walk in humility, I will have the caution and wisdom of one who does not want war. I walk between perfectly shaped bushes, too shaped, like history. My eyes are many, vigilant, loving, restless. They are at work under the stars of the **solo mujeres** solstice night. **I am breathing in rhetoric, in the never ending process of hope.**†

FIRST BEND
the sea creates fissures in political life

life teaches us to use pronouns well. To set them all about the I in order to recognize, within us, the others, without too many collisions.

[ ] Para mi la politica es una grand passion. Es la passion de la libertad y de la verdad.
[ ] My politics have brought me as far as I could dream but being politically correct doesn't seem to improve my writing.†
[ ] A political statement is always a statement of principle on which it is easy to graft solidarity and slogans, intolerance and lies. Life is a principle that wears itself out in anecdotes.

---

†Dagger indicates English in the original.

[ ] Creo que para una feminista, la politica es un methodo practico de eleminar la mierda de los hombres y creo tambien que para una lesbiana, la politica es un methodo practico de abrazar las mujeres de sus brazos ardientes.

[ ] Life is not in the principle of life, but in the mouth that speaks the principle. Saliva, bacteria, tongue, mucus, palate. Life is transmittable like illness, knowledge and power. Thus it is in your mouth that I must seek the principle.

[ ] Political life can be like a spell if you can't spell your name with a woman in mind. †

the sea creates fissures in the political life of pronouns and the pronouns, some faces within us more than others, are one day transformed in turn into essential figures. Thus there is no I who is untouched by memory and the figurative meaning that enters into the composition of our political choices.

SECOND BEND
questions that follow on one another in archipelagos

first, there was the tranquil water of my childhood. Then life began giving its heterosexual explanations on art, love, nature and history. Naturally, life took its course, but each time I addressed questions to art, love, nature and history, these questions became pebbles. In continuing to question, I finally found myself on an island composed entirely of question-pebbles which I had trouble walking on, at first. But in trying to soften the pain caused by the pebbles, other questions came to me, so many that they in turn formed another island. One could have said that I was **here and there** at the same time, here on the now familiar ground of the first island, and there on the still foreign ground of the second one in view. The islands multiplied and created a beautiful archipelago. Over the years, I learned to travel with ease from island to island. My questions created new islands, my answers served to move me from one to another. Between the islands, I could now make incredible leaps that were soon transformed into beautiful silent gliding flights. And with that my vision changed. From terrestrial and partial, it became aerial. It was at that time that I multiplied the trips between the islands until the day when, from all evidence, I realized that I had finally succeeded, thanks to the archipelago, in diverting the normal course of tranquil explanations that life had once given me about art, love, nature and history.

THIRD BEND
the blue shawl slipping from Simone's shoulders

the image is a vital resource that forms complex propositions from simple and isolated elements. Each time an image relays desire, this image thinks, with unsuspected vitality, the drift of meaning. So it is that images penetrate the solid matter of our ideas without our knowledge. Here at the third bend, I must decide on the meaning of the image, on the direction that the blue will take, when we do not yet know if the blue comes from the colour of Simone's eyes or if it has some symbolic value. Decide also if the shawl should fall here and no longer interfere with Simone's gestures, or if between Simone's eyes and her bare shoulders, I discover my intentions. The image is a powerful allusion that slips silently into our thoughts. Without the shawl and its slowly freeing movement on Simone's shoulders, would the beauty of her shoulders have blazed its way into me with such intensity? In the very carnal night of solstice, is the image lesbian because in reproducing it I want it to be so, or should one simply assert that this image is fruit that is not of chance. The image slips, surprising re/source that slips endlessly through meanings, seeking the angle of thoughts in the fine moment where the best intentions guiding me, worn out by repetition, seem about to close in silently on themselves. The image persists. It is blue in the green night like a made-up story. It goes against chance, fervent relay.

FOURTH BEND
the ability to bypass the word country

we are all born young between a woman's legs. We are also born young in a country where the males sow women with repetition and tradition. Each one of us loves a country and knows that every war is hateful.

the country that enters into us through the senses, music and colours, is a country that is shared like the memory of fruit, seasons, heat, rain and storm winds. The country that enters into us through history and its violence is a country that divides us in memory of the pride of the conquerors and the pain of the conquered. The country that enters into us through the mouths of men of law is a country that denies our rights. The country that enters into us through the face of God and his heroes is a country that brings us to our knees. The country that enters into us through the language and tongue of a lovher is a country that unites us. The country that enters into us through the beauty of trees, the fragrance of flowers and the shared night is a country that transforms us. The country that enters into us through male politics is a country that divides us. The country that enters into us like dreaming into life is a country that invents itself.

is there then a single country that is not an affair of vestiges and nostalgia? **Sometimes, I wonder.**† My love, speak to me in the tongue of the un-subjected. The full hour that leaves us without country prolongs our lesbian lives.

FIFTH BEND
when snowflakes fall on your forehead

this image leaves me perplexed. See how already it becomes two, vertical in the joy of the first snow, horizontal in death and silence. I would like to be peaceful and take pleasure in telling you how this morning, at the simple contact of the air, I expected snow, an embrace in the snow. I would also like to tell you how, in writing *your forehead*, I was seized by the thought that a lovher in her final rest takes with her some of the eternity that sleeps within us. I would like to be peaceful and share with you the sensation of that very particular humidity, just before it snows, that turns senses and memory in-side out. Death is impartial, I know. She would touch, they say, the imag-inary zone in us that is most difficult to transpose, most difficult to share; the zone, they say, that helps us recapture our destiny.

i also add this paragraph: the snow falls and traces a series of images in the air, air that we sometimes lack when trying to translate **bonheur de l'instant**. It is extremely soft and peaceful and our cheeks are made ever wetter by large snowflakes that are destined, when they fall on our cities and meet the warmth of our faces, to be confused with tears.

i would like to be that peaceful when one of us escapes definitively from representation.

SIXTH BEND
life is in the mouth that speaks

multiplying ideological anchors, escapes ahead, syntheses, feints and perspectives, always seeking a mirror, drifting on a word, butting up against another, obsessive or distraught, thought remains the most modern of the language games that unleash desire. In one's mouth, thought is living proof that life is a statement that experiments with the truth of **je thème.**[1]

thus, the lesbian **I love you** that unleashes thought is a speaking that experiments with the value of words to the point of touch, stretching them out so that they can simultaneously caress their origin, their centre and the extreme boundary of sense.

in the lesbian mouth that speaks, life discerns itself by the sounds pleasure makes as it rubs up against a speaking.

SEVENTH BEND
between history framed in visions

i have been walking in the labyrinth for more than two hours now. I think I have passed the same place several times, but I am no longer sure. Each bend resembles another. All as green as the night. Breeze, hints of fragrance, vertical silence. Shoulders that rub up against the night like an absolute **in the never ending process of hope.**† I no longer know if I seek the centre or the exit, I know only that in the distance, between the beautiful bushes of the jardin del laberinto, I see the first French ships that sailed up the St. Lawrence River. I watch them brush against the whales and the horizon, I see them on the shore, unloading—in the midst of provisions, weapons and tools—a French language that will soon be used to describe the aurora borealis, the North wind and the vertical silence of snowy shores. That was a long time ago. My eyes no longer know where to look, to the river and the rhythm of the waves, or to the **solo mujeres** night and the rhythm of dancing bodies. My eyes seek the long black eyebrows of Frida Kahlo, the piercing eyes of Gertrude, the floating body of Virginia. Then the ships returned, this time filled with rondos, sonnets, madrigals, odes, books of fables and parodies that resisted the successive snows. I am now surrounded by whales and moose, by a flock of seagulls; I enter into the torment of shapes, swimming suddenly in my rising desire to see, between my lips, my tongue slipping on the very tender flesh of the word clitoris. **Breathe your silence, respira en tu memoria,** impregnate rhetoric. In history and the present I am shaping the subjectivity of she whose mouth resembles mine.

EIGHTH BEND
mysterious signifiers in the curve of lips

the process is always the same: it is in wanting to precipitate the necessary word that mysterilaugh signifiers apparaissent au coin des livres. Comme si un choeur entier se levait en nous pour entonner une passion secrète et lécher publiquement chaque mot sous tous ses angles, dans tous ses états de rire et de rût.

la langue de rue que l'on parle aux habitués en traversant la vie hétérosesexuelle se charge de signifiants mystérieux quand la pensée sucrée de la sacrée amoureuse qui aime parier d'amour sur les mots s'aventure dans la bouche nacrée du désir.

la procession des perles dites signifiantes déjouent les gens d'armes. C'est en quoi les dites dykes enclines dans l'herbe et les grands jardins à courir les perles n'ont jamais peur de se tremper dans le plaisir.

le processus est toujours le même si en voilant les précipices de la parole nécessaire, on se précipite au coin des rues pour apparaître. Le coeur lâche pudiquement des sons secrets qui étonnent et sécrètent en chaque mot des mets sucrés que les habitués de l'état ne sucent jamais. Seule, l'amoureuse sucrée tourne dans sa bouche les perles d'éclat comme on décline un verbe sans jamais avoir peur de se tromper.

NINTH BEND
I am breathing in rhetoric†

i am writing this text on several levels because reality is not sufficient, because beauty is demanding, because sensations are multiple, because putting a great deal of oneself into language does not eliminate the patriarchal horror, does not explain the composition of my subjectivity and all these images that move like a woman in orgasm. Energized by the raw material of desire, I write. Word matter, when it is too cold or too soft or so crazy that it is hard to contain in our thoughts, this matter that is eternally contemporary with our joys and energized bodies, murmurs and breathes, opens us to the bone and sews in wells and depths of astonishment. I exist in written language because it is there that I decide the thoughts that settle the questions and answers I give to reality. It is there that I signal assent in approving ecstasies and their configurations in the universe. I do not want to repeat what I already know of language. It is a fertile ground of vestiges and vertigo. Depository of illusions, of obsessions, of passions, of anger and **quoi encore** that obliges us to transpose reality. I am even more unwilling to retrace my steps since, in this very beautiful fragrant labyrinth of the solstice night, I owe it to myself to not erase the memory of my path, to not erase the strategies and rituals of writing that I had to invent in order to survive the customs and phallic events of life.

TENTH BEND
in the eternal process of tears

whoever writes must imagine that the imaginary has already gone through it, traversed her city and her tongue, and must fully weep her hope at the end of sentences. The body of men needs tears because for centuries his hard thinking has dried up women's life. The body of women keeps her tears even after dying. Lesbian cyprin[2] continues to sing long after death, approving ecstasies and their configuration in the universe. Life does not come through the neuter. At the far end of great fields of interlaced signifiers and signifieds, each generation marks the horizon, eyes filled with tears, arms filled with myths. Here in this labyrinth where the only horizon is a spiral of desire, I have no time to weep and yet I can, endlessly, at each bend or in remaining still, too much. Too much is a safe port where feeling returns full of images and the unsuspected vitality provided by certainty. Certainly tears have, for each woman among us, a short sentence to propose: **breathe in your memory, your anger, your desire/for women only/the silk/self road**. Even when they use no verbs, tears, when they propose, put what is necessary at our disposition.

ELEVENTH BEND
for women only

now is the time to reaffirm that in surrounding themselves with women, lesbians constantly pose the question of representation, identity and seduction. The **for women only** that takes shape with each generation of lesbians is a power of dreaming that extends the creative life and love of every lesbian. Space, free movement and energy come from a **for women only** that safeguards the lively and proud spirit of the lesbian traveller. I am forgetting here the word territory because every territory has its barbed wires and men of arms: sooner or later you have to give the right password or bare your fangs. Let us say that I think there are places and space and that each time a woman approaches a lesbian with mysterious signifiers in the curve of her lips, they invent a **here and there** that is called presence of spirit.

It is a story. I did not see the night. I came out of the labyrinth at dawn and found women had become couples, shoulders and arms ardent among the cypress. The taxi let me out at Las Ramblas, near Ferran street. I walked, thinking that there was too much description in books and that the time had not yet come to tell my life like someone taking off her shoes before going to bed. I thought about how tomorrow each of the women in the labyrinth park night would go back to a country in which she would have to choose between the battle of the sexes and exile.

Thus, well before the solstice night began, knowing the existence of the labyrinth and knowing that I could not avoid it, knowing that that night I would risk all for everything and that I would look at the same sky a hundred times, astonished at what anguish and solitude do to humans, in that afternoon preceding the green night I took the precaution of loving long and well a woman who, like myself, had dived into many books, without ever being afraid of drenching herself in dream and reality.

WRITER'S NOTE

On June 24, 1990, four hundred women gather in the Park d'Horta to celebrate the last night of the IV International Feminist Book Fair. Many are lesbians, which tips the celebration to the side of the orchids. Most of us had taken the metro at Drassens station. At each station we had left behind a goddess who now watches over women travelling alone. Over the years and generations, a natural curiosity develops about texts and how they are made. Such curiosity is completely legitimate because it is good to be able to imagine that what we are reading is not simply a matter of imagination. It is always pleasant, during a reading, to recognize a name here, a place there, a tree here, "the truth" there. It is good to know that reality exists. So I think it is fair to tell whoever will read this text that at no time during the night did I enter the labyrinth. As for the afternoon preceding solstice night, I spent it alone, walking in Old Barcelona. Except for a brief encounter with Angela Hryniuk, I spoke to no one before 7:00 p.m., when I met Rachel Bédard, Lisette Girouard, Ginette Poliquin, Louise Cotnoir and Ginette Locas for dinner. You will now believe that from sentence to sentence, I was lead to speak the truth. It is true that when a story can be followed mechanically it gives this impression. But this is not a story. It is the soft flow in present time of a sharing and an immense love for every woman's creativity.

NOTES

1. Translator's Note: **Je thème**, translated literally, means "I theme." However, it is also pronounced the same as **Je t'aime**, "I love you."
2. Cyprin: female sexual secretion. From the French *cyprine*, from the Greek Cyprus, birthplace of Aphrodite, goddess of love. Created by Susanne de Lotbinière-Harwood in her translation of Brossard's *Sous la langue/Under tongue*.

SELECTED PUBLICATIONS

BOOKS IN TRANSLATION

A Book (Un livre). Toronto: Coach House Press, 1976. Translated by Larry Shouldice.

Turn of a Pang (Sold-Out). Toronto: Coach House Press, 1976. Translated by Patricia Claxton. Out of print.

Daydream Mechanics (Mécanique jongleuse). Toronto: Coach House Press, 1980. Translated by Larry Shouldice.

These our Mothers or: The Disintegrating Chapter (L'Amèr). Toronto: Coach House Press, 1983. Translated by Barbara Godard.

Lovhers (Amantes). Montreal: Guernica Press, 1986. Translated by Barbara Godard.

French Kiss (French kiss). Toronto: Coach House Press, 1986. Translated by Patricia Claxton.

Sous la langue/Under tongue (bilingual). Montreal: L'Essentielle, éditrice and Charlottetown, Canada: gynergy books, 1987. Translated by Susanne de Lotbinière-Harwood.

The Aerial Letter (La Lettre aérienne). Toronto: The Women's Press, 1988. Translated by Marlene Wildeman.

Surfaces of Sense (Le Sens apparent). Toronto: Coach House Press, 1989. Translated by Fiona Strachan.

Mauve Desert (Le Désert mauve). Toronto: Coach House Press, 1990. Translated by Susanne de Lotbinière-Harwood.

Picture Theory (Picture theory). Montreal: Guernica Press, 1991; New York: Roof Press, 1991. Translated by Barbara Godard.

CO-AUTHORED BOOKS

With Daphne Marlatt. *Mauve* (bilingual chapbook). Montreal: NBJ (collection Transformance) and Writing Presses, 1985. Out of Print.

With Daphne Marlatt. *Character/Jeu de lettres* (bilingual chapbook). Montreal: NBJ (collection Transformance) and Writing Presses, 1986. O.P.

EDITED BOOKS

The Story So Far/Les Stratégies du réel (bilingual). Toronto: Coach House Press, 1979. O.P.

CO-EDITED BOOKS

With Lisette Girouard. *Anthologie de la poésie des femmes au Québec (1677-1988)*. Montreal: Les Éditions du Remue-ménage, 1991.

INTERVIEWS IN ENGLISH

Jean Wilson. "Nicole Brossard: Fantasies and Realities." *Broadside* (June 1981): 11, 18.

Clea Notar. "An interview with Nicole Brossard." In *So to Speak: Interviews with Contemporary Canadian Writers*, edited by Peter O'Brien. Montreal: Vehicule Press, 1988: 123-43

Ingrid Joubert. "Continent of Women." *Prairie Fire* 10, no. 3 (Autumn 1989): 44-45.

Janice Williamson. In *Sounding the Difference: Interviews with Canadian Women Writers*, edited by Janice Williamson. Toronto: Univ. of Toronto Press, 1991.

IV

Questions Beyond Queer

Forging a Woman's Link
in "di goldene keyt"

Some Possibilities for Jewish American Poetry†

IRENA KLEPFISZ

I began writing seriously in my teens. This was in the mid- and late fifties. I don't remember the content, but do remember writing poems in the voices of old men. I thought poetry should be wise and wisdom resided only in old men who walked down long roads. In the eighth grade I'd been forced to memorize the first ten stanzas of "The Rime of the Ancient Mariner," so perhaps I was imitating Coleridge.

This period is vague. I wrote a lot, but never showed it to anyone, though I did tell people I wanted to be a writer. Against all school counselors' advice and the prognoses of aptitude scores, I chose to be an English major in college. Everyone wanted me to be a science major, to study engineering like my father who'd been killed during the war. But I was drawn to literature, loved to read, loved to write, and persisted, despite undistinguished, sometimes poor, grades. I did eventually make it into the honors English program at City College and won third prize in a short story contest. My

---

†This text was written for *Conversant Essays: Poets on Poetry*, edited by James McCorkle, Wayne State University Press, 1990.

image of a poet was Dylan Thomas, dead drunk in a bar on the Upper West Side, talking about being "a windy boy."

I decided to go on to graduate school and ultimately received my M.A. and Ph.D. from the University of Chicago. This was during the sixties, a difficult period for me. Right after I graduated from college, a close friend, another child survivor [of the Holocaust] four years my senior, committed suicide. Elza was in many ways my role model. She was brilliant in languages, translated Latin poetry, wrote her own poetry and fiction, had gone to Cornell and then graduate school. It was partly because of Elza that I wanted to write and distinguish myself. She too had admired Dylan Thomas and for my eighteenth birthday had given me a record of him reading his own work. When Elza died, I was left with a lot of questions and fears.

More than anything I wondered if our similar backgrounds, similar interests, and the very nature of being a poet indicated that I too would be a suicide. Was it a question of time? I wrote a great deal during those six years, almost exclusively about the Holocaust, about Elza. I wrote out of pain and terror. I abandoned the old man's voice and instead frequently wrote in Elza's voice — the dead poet, the child survivor, the woman incapable of being rescued. I wrote from within what I imagined to be her madness. It was an easy voice to take on. I reworked much of this poetry, but never had it completely under control. It just poured out — one depressing poem after another, one atrocity after another, death always the central motif. I suspect that it was solid therapy, that it saved me.

I am not sure how or why this changed. Either I was through with it or I learned something or both. I came to New York to teach and, in the early seventies, had contact for the first time with a young poet. He was neither obsessed with death nor planning an early demise. It suddenly occurred to me that writing poetry could actually be a way of living. At the same time, I was teaching in a department with a number of poets and they too, though all male, gave me a glimpse of possibilities, a way of being a poet in the world. I began rewriting in a different way. The act was no longer therapy; it was less concerned with releasing pain and more with shaping a poem. I developed a way of laying words out on a page and surrounding them with a lot of empty space — the poems were sparse, the words far from each other. They were as much about speaking as about silence. I was not aware of this, but silence had become and remains a central theme in my writing.

During this period when I was beginning to develop what I now recognize as an identifiable voice, I worried that the sole significant topic of my poetry was the Holocaust. I felt that my strongest poems were "death camp," " herr captain" and "about my father." I wondered how long I could keep writing about this and if I wanted to. I was very determined not to play into the commercialism with which the Holocaust was becoming increasingly surrounded. I wanted true poems, but was also drawn to write about other things. And it was during this period that I first became conscious of feminism and gay issues.

I had, of course, written poems about the present — responses to places and events, to people and lovers. I always felt, however, that these were dwarfed by my Holocaust poetry and had little significance. But when I came out, I suddenly found myself confronted with material that was unacceptable and taboo. Feminist ideas, women's lives, lesbian love, the whole gay world — all were subjects that had few outlets. It was with this consciousness that I self-published in a cooperative venture with four other lesbian writers my first book of poetry, *periods of stress* (Out & Out books, 1975). The book reflected the strict divisions between my Jewish and lesbian life. Soon after, in 1976, I helped co-found *Conditions* magazine. Open to all women and committed to women usually silenced and kept out of the mainstream, *Conditions* emphasized writing by lesbians. Helping to start a feminist press and a magazine made me begin to view writing and my present life in a more complex political and historical context.

But this sudden expansion had a surprisingly restrictive effect on me. As a lesbian, I felt alienated from the community of my roots. The original Jewish impulse behind my early poetry was still there, but it suddenly seemed out of place. I did not feel comfortable presenting my Holocaust poems in the lesbian community, and I felt to some degree unwelcome in the Jewish community. (Both communities have undergone significant changes in attitude since then.) It was a confusing time. The confusion and economic pressures and work on the magazine were not very conducive to creativity and I wrote little in this period. What I did write, like "From the Monkey House and Other Cages" was very Jewish — a direct outgrowth of my Holocaust poetry — but now the primary focus was women. My feminism led me also to write about office work. In 1973 I lost my teaching job as a result of economic circumstances that were to affect thousands of Ph.D.'s in this country. I was frequently forced to do office work to support myself. This work experience was predominantly a female one, a subject that I realized could be explored further in poetry. No doubt, my Jewish socialist background helped in my ability to understand this — so did feminist writers like Tillie Olsen and lesbian poets like Judy Grahn. So I wrote "Work Sonnets." Again the material was informed by my Jewish upbringing, but did not overtly deal with Jewish themes.

With "The Monkey House" and "Work Sonnets" I was also pushing boundaries of form and language. In the first I tried to deal with nonverbal beings expressing feelings through gestures; I pared down the language as much as possible. I did the opposite in "Work Sonnets" where I alternated between prose and lyrics. I stretched the sonnet to fifteen lines and explained in an epigraph I ultimately discarded: "Under these conditions don't expect the perfect form." I forced more prose into the poem by adding two sections after the sonnets themselves: "Notes" by the writer doing office work, and "A Monologue about a Dialogue" in which the "career" secretary reveals her perceptions of the feminist she works with. I knew the sections were not poetry, yet they clearly belonged with the sonnets. These experiments taught me that new content frequently demands new genres, definitions and boundaries.

It seemed, for a while anyway, that I had abandoned explicitly Jewish subjects. Ironically, it was activism within the lesbian and feminist movements that pushed me back to earlier themes. The publication of *Nice Jewish Girls: A Lesbian Anthology* in 1982, Israel's invasion of Lebanon, a more palpable anti-Semitism emerging outside and inside the women's movement — all contributed to my turning again directly to Jewish themes and the subject of the Holocaust. But this time the approach was not exclusively private or experiential. Now I tried to untangle both past and present issues as faced by a contemporary Jew in America. In addition, the Jewish content was informed by my feminism.

Three long poems — "Glimpses from the Outside," "*Bashert*," and "Solitary Acts" — focused on women in my family and other women in my life. I was using everything I had learned in the feminist movement and applying it to the Jewish experience. Thus, all the figures in the last section of *Keeper of Accounts*, "Inhospitable Soil," are women who struggled to survive in Europe, women who struggle to survive here. Without realizing it, I was beginning to think from a Jewish feminist perspective, helping make visible a woman's link in the chain of Jewish history.

For these poems I chose a variety of formats — prose poems, plain prose, ritual repetitions. I wanted to push the prose limits of poetry as far as possible. I did it to such a degree that I became afraid I would never be able to return to more rhythmical free verse. The result was "Solitary Acts," which by contrast is quite lyrical and formal. I also began to include in a more deliberate way non-English words. The central poem of that last section, "*Bashert*," uses some Yiddish (the word *bashert* means predestined or inevitable). I used the Yiddish word as the title because I realized there was no English equivalent to express a certain quality of Jewish experience.

Unlike my first book, *Keeper of Accounts* laid itself out almost chronologically and felt completely integrated. It seemed an accurate reflection of my expanding consciousness and is highly autobiographical. It reflects my internal development as a poet, a feminist and a Jew. It solidified for me certain aspects of writing, of the use of words in isolation and in large unwieldy clumps. I felt I had gained greater technical control over my material. With the completion of that book, I experienced a sense of closure, particularly with "*Bashert*" and "Solitary Acts."

I began looking around for new territory. Again my political activism pointed the way. Together with Melanie Kaye/Kantrowitz, I had been giving a lot of workshops on Jewish identity and for a number of years had worked with her on a Jewish women's anthology which would ultimately appear as *The Tribe of Dina* in 1986. I was thinking a great deal about assimilation, about the effect of the Holocaust (rather than the historical events themselves) on current and future generations. I was drawn to examine my own development and consciousness and began to realize the importance of *yidishkayt*, Yiddish culture, in my life. It had always been there. I'd been raised with it and had internalized it to such a degree, I was barely conscious of its great influence. Certainly I had never thought I had any active role to play in its preservation. But now I began to think more about Yiddish itself and how I might use it in my own writing. I began to think of how the Holocaust had robbed my generation of the language and culture which should have been our natural legacy. More than sixty years ago, Kadia Molodowsky, in the first poem of her series "*Froyen lider*" (Women poems) had lamented that "*mayn lebn [iz] an oysgeflikt blat fun a seyfer/ un di shure di ershte farisn*," her life as a woman was a torn page from a sacred book and the page's first line was illegible. I realized that for me and for many of my generation—as Jews and especially as Jewish women—*di sforim un di bikher*, the sacred and secular books, were lost altogether.

I was struck that as a poet, someone who is intensely involved in language and believes that the kind of language used should reflect what is being expressed, I had never thought about the discrepancy between *di yidishe iberleybungen*, the Jewish experiences I was trying to write about, and the

language I was using. (The use of "*bashert*" was the beginning of that realization.) I was also struck by the fact that I had been intimately tied to Yiddish
(I had attended Yiddish schools, studied it in college, had even taught it)
and yet I had never considered incorporating Yiddish into my work. I began
to try to conceive of ways of doing that. Chicana writer Gloria Anzaldúa, who
mixes Spanish and English in her writing, was very influential in this process. And so I began experimenting with bilingual Yiddish/English poetry.
"*Di rayze aheym*/The journey home" was one result, a poem in which I try to
duplicate in language and form the thematic conflict in the poem itself—the
loss of language and voice, the efforts to regain them. "*Etlekhe verter oyf
mame-loshn*/A few words in the mother tongue" is an attempt at total
integration—to merge feminism, lesbianism and Yiddish language into one
piece.

But I realized that being the only poet using Yiddish was not particularly
gratifying, since such isolation defeats what I want the very use of Yiddish to
represent. I wanted a context within which this poetry would grow *tsuzamen
mit di lider fun andere froyen*, together with the poetry of other women, a context incorporating the present and the past. I wanted to search for *di bikher
un sforim* from which Molodowsky's page might have been torn. I naturally
felt a need to know more about Yiddish women writers, particularly immi-
grants, who faced some of the same issues I faced when I first came to the
States. I was interested in how they dealt with assimilation, the language issue, and if they were conscious of feminism. But Yiddish cultural legacy, *di
goldene keyt*, which had been passed on to me was strictly male. As much as
I loved such Yiddish writers as Morris Rosenfeld, Avrom Reisen, I.L.
Peretz, H. Leivik, Sholem Aleykhem, and Chaim Grade, I was aware they
were presenting male perspectives on Jewish life. I wanted to find out *vos di
froyen hobn getrakht un geshribn*, what the women had thought and written. I
was looking for a link to *yidishkayt* and to *yidishe froyen*. This could be in
part done by establishing a dialogue *mit der yidisher fargangenhayt*, with the
Yiddish/Jewish past, a dialogue that would have to include women. It would
be presumptuous of any of us to act as if nothing came before us. And what I
also realized was that I had to find the women myself—much as I did Fradel
Schtok—pick them up through references in my readings, and in planned
searches.

I knew that there were a lot of women writers, but aside from a handful of
poems (and these mostly by Kadia Molodowsky) no women prose writers
have been translated or are known to American Jews. So I began to look

through the literature and the *Leksikon* as well as articles and anthologies. The work of Norma Fain Pratt was of particular use. Having become better acquainted with some—Rokhl Luria, Kadia Molodowsky, Fradel Schtok—I became committed to translating their work, and making them available to American Jewish women. (A couple of these translations appear in *The Tribe of Dina*.) One poem which resulted from my reading was "Fradel Schtok," a dramatic monologue in which I take on the voice of the writer as she expresses her confusion about adopting English and abandoning Yiddish. I hope to do more writing in this vein.

I am not completely satisfied with how I have used Yiddish in some of my poetry and am unclear how Yiddish will manifest itself in my future writing. My sense is that the bilingual mode is too artificial to maintain. I expect a strong Yiddish element will remain, however, because I feel deeply connected to that literary tradition and culture and this must inevitably find expression in my work. With all the talk about Yiddish being a dead language, I feel it is important to use whatever Yiddish is available to me, even if at times it is fragmentary. Currently I am using simple phrases in what are virtually exclusively English poems. Context usually explains the Yiddish and the Yiddish, I hope, seems appropriate because of what is being referred to. For example, in the poem "Warsaw, 1983: *Umschlagplatz*" about my trip to Poland and what I experienced there, it seemed natural to use Yiddish when referring to a plaque written partly in Yiddish. In addition, I used an epigraph from a poem by the Yiddish poet H. Leivik. The desire to use the epigraph, a phrase I had heard all my life—"*In Treblinke bin ikh nisht geven*" (I was never in Treblinka)—was but one small attempt to begin the dialogue.

Purists might ask: *Farvos shraybstu nisht bloyz oyf yidish?* But why not write only in Yiddish? I don't feel as in control of the language as I do of English. But there are other considerations. I want to remain accessible to as many people as possible and the fact is that using Yiddish exclusively would bypass the very audience which has appreciated and responded strongly to the presence of Yiddish in my work. The intensity and emotionalism of that response still takes me aback. Just a few Yiddish words, the very sound of the language evokes very strong feelings and memories. So I am determined that Yiddish will never be a barrier, as it has been for many Jews whose parents spoke it only *az di kinder zoln nisht farshteyn*, so the children won't understand. I realize I need to find ways in which I can use Yiddish, intertwine it with the English so that it is not directly translated, yet is intelligible. This can be done by repetition, inference, paraphrasing, etc. I'm beginning to consider more formal poems (such as the pantoum) which, because of their forced repetitions, would make integration of the two languages easier. I am still experimenting.

So the impulse for my writing at this stage is very different than it was when I wrote in my early twenties. I am more deliberate about choosing subjects and I find myself needing to read, research, and internalize what I learn. I frequently start with an idea, as in the case of the pantoum. Here the form is the idea. Often the content—a desire to create something about a certain subject—is the idea, as in "Fradel Schtok." Language, form, and content take on new meaning for me at this stage.

My perception of Jewish content has, I believe, broadened. I no longer view the Holocaust as dwarfing my new themes. The present and the more distant past seem significant subjects for poetry. And this includes everything in the present—whether cultural issues such as Yiddish and Yiddish literature, forms of secular identity, relationship to the past, assimilation, Israel and the Palestinian struggle for self-determination—all are fitting subjects for contemporary American Jewish poets. By turning to these, by framing them in the present context, by presenting them from a feminist perspective, we can create a viable American Jewish poetry and poetics, one that is linked to the past and contains a legacy for the future.

I often ask myself who I am writing for and who is interested in Jewish poetry and poetics with a feminist or lesbian perspective. I feel some confusion at this point about the different audiences for my work. I am deeply committed to the lesbian and feminist movements, to Yiddish and *yidishkayt*, to the Jewish community, to radical politics. How to reach all these audiences, through which journals and magazines, are the questions I have not answered. I am working on the answers in the same way I am working on my poetry.

What I am certain of is that my political work—consciousness raising on feminist, gay and Jewish issues, building Jewish awareness of *yidishkayt*, teaching Yiddish, translating significant material, working towards a peaceful solution in the Middle East—has become as important to me as my writing. And this surprises me, given how I began writing in such complete isolation. But my commitment to these political causes has become very deep and I could never again think of poetry writing as the sole and central preoccupation of my life. I, of course, don't want to abandon entirely the personal, private inner life which was often the impulse behind my early work. But I have a keen sense of the present as historical, a turning point — Jews are shaping their future now. How we preserve and recast Yiddish culture and sensibility on American soil are questions I feel compelled to address both in my political activism and in my poetry.

SELECTED PUBLICATIONS

BOOKS

Periods of Stress. Brooklyn: Out & Out Books, 1976. Out of print.

Keeper of Accounts. Watertown, Mass.: Persephone Press, 1982; Montpelier, Vermont: Sinister Wisdom Books, 1983. O.P.

Different Enclosures: Poetry and Prose of Irena Klepfisz. London: Onlywomen Press, 1985.

A Few Words in the Mother Tongue: Poems Selected and New. Introduction by Adrienne Rich. Portland, Oregon: The Eighth Mountain Press, 1990.

Dreams of an Insomniac: Jewish Feminist Essays, Speeches and Diatribes. Introduction by Evelyn Torton Beck. Portland, Oregon: The Eighth Mountain Press, 1990.

EDITED JOURNALS

Yedies/News of the YIVO (quarterly Yiddish/English newsletter). New York: YIVO, 1974-76.

CO-EDITED BOOKS AND JOURNALS

Co-founder and co-editor of *Conditions*, a feminist magazine of writing by women, with an emphasis on writing by lesbians. Brooklyn, 1976-81.

Co-edited with Melanie Kaye/Kantrowitz. *The Tribe of Dina: A Jewish Women's Anthology*. Montpelier, Vermont: Sinister Wisdom Books, 1986; Boston: Beacon Press, 1989.

Co-founder and co-editor of *The Jewish Women's Peace Bulletin*. New York: The Jewish Women's Committee to End the Occupation of the West Bank and Gaza, 1989.

Co-edited with Rita Falbel and Donna Nevel. *Jewish Women's Call for Peace: A Handbook for Jewish Women on the Israeli/Palestinian Conflict*. Ithaca, N.Y.: Firebrand Books, 1990.

ANTHOLOGIES

"The Journal of Rachel Robotnik." In *Lesbian Fiction*, edited by Elly Bulkin. Watertown, Mass.: Persephone Press, 1981. O.P.

"The monkey house and other cages: monkey II." In *Seis poetas norteamericanas: Contestame, Baila Mi Danza* (Muriel Rukeyser, Denise Levertov, June Jordan, Diane Di Prima, Adrienne Rich, Irena Klepfisz, Barbara Deming), edited by Diana Bellessi. Buenes Aires: Ediciones Ultimo Reino, 1984.

"Dedications from *Bashert*," "*Etlekhe verter oyf mame loshn*/A Few Words in the Mother Tongue," "Royal Pearl." In *Early Ripening: American Women Poets Now*, edited by Marge Piercy. London: Pandora Press, 1987; New York: Routledge, Chapman and Hall, 1987. O.P.

"Women without children/Women without families/Women alone." In *Politics of the Heart: A Lesbian Parenting Anthology*, edited by Sandra Pollack and Jeanne Vaughn. Ithaca, N.Y.: Firebrand Books, 1987.

"Feminism, Consciousness and the Girls at the Office: An Essay in Fragments." In *Out the Other Side: Contemporary Lesbian Writing*, edited by Christian McEwen and Sue O'Sullivan. London: Virago Press, 1988; Freedom, Calif.: The Crossing Press, 1989.

"Solitary Acts," "Royal Pearl," "Fradel Schtok," "East Jerusalem, 1987: *Bet Shalom* (House of Peace)." In *Decade: Poetry and Commentaries: 1980-1990*, special issue of *New Letters*, edited by Trish Reeves and Robert Stewart. Kansas: Univ. of Missouri — Kansas City, 1989.

"Fradel Schtok" and "Cactus." In *An Ear to the Ground: An Anthology of Contemporary American Poetry*, edited by Kathleen Aguero and Marie Harris. Athens, Georgia: Univ. of Georgia Press, 1989.

INTERVIEWS

Diana Bletter. In *Invisible Thread: A Portrait of Jewish American Women*, edited by Diana Bletter. Philadelphia: Jewish Publication Society, 1989.

Esther Helfgott. *World Focus: Jewish Feminism 14* (video interview). Seattle: Univeristy of Washington, November 1990.

DRAMA

Bread and Candy: Songs of the Holocaust (a one-act play for five voices). Produced at the Jewish Museum, New York City, September 1990. Forthcoming in *Bridges* 2, no. 2 (Fall 1991).

Troubled Times†

Interview by Andrea Freud Loewenstein

SARAH SCHULMAN

AL: *You said recently in* Gay Community News *that just doing art as a political action isn't enough. Why isn't that enough, and why does an artist have to be doing other kinds of political action as well?*

SS: When I started writing novels I didn't know anybody who wrote books. I was working as a waitress. And then in 1986 I got admitted to the McDowell Colony for two weeks. I waitressed the day before I left and I waitressed the day I came back; but those two weeks were the first time in my life that I'd ever been treated as an artist, called an artist, and surrounded by artists. After that I began to get more involved in the art world, after having been involved in politics and in the gay community most of my life.

And what I found was really appalling to me. I found this group of people

---

†Sarah Schulman's novel *People in Trouble* is the story of a love triangle between Kate, her husband Peter and her lover Molly, written against the background of the AIDS crisis. Novelist Andrea Freud Loewenstein talked to Sarah Schulman about *People in Trouble*, the AIDS crisis and the politics of fiction. This interview was published in the *Women's Review of Books*, July 1990.

2 1 8   I N V E R S I O N S

who really felt that they were better than other people, more important than other people, and who looked down on other people and didn't feel any responsibility. In fact they felt that the world had a responsibility to them.

This is the New York City art world, so they're people who are surrounded by the lure of money and potential for fame. And I heard a lot of rhetoric about how "My art work is my political work"; "Challenging form is radical because it challenges the way people look at things" — all this type of rhetoric that I had never heard before, from people who were basically very conservative and actually in enormous complicity with dominant cultural values.

When I came to ACT UP† I came to it as an artist, wanting to bring the arts community which was being affected by AIDS into activism, and I found that the only way that people would do that was to perform their work at a benefit, or mention AIDS in their work. And that was very few people, that was only gay people. But straight artists refused to walk into a room of 500 homosexuals, or stand on the picket line with them, or go to a demonstration with them. They refused to make a stand with them, under this pretense that their artwork was equal to everyone else's humanity. And it's not.

I was really angered by that whole perspective. There's no other group of people who claim that just doing what they want to do is a political action.

AL: *In* People in Trouble, *was "Justice" supposed to be a portrait of ACT UP in some way?*

SS: Well, it's a tricky thing. I started writing the book four years ago. When I started it, I thought, okay, I'm going to make ACT UP be the kind of organization I want it to be. I felt that they weren't being radical enough. However, in the interim ACT UP has outwitted me, and become more than even I imagined. So for example, in the book I imagined these forty timid men nervously disrupting a service in St. Patrick's Cathedral. Well, the reality was, right before the book came out, ACT UP had this huge demonstration of 7000 angry people at St. Patrick's Cathedral.

---

†ACT UP, the AIDS Coalition to Unleash Power, is an organization committed to direct action to end the AIDS crisis. It was founded in New York City and now has branches across the U.S., Canada and Europe. Sarah Schulman has worked with ACT UP on and off for almost three years, and has written on the exclusion of women from experimental drug trials for the *Village Voice* and on AIDS and the homeless for *The Nation*.

AL: *There's a place in the book where Kate gets involved in "Justice" and Peter says, "Well, why can't we do Nicaragua, we can both participate in it?" Were you saying our priority is AIDS now, and it's less important to do other kinds of actions—is that how you feel, that this is the kind of action that we as lesbians and gay people should be doing now?*

SS: Actually, what I was commenting on there is that in ACT UP/New York there are 500-600 people, and there are probably three straight men. I was commenting on how straight men are willing to march for any nation in the world, but they will not walk into a room full of homosexuals who live next door to them and are related to them.

AL: *How conscious was it to decide to write this novel, and what it was going to be about—especially the AIDS part of it? I'm interested in how a novel happens for you.*

SS: I usually write by collecting fragments for about a year—one sentence, phrases, or whatever. Then I usually write one scene. And then a few months later I write another scene. Then you have two points and then you connect them. And gradually I put all the fragments together and I usually end up with a first draft that's about 80 pages from beginning to end. Then I do about twelve drafts over a three year period. Each time it gets bigger and bigger and bigger; so I have a total structure for the first draft and then I fill it in inside.

A major theme in *People in Trouble* is that it has become impossible to write a gay book without discussing AIDS in some depth. I write about New York City. New York is a very socially stratified city, and your layer of protection determines your sense of responsibility to the crisis—because that's the disease of how Americans live, people don't care about something unless it affects them personally. So marginal people know how they live and they know how the dominant culture lives. Dominant culture people only know how they live. The people who have the most power have the least information and the smallest sense of responsibility.

So I constructed these three characters, none of whom has AIDS, but all of whom have different levels of social vulnerability, different levels of proximity to the AIDS crisis: a straight man, a bisexual woman and a lesbian. And because of their differential in social power, they have different consciousnesses, which lead them to draw different conclusions about their responsibilities to other people. I think that people who are vulnerable feel more responsible, because they need each other more. When a straight man says to me "I don't believe in groups, I'm not a group person," well, he belongs to the group that's not called a group. He's unaware of the structure that he's living in. He doesn't feel the responsibility because he feels normal.

Though it appears to be a book about AIDS, it's actually a book about male power and homophobia. The principal idea behind it was how personal homophobia becomes societal neglect.

AL: *It sounds quite conscious—you were saying that you do a scene here and a scene there, but at some point you decided to have these characters who would represent different layers of privilege. So you had written a few scenes, and then you decided that this was going to happen?*

SS: No, that was happening anyway. Each of the books that I've written has been a response to the other gay literature of its time. What this book responds to is that lesbian writers have still not written about men. And I really have a lot to say about men. And frankly, I think that white heterosexual male writers have very little to say at this point, and that we all—everybody else—have a lot to say about them. So addressing men, male power, the male image in literature, all these issues, is where I really have to go. I'm seeing a lot more lesbian writers who're doing that. I just read a novel, *The Passion*, by Jeanette Winterson, the British writer, and she's doing that; I saw a play by Eileen Miles, *Modern Art*—she's a wonderful lesbian poet, and she's doing that too.

AL: *Peter, the straight man in the novel, is a really interesting character. I like all the characters, but I was very drawn in by him even though I didn't like him, and I kept wondering what a straight man who read this would think.*

SS: He's the kind of character where lesbians read and they go "Oh, that guy is such a drip"—we recognize that guy. And straight men read him and go "Oh, he's really trying."

AL: *How did you do him?*

SS: I started to write him and I discovered all these things about having never written a straight male protagonist before, and having no one I know who'd done that. It was kind of a mystery.

AL: *Do you know a lot of straight men?*

SS: I know a lot like him. I mean, I live here, it's not an isolated community. But a straight male character walks into a book the way a straight man walks into a room, and he's subjected to a very low standard of judgment. As long as he's not a brutal rapist, he's a hero.

AL: *Depending on who's reading it.*

SS: If a woman behaved the way Peter did, she would have been judged really differently. But because he wasn't a pig, people liked him. The standard is very low.

AL: *Even for lesbian readers?*

SS: That's another issue. The generic reader, the spectrum of people who read books, recognize that character as a good guy. He's not an evil person. Even though he is apathetic, he doesn't take care of other people, he doesn't recognize his own power — still he's benign, he's a nice guy, you know, he's trying, so he becomes good.

A lesbian character has a very high burden of proof. She has to be really kind, really good in bed, really intelligent and very gracious in the face of oppression. It's a very big thing for someone else besides a lesbian to accept her as a character. Now trying to balance these two characters is virtually impossible, because he can do anything and she can't do anything. But I had to balance them.

So first I thought, okay, I'll go back and look at books where straight male characters and lesbians have appeared together. Well, there are hardly any, not unless one is a vile stereotype. And the reason is that these two people live in different universes. They cannot coexist in the same book. Either you see them from his point of view or you see them from her point of view. There's no objective point of view. What's called the objective point of view is his point of view. They have completely different values. This really angered me, to see how much the world of fiction is the outside world, that we bring the same values to it. It was very much of an eye-opener.

But I also knew that I was really vulnerable to the accusation "She's a lesbian, she hates men." So I had to make Peter be better than I really believed him to be. It's the only time in my life I've ever lied about a character. What I did to "humanize" him was make him be me. I put all of my personal stuff into him. I gave him the most attention, and so he's the most developed character.

Although now I'm publishing with a mainstream publisher, reviewed in the mainstream press, I'm not a valued person, I'm a deviant person. Reviews that I now get say things like "This isn't a gay book, this is a universal book." That's called a good review; because if it was a gay book, there'd be something wrong with it. How I have experienced men in my life, and male power, and how all the people who I love and take care of and care for have experienced that in their lives, is not a valid perspective in the mainstream world. It's okay if you're talking about women, because women are a secondary subject-matter. But once you're discussing the important topic, which is men, men's life and men's power—if you have this other view, you get dismissed. And I reacted against that by making Peter better than I experienced him to be.

AL: *Now to me Peter was bad, even though as a reader you get involved in him. But the gay men who are struggling with AIDS in some way or another in the book are very heroic. There isn't one who's becoming hateful and paranoid and bitchy. How about that?*

SS: Well, I think that that's realistic. What the gay community has done is so unparalleled. You know there's this push for domestic partnership laws, for gay marriage. But if the gay community was divided up into privatized marriage family units, and wasn't a community, the response to AIDS would never have been what it has been. The amount of love and courage that people have put out. . . It is heroic, it's hugely heroic, especially given the level of neglect that permeates American culture right now.

AL: *One of the things I think you write about better than almost any lesbian writer I know of is sex. Is that hard to do?*

SS: Well, it's always changing, because the things that I started out with are things that I don't want to do anymore, and I am trying to get a more imagistic way of writing about sex. When I started there was no "lesbian sex" phenomenon, and now there is all that. And so the need to describe acts, or body parts, is no longer relevant, because there is this whole lesbian porn industry now.

AL: *That's a little different, though.*

SS: It's different, but it changes the terms of what needs to be done.

AL: *You mean it's not as necessary to be concrete.*

SS: Yes, you don't have to say certain things. At one point, using "sex talk" or being able to say certain words was important, because words like "cunt" and "pussy" weren't acceptable in literature. Now they're the norm of the sex literature. Magazines like *On Our Backs* have created a new norm, or a new establishment. I'm trying to find new ways of writing about sex and sexual experiences that are more imagistic.

AL: *You've obviously also thought a lot about how to write about AIDS.*

SS: Developing a vocabulary for AIDS fiction is a really major part of this book. When I started writing there was no way to talk about AIDS, there was no language, I didn't know how to talk about it. The first thing that I did was to go back to fiction that had been written about large disasters, like Holocaust fiction, Hiroshima, the plague; and what I found out is that very, very little fiction was written about those events at the time they happened or even within the next forty years or so after them. Mostly what people wrote was survivor memoirs and journalism. I think that a lot of the reason is that fiction is in some ways not an appropriate form for very huge events. Fiction is a really limited form. And there are certain things that you cheapen when you represent them, because you make them palatable.

AL: *You think so?*

SS: Yes, I do think so. That's why I would never write a rape scene in a book. When you describe torture, when you describe mass death, which is what AIDS is, you sum it up, it becomes something that's comprehensible, that you can understand — but it can't be understood; it can't be defined. That's the reason, I think, that people don't go first to fiction: because non-fiction is so much larger. So I understood that limitation, and ultimately I think that that's one of the problems of the book.

We're the first generation of AIDS fiction writers, there is no really great novel that has come out of AIDS yet. What we can do is start to establish a vocabulary that future writers can use as a foundation to build on to discuss the issue.

Writing about AIDS isn't like writing about love, which is something that people have written about for millennia. We're describing the final experience of life, dying, the only experience where there's no retrospect. And we're describing mass death, in a community, and reviewers and critics and readers have to understand that we're just learning how those issues are addressed in fiction.

Establishing the vocabulary that I was going to use was a whole project before the book could be written. I did things like make lists of details of the crisis, and ended up picking fifty details that I'd use. There were things like watch alarms going off in public places so that people could take their AZT, you know that's a detail that people will recognize later. There are hundreds of these things, and I picked fifty. Then there are also terms that I had to decide not to use, because there's a lot of language around AIDS that's very distorting, like "general population" or "innocent victim." Another word that I rejected is "Holocaust," because I don't feel that that's appropriate. There's a lot of word choice that's really important.

AL: *Do you make a living from your writing?*

SS: I'll tell you what I make. On a hardcover book I make one dollar, and I make fifty cents on a paperback. *After Delores*, for example, has sold five thousand hardcovers and twelve thousand paperbacks; that comes to eleven thousand dollars. That's for three years of work, and it's been out for two years. That's five years, and I got a five thousand dollar advance on that book. So, that's not a living. For *People in Trouble*, I got seventeen thousand dollars for both hardcover and softcover rights, and that was in 1987 or '88, so I would have to sell 17,000 hardcovers to break even on my advance.

AL: *So how do you write so much if you have to work? How much do you have to work at your other job?*

SS: For my first two novels, I worked full-time as a waitress while I wrote them. Now my writing brings in enough to only work part-time.

AL: *And how do you do that and have a life too?*

SS: I am a very, very economical and efficient writer. I think about it a lot, and by the time I sit down it comes out really clear. I rarely have to be at the typewriter more than two hours a day.

AL: *And do you make the choice of not doing work that's directly connected to writing? At this point you could certainly get a job teaching creative writing.*

SS: I'm trying.

SELECTED PUBLICATIONS

BOOKS

The Sophie Horowitz Story. Tallahassee, Fla.: Naiad Press, 1984.

Girls, Visions and Everything. Seattle: Seal Press, 1986.

After Delores. New York: E.P. Dutton, 1988 (hardcover); New American Library, 1989 (paperback).

People in Trouble. New York: E.P. Dutton, 1990 (hardcover); New American Library, 1991 (paperback).

Empathy. Forthcoming. New York: E.P. Dutton, 1992 (hardcover); New American Library, 1993 (paperback).

ANTHOLOGIES

"Rosie and Me." In *The Things That Divide Us*, edited by Faith Conlon, Rachel da Silva and Barbara Wilson. Seattle: Seal Press, 1985.

"When We Were Very Young: Radical Jewish Women on the Lower Eastside, 1879-1919." In *The Tribe of Dina: A Jewish Women's Anthology*, edited by Melanie Kaye/Kantrowitz and Irena Klepfisz. Montpelier, Vermont: Sinister Wisdom Books, 1986; Boston: Beacon Press, 1989.

"The Penis Story." In *Women on Women*, edited by Joan Nestle and Naomi Holoch. New York: New American Library, 1990.

ARTICLES AND REVIEWS

Kinky Friedman. "She Considered Boys for About Five Minutes." *New York Times Book Review*, 15 May 1988.

Kathy Acker. "Love Stinks." *Village Voice*, 30 August 1988.

Johnathan Mandell. "AIDS Activists, in Fact and Fiction." *New York Newsday*, 7 February 1989.

Patricia A. Roth. "Mean Streets: Obsessiveness Obtains in the Crossover Success Novels of Sarah Schulman." *Bay Windows*, 1990.

DRAMA

"Breaking and Entering." *Out/Look*, (Winter 1989): 32-33.

"My Suggestion." *Taos Review* 3 (1990).

My Work

BARBARA WILSON

W hen I was growing up there would sometimes appear, on the narrow strip of grass that separated our driveway from that of the Bear family next door, a bunch of bananas. Not a small bunch with the six or eight bananas you find in grocery stores; this was a stalk of bananas, a hundred bananas on a thick stem, and Barney Bear had put them there for us and everyone else in the neighborhood to take and eat. Barney Bear was a longshoreman at the Port of Long Beach, California.

Our neighbors on the other side were the Krebs. John Krebs was a car mechanic who had a habit of tinkering late into the evening on cranky racing cars in his driveway, while Mary Krebs was a night nurse who demanded absolute silence during the day from her sons Johnny and Jamie. Across the street Mr. Young worked as a pill salesman for the delightfully named Upjohn company, and next to the Young family lived the Shabiccas. Mr. Shabicca was in construction and wore a hard hat. Leah, the neighborhood spinster, lived with her mother during the summer and taught high school in Alaska the rest of the year, while the red-headed, freckled widow, Peggy Sprague, the mother of my off-again-on-again friend Suzanne, taught at another elementary school than the one we went to. (Johnny Krebs and I speculated that that's why Suzanne was so pink and white and well-behaved.)

I was interested from an early age in what people did for a living. Some of the women in the neighborhood, like my mother, did not have paid jobs; they were usually involved in church work instead, like Dolores Bear next door, who trilled arpeggios all week long in preparation for her Sunday solo at the Baptist church, or my mother, who helped fundraise the building of the our church and who was head of Sunday School. But almost all the mothers had worked at paid jobs before they got married and somehow I knew about that work too. My mother had come out to California from Michigan with her two best friends, Harriet and Gertrude, and all three had worked as kindergarten teachers.

Of course we learned about jobs in school — we were, after all, being readied for long lives as workers and the wives of workers. Boys could be firemen, train conductors, pilots, the president; girls could be nurses or teachers before they got married. The *idea* of being something, of having a social role in the world was always of great interest to me; I never thought of being a nurse or a teacher, however. From the age of eight I knew that I wanted to be a writer who would write the kind of books I liked to read, but that never stopped me from fantasizing about other occupations. I was always hearing, after all, that writers needed experience of the world, and experience — to me — meant work.

It has been a given to me as a fiction writer that my characters would have livelihoods, social roles and relationships with their co-workers. Until I was asked to write this essay, and began to think about areas of invisibility that I experience as a writer, I never considered that it is generally the working — not the sexual — lives of my characters that go unacknowledged by reviewers. Perhaps because I have been an explicit feminist and lesbian almost as long as I have been publishing, the lesbian-feminist content of my writing has never been ignored. In my Pam Nilsen mysteries especially, I marked out my territory: the lesbian and leftist subculture. My books have long been "seen" in terms of their political and sexual content — not only by lesbian-feminist critics, but also by sometimes more and sometimes less sympathetic straight critics in the national media. The headline might read "Too Much Sex, Not Enough Mystery," but the reviewer does deal with the lesbian characters. Of course this means that sometimes my books don't get reviewed, but it also ensures that when they are, women as lesbians will be there. But quite often, lesbians as workers will not.

My class background is mixed, and the contradictions I've experienced have enriched my writing as well as provoked personal anxieties about money and position. One of my grandmothers was born in Stockholm and immigrated at a young age to a Wisconsin farm. She married at sixteen and died in childbirth at twenty. One grandfather was brought up in County Cork in Ireland in extreme poverty and ran away to Boston. My father was orphaned, adopted, and orphaned again, all before the age of fifteen. My mother grew up lower-middle class and religious in a small town in Michigan. Both my parents came out to California during the war and experienced the post-war boom. While my mother tried to instill in us her own upwardly mobile values, my father remained convinced that poverty lay right around the corner. He never quite believed in our temporary suburban affluence and was never surprised when things went badly for him. My father liked nothing better than to tell us stories of the Depression. There had been work on the farm, the heavy labor of plowing and harvesting; there had been numerous jobs while he put himself through high school and college: grill chef, swimming pool attendant, farm laborer. My mother might be indifferent about cooking and cleaning, but my father would grab a can of Ajax in one hand and a rag in the other and give my brother and me a vigorous demonstration of "elbow grease" as applied to the bathroom sink. It was his firm conviction that my brother and I had no idea of what hard work really was.

Some parents have career plans for their children. Mine never seemed to. My mother, who had always encouraged my drawing and writing, died when I was twelve. My father sighed when I stubbornly said I didn't need to take business or technical courses: I'd support myself as a writer. It was a mystery to him where I could have gotten such an idea, for there were few books in our house other than the Bible. "I guess you could always become an English professor," he said doubtfully. "But it would be better to get into a field where there isn't so much competition."

My father may have lacked a vision for me, but he taught me some important things about how to love what you do. Some of my earliest memories are of visiting the business and technical college classroom where he taught basic accounting. I remember how from time to time he'd forget his lunch, and my mother, little brother and I would drive downtown to deliver it. Invariably my father, so jocular and hearty in those days and much-beloved by his students, would draw us into the room. He always introduced us and once, I remember, stood me on the big desk in front of rows of students. I laughed and waved my arms about: So this was teaching! To be the center of attention.

I'm not romanticizing work. All the same I have been fascinated with occupations and have had numerous jobs, most of which I've enjoyed — at least I enjoyed my co-workers when I didn't enjoy the work — and all of which I've learned from. I've worked on assembly lines and at fast-food counters, I've managed a souvenir shop and washed dishes on a ship; I've clerked and stocked in discount stores, worked as an aide in a nursing home and as a ward clerk in Pediatrics and Coronary Care. I've sold encyclopedias in Arizona, taught English in Spain and taken care of children in Norway. I was a maid in Germany and a furniture saleswoman in Connecticut. I held numerous miscellaneous, brief jobs as a filing clerk and typist.

In 1976 Rachel da Silva and I started Seal Press with just over a hundred dollars. We both had other jobs for years, and just about killed ourselves; still, I feel that we were lucky. We taught ourselves how to do everything from book packing to selling rights, from designing books to promoting them, and somehow, we succeeded. Over the years, with the help of many women and a network of bookstores, periodicals, distributors and readers, Seal Press became a going concern that employs a staff of eight and publishes ten to twelve books a year. In 1984, when we published my first murder mystery, I was finally able to quit my other job at the hospital.

In every way my life as a creative artist has been informed by the occupations I've held and the work I've done. Having one foot in the marketplace has given me an additional social role to that of author; being in business, I have found, creates endless opportunities for experiencing the melodrama of money. Of greater interest to me is what I've learned about work relationships. My business partnerships have been two of the most complex and rewarding connections in my life. The community of workers we have been able to build at Seal in the last few years seems quite as important to me as the books we publish.

I have been an employee, watched by eagle-eyed supervisors, and an employer, trying hard to be fair, yet caught sometimes in the coils of hierarchy. I have been a collective member on a newspaper, and part of a team during a hospital crisis. As a writer I've spent endless hours alone in front of my typewriter; as a translator of Norwegian I've experienced the fascination of working in collaboration with another writer, shaping two vocabularies into one. I have wanted to put some of the things I know about work into my fiction.

My characters work and their relationships with other characters are often based on work. Much of *Ambitious Women*, my first novel, is a study of the business partnership of Holly and Allison and what happens when work and politics intersect and collide. Allison is a single mother from a lower-middle class family while Holly's family was well-off, though she sank into poverty with her first husband. Middle-class white liberal Pam Nilsen, the epitome of the laid-back Seattle Left, and the amateur sleuth of three mysteries, is firmly planted in the midst of her printing collective, which includes her twin sister Penny and Penny's boyfriend/husband Ray. Pam's detective activities lead her through a variety of non-middle-class milieus. Many of my short stories, more autobiographical than my novels, have women working at a variety of jobs: maid, factory worker, nurse, door-to-door salesperson. In my latest book, the comic thriller *Gaudi Afternoon*, my itinerant hero Cassandra Reilly, a working-class Catholic girl from Kalamazoo, Michigan, is translating a Spanish potboiler the whole time she's investigating various disappearances and thefts in Barcelona.

A novel published several years ago, *Cows and Horses*, usually referred to by reviewers as the story of the break-up of a ten-year relationship, is also the story of the break-up of a long-term retail business. Norah's desire to make Flexible Futons more commercial is not just symbolically tacked on to her penchant for sexually betraying Bet. It is another equally important aspect of what is driving her and Bet apart. Yet few reviewers made much of a point of the fact that Bet and Norah had been in business together and that that was a major part of their relationship.

My minor characters have livelihoods as well. In *Cows and Horses*, for example, Kelly is a welder at Texaco; Marianne keeps a dairy farm; and Sylvia works at the phone company while running an upholstery business on the side. The characters don't talk about their work as much as characters in *Ambitious Women* perhaps, but their jobs are absolutely core to my understanding of them and to my understanding of the world.

I write about class directly and indirectly — sometimes through the occupations my characters hold, sometimes through what possibilities they see open to them. Pam Nilsen, for instance, is solidly middle class in upbringing and lifestyle. She grew up in a safe neighborhood in Seattle, had a secure family situation, and never, in any of the books, worries one bit about money. Her lover, Hadley, has inherited wealth, while other characters, such as June, a Black worker at the printing collective, are working class. I don't identify with Pam's background; Allison's, in *Ambitious Women*, seems more familiar to me, and Bet's, in *Cows and Horses*, is most familiar of all. I frequently write about characters who, often with others, run their own small businesses. Not only is it a situation that I know intimately, but I find it a useful way of bringing together characters from different social and class backgrounds who have contradictory feelings about money, power and entitlement.

One of the things I do in my fiction is split up my own class and work experiences and give them to various characters, so that they can play out the contradictions I feel in myself. I give some characters more money and privilege and some less; I give some alternative jobs and some jobs as employees. Some of the characters love their occupations and others are searching for something to do that has meaning.

There are class conflicts all through my writing: Bet's with Norah; Pam's with Hadley; Allison's with Holly. They tend to be implicit rather than debated, but they affect, in a very clear manner, the ways in which these characters relate to the work they do. Bet, for instance, feels that Norah is capable of doing anything she wants with their futon business — that she's going to turn it into an import shop and make lots of money with it — while Norah, who is from a middle-class, well-educated background, is impatient with Bet's constant sense of limitation. Norah is leaving Bet behind, by finding a professional woman as her new lover, by decorating the shop with upscale merchandise. Some of the grief in the novel is class grief.

Too often writing about work is assumed to be something only a working-class writer would be interested in. For a writer to say that work is a major theme in her writing is for people to assume that, in fact, class is her main subject. To even mention the word "class" in North American feminist circles is for people to assume you mean to assert your working-class background and rights (upper-class women hide their backgrounds, while middle-class women just assume everyone shares theirs). Yet writers who write from a working-class background don't always write about work — nor should they be expected to. Often by the time working-class women have become published writers they have left behind the work of the working class and are dealing with the class aspects that make them feel so uncomfortable and not-at-home in the primarily middle-class feminist movement.

For me, the work my characters do, like the class they belong to, is paramount to my knowledge of them, and to what I want to say about the world in my novels. Yet I don't find that to be true of many lesbian novels. In over ten years of having my fiction reviewed and reading the reviews of other writers, I have found that a character's occupation or her class is rarely commented on, much less discussed with the attention it deserves.

Why *is* work so invisible in contemporary lesbian literature? Why is it often missing from our writing? Why don't critics see it when it's there? Why don't they see when it's *not* there?

Of course there have always been lesbian writers who have provided their characters with real jobs, starting with Beebo Brinker as an elevator operator. Others who come to mind are Andrea Carlisle in *The Riverhouse Stories*, Maureen Brady in *Folly*, Andrea Freud Lowenstein in *This Place*, Isabel Miller in *Patience and Sarah* and *The Love of Good Women*. Lee Lynch and Valerie Miner in the U.S. and Caeia March in England are working-class writers who write with respect and insight about women as workers and about the often difficult trade-offs that come with upward mobility and "cross-class travel." Jane Rule has always given us a variety of characters whose occupations have everything to do with who they are and how they live their lives. *Desert of the Heart* is the obvious example, with its gorgeous descriptions of Silver and Ann working in the casino, but all Rule's work is rich with people who care about what they do. Yet I've never heard Rule described as a writer who writes well about work. I've never heard any of the above writers praised, in fact, for their descriptions of waitressing, factory life, teaching or working as an electrician. At most Lynch, Miner or Brady will be cited as a working-class writer; more likely each will not only have to claim that classification for herself — she'll also have to explain what it means.

I'd like to say the situation is better in literature in general, but lesbian literature too often mirrors rather than contradicts what's being written in mainstream North America. It's as rare in New York publishing to find a novel like *Spartina* by John Casey, which evokes the world of fishermen in Rhode Island, as it is to find a gripping, meticulously researched and felt story of class struggle on the lesbian bookshelf. Lesbians tend to be among the poorer strata of society — yet it's amazing how many bland but securely employed professors, lawyers, journalists and therapists one finds in our novels. Why no gill-netters or telephone repair workers? Why no secretaries who enjoy their jobs or nurses who take pride in their skill? For that matter, why no women CEOs? Most of the women in lesbian literature who own their own businesses make jewelry.

The issue is, of course, that work isn't seen as a legitimate theme in the literature of the late twentieth century. Depression-era feminists and socialists such as Meridel Le Sueur and Tillie Olsen are written about but rarely emulated. Popular lesbian fiction today tends to be about romance, recovery and sex. Work is merely background; a character's occupation means little more than the color of her hair. That's true in the lesbian *Bildungsroman* as well, which explores the struggles of a writer or artist to create without adequate time, space or recognition. In these works of fiction the protagonist often has a menial job that saps her energy and humiliates her talent. She's a file clerk, a waitress, a migrant assistant professor, something temporary, something *beneath* her (most *Bildungsromans* are, not surprisingly, written by middle-class writers). Extremely experimental lesbian writing avoids the question of making a living completely, and is much more focused on criticizing patriarchal language than the patriarchal workplace.

There are reasons for all this, and to explore them is beyond the scope of this essay. But I do know that traditionally the writer feels apart from ordinary people; the reality, as well as the myth, is that creative people *are* alienated from mass culture. It's also clear that most jobs are not fulfilling in any way. To answer the phone or sit in front of a typewriter or to ring up sales or to place a fork on a napkin as it slips by on a conveyer belt (all of which I have done) is not challenging and is never well paid. One might also say that lesbians in particular are almost always underpaid and exploited on their jobs, and that at night they want to read about something other than their stupid clerical jobs. Lesbian writers, even more than most writers, or most lesbians, have to struggle with poverty and temp jobs and with trying to make a little place, a little space for themselves to write. One could say that it's not that most lesbian writers are against work or contemptuous of it, it's that they are never paid for the work that they do, and the work they do is writing.

All the same, I hunger for stories of work. They're stories I want to tell and stories I want to read, and I don't always know where to find them. Recently I picked up an anthology of working-class women's writings, *Calling Home*, but to my surprise I found that the section "The Job" comprised only thirty-seven pages in over 300; there were only six writers out of seventy-five, and none of them were writing about lesbians. A wonderful anthology was published last year by Papier-Mache Press. Already *If I Had a Hammer*, with its bold subtitle "Women's Work in Poetry, Fiction, and Photographs," has become a favorite of mine. I feel encouraged by the love and care that went into producing such a volume and by the number of writers who contributed to it.

Like any writer, I want my work to be recognized for all that it is. I'm fascinated by plot and structure, by genre subversion, by history. My overall fictional intent could be described as one long meditation on death and loss. There are many things I want to do in my writing, many things I want to have readers and critics notice: my images, my obsessions, my narrative strategies, my humor. Yes, I want very much for my work to be recognized, but also my *writing about work*. And I worry that most critics are too middle class to see that, that many of them have never worked at jobs outside academe, that they share the prevalent contempt for both blue-collar work and for work in general, unless it is glamorous, highly paid and prestigious.

The paucity of description and discussion about the work we do and about our relationships with other women and men as co-workers is a serious lack in the growing field of lesbian literature. It intrigues me, it concerns me, it disappoints me. It tells me that there are other ways to be invisible than to be a lesbian.

SELECTED PUBLICATIONS

BOOKS
Thin Ice and Other Stories. Seattle: Seal Press, 1981.
Ambitious Women. Albany, N.Y.: Spinsters, Ink, 1982; Seattle: Seal Press, 1985.
Walking on the Moon. Seattle: Seal Press, 1983.
Murder in the Collective. Seattle: Seal Press, 1984.
Sisters of the Road. Seattle: Seal Press, 1986.
Miss Venezuela. Seattle: Seal Press, 1988.
Cows and Horses. Portland, Oreg.: The Eighth Mountain Press, 1988.
The Dog Collar Murders. Seattle: Seal Press, 1989.
Gaudi Afternoon. Seattle: Seal Press, 1990.

TRANSLATIONS FROM NORWEGIAN
Cora Sandel: Selected Short Stories. Seattle: Seal Press, 1985.
Nothing Happened, by Ebba Haslund. Seattle: Seal Press, 1987.

CO-EDITED BOOKS
With Rachel da Silva. *Backbone* 1-4, anthologies of Northwest women's writing. Seattle: Seal Press, 1977-1982. Available on a limited basis from Seal Press.
With Faith Conlon and Rachel da Silva. *The Things That Divide Us*. Seattle: Seal Press, 1985.

ANTHOLOGIES
"We Didn't See It." In *Lesbian Love Stories*, edited by Irene Zahava. Freedom, Calif.: The Crossing Press, 1989.
"Murder at the International Feminist Bookfair." In *Reader, I Murdered Him*, edited by Jen Green. New York: St Martin's Press, 1989.

"Is This Enough For You?" In *Lesbian Love Stories, Volume 2*, edited by Irene Zahava. Freedom, Calif.: The Crossing Press, 1991.

"The Erotic Lives of Fictional Characters." In *An Intimate Wilderness*, edited by Judith Barrington. Portland, Oreg.: The Eighth Mountain Press, 1991.

"Theft of the Poet." In *A Woman's Eye*, edited by Sara Paretsky. New York: Delacorte Press, 1991.

"The Death of a Much-Travelled Woman." In *The Fourth WomanSleuth Anthology*, edited by Irene Zahava. Freedom, Calif.: The Crossing Press, 1991.

INTERVIEWS

June Thomas. *off our backs*, January 1990.

Victoria Brownworth. "Making the Political Personal." *Outweek*, 9 January 1991, 68-70.

Sheila MacIntosh. *Sojourner*, June 1991.

Askenet

Meaning "Raw" in My Language

CHRYSTOS

Staring out the foggy window over my typewriter, I want confidence that this new book[1] is good, will be as well received as *Not Vanishing*. I'm pushing at the boundaries of censorship with it — not those of hell-bent helms, which don't interest me — but the covert ones of the Native and Lesbian communities concerning what is acceptable to say. I wonder if the boundaries are actual or my own paranoia. Fighting depression, numbness. I'm not good enough. It will fail. I can't do it. Everyone will laugh. I'll be rejected. Each book becomes more of a risk. The acclaim for *Not Vanishing* has opened a craving for acceptance; the desire to preserve the little I've gained. The new book could deprive me. Fear of failing my Indian people, of their possible discomfort with my blatant sexuality. Fear of failing Lesbians, of their discomfort with my insistence on a different world view, on respect rather than exploitation as a goal (in a dominant culture which exploits everything & everyone, including children). Fear of telling the truth because it is not pretty or flattering or easy. Maybe no one will want to read me anymore. Then I'll have to go back to being a maid full-time, which will kill my spirit (or cause me to kill someone I clean for).

I begin to understand why P. wrote less and less as time went on — she was afraid she couldn't live up to herself. The more one writes, the more closely that writing is scrutinized. The more one becomes known, the more one arouses inevitable jealousy, which can be expressed in devastatingly hideous ways. The more one gives to the audience, the more they demand. Fiction writers can pretend that they write fantasy, with no reference to their own experiences, but poets of my genre (and P.'s) are writing from our very lives. How can we protect ourselves & our loved ones from intolerable judgments? What IS permissible to write? Who has the "right" to our stories? Can I criticize my own? Is my work bringing us a good future? Am I asking the important questions? Am I just a self-centered brat demanding attention? Sometimes I feel my writing is too real to publish.

I've recently developed an idea about writing down every racist incident that I hear about, that happens to me or that I see. I want to examine how each one occurs & what it feels like, even the "petty" interactions that People of Color are forced to ignore/swallow or risk ending up in jail. Writing down the invisible toll on all of us has changed me in good ways. I'm stronger & less vulnerable. It's easier to stay sober & my blood pressure has gone down. I eat compulsively less often. I'm beginning to form more healthy personal ties. Acknowledging the overwhelming variety of assaults on us is a relief. It isn't in our imaginations & it doesn't get better if we just behave & shut up. It has also helped me to think about how the dynamics of racism affected my family (& thus, shaped me). I realize that racism is one of those "Oh no here she goes again with *that*" subjects, & that many feel it is all fixed or doesn't affect them, but I know it is one of the cornerstones of the cultures we live in & is so deeply embedded in our lives that it is often invisible, like the glass ceilings women executives describe. None of us are healthy because of it.

The longer I'm sober, the more that I heal & the more that I face my own scars — instead of projecting their pain onto someone else — the better I become as a writer. It's hard to fight the fame disease, to remain open & down-to-earth, to resist exploitation, to remain an ordinary person rather than a freak. I didn't understand these complications of publishing before I became well known. I was very naive & excited that someone at last wanted to listen to me. I've learned a lot about how to use the english language since I began speaking publicly, especially how to protect myself from sounding uneducated (this is glaring in some of my early interviews). I haven't been polished by the college system, which is where most writers learn how to present themselves as intellectuals, so there are times when I don't fit in or I feel as though my writing is too raw to be read with other writers, who are more academic. I also understand that my rawness is exactly what makes my writing accessible to many people who claim to hate poetry (but like mine).

Many reviewers & audiences have seen me almost entirely as an "angry" poet, which is very frustrating, because less than half of *Not Vanishing* is about anger. I think this labeling is due to the fact that anger is a verboten emotion in western culture, unless it is directed at someone less powerful than oneself. It doesn't make money, it doesn't maintain hierarchies & it might interrupt the flow down the assembly line. I hope that my turn toward sarcasm in *Dream On*, as a method of making my points, will change this stereotyping of my work. I also can't understand how anyone could expect me to *not* be angry about the facts of our lives as Indigenous People, as Women, as Lesbians, as Workers, as Survivors of abuse of all kinds. I've never been rewarded (or accepted) as a nice girl, so I have less need to be one.

I've used writing as a way to box up pain & make it bearable. It's always a struggle for me not to cry on stage. I cry very easily at other times & am not innately ashamed of tears. But I know that the dominant culture thinks that tears are a sign of "being out of control" or not being "cool." My main purpose is to convey our situations — to make our political realities known widely — not to be pitied by audiences. I get a lot of headaches from putting my body through this. Because performing is more satisfying to me than books are (it is closer to my oral tradition), I fight myself in this battle to reveal emotion through my work without being wiped out by it. Some of my work DOES wipe me out. For example, I wrote "For Eli"[2] in one sitting & hung it up by a safety pin in my kitchen for over nine months before I could look at it again. When I was trying to type it for the manuscript, I made so many typos from tension that it took me several days to get a clean copy. It's important to me to say this because I want to explode the myth that writing is something one is in charge of. Often a piece has me by the throat & I wish it would leave me alone.

I've wondered if my writing is mistaken for being powerful when it is perhaps desperate. I can still be devastated for months by a critical remark, which makes publishing an excruciating experience. My loneliness increases when it is assumed that "my crazy grandfather" or other subjects in my writing are metaphors. They aren't. There hasn't ever been enough space for me to write anything else BUT my actual life. The stories I amuse myself with as I work don't see print, nor do the stories I hear in my mind that come from elsewhere. I'm envious of those who have the time to create something other than their own lives in print; at the same time I'm suspicious of "characters" who can so easily reflect aspects of colonization & exploitation without commentary. Native People do not share the same world view as Eurocentric People. We don't share the same assumptions about the nature of reality, the same stories, values or beliefs. Even our most honest attempts at communication can be misinterpreted or ignored because we lack a common ground. Though writing IS communication, it is often used/abused for obscuring reality, as all culture can be used. The "reality" of books in print is still primarily white, middle or upper class, male, heterosexual & connected seamlessly to dominant western cultural values. There is very little room for our voices unless they are pleasantly modulated & charming. Even in the radical fringe world of Lesbian Feminist publishing, books appear with demeaning uses of the words "pow wow" or "peace pipe." Or a character is defined as "Native" in one sentence, but thinks & acts like a white person throughout the book. If you miss that one sentence, you assume the character IS white. The word "blind" is still used to mean ignorant or insensitive, which is inexcusable, especially after all the hard work of women with disabilities.

Many of the books I read, which aren't written by People of Color or writers from other countries, seem superfluous & self-indulgent — if not actively offensive. Most of popular Lesbian culture I find boring (particularly a great deal of the music). I feel guilty that I prefer reading writers from other countries, even (shock) heterosexual males. I am sick of the Lesbian Cultural Ghetto which idolizes certain performers who are slick & mediocre rather than passionate & politically astute. What is the political implication for Lesbian Country of the fact that the hottest-selling books in feminist book stores are sappy, happy-ending romances, so poorly written that Agatha Christie is preferable? What does it mean when I consider writing one because I'm broke, using an assumed name?

I have several concerns as a writer which fall outside the realm of accepted discourse. I want to examine the unspoken rules which operate inside our writing. Some of these are: Women are good, or only bad because men have made them bad; that by their very nature, Lesbian relationships are more equal than heterosexual ones; that other cultures exist for our enjoyment; that we, meaning the united states, are the center of the universe; that when another Lesbian is violating our community standards, the best thing to do is shut up & hope it goes away. These are kinds of self-censorship which are more frightening to me than those of a sexual nature (which I tend to ignore).

I want to face serious issues as a writer. What is ethical to tell? This is especially complex when one is a part of oppressed groups, who stand to have any negative information used against them by the dominant-white-male-christian establishment. Because words now travel all over the globe & because people read who even fifty years ago did not, the questions of responsibility deepen. A writer can no longer, in good conscience, "take over" the experience of those whose own voice is fighting to be heard. I'm still angry when a man publishes a book supposedly written from the female point of view (even when I enjoy the writing), as well as when work by caucasians is purportedly written from the viewpoint of People of Color. This is a disgustingly prevalent trend concerning Indigenous People. What does this mean for me in regard to fiction, which I haven't written yet because my own experience has been so overwhelmingly in need of a voice? The debate which raged at the 3rd International Feminist Book Fair (Montreal, June 1988) concerned the "right" of the author to write anything she could imagine. I don't agree because writing is a responsibility, not a right. But I cannot explain how I would draw appropriate lines. Indeed, it would be rude in my culture to enforce my sensibilities on another writer. I joke bitterly that I'm going to write a novel completely about white people, (in which no one else appears) as a satire on their world view & to illustrate that I see them better than they see themselves.

How does one write so that it is not embarrassing to reread one's work in ten years, given the nature of our beings to change & outgrow ourselves?

How can one write honestly about an experience which is outside of one's life? My experience of motherhood is one of observation, so though I'm acutely aware of the pain on both sides of the maternal connection, I hesitate to write about it because it seems presumptuous when I've never faced the incredible hardships of raising children in the anti-child dominant culture.

Because I travel widely doing readings, I'm told many stories that I'm not at liberty to repeat, but which weigh me down because many of them are so painful. What can I do with these psychic wounds that are not my own, but become part of me through listening?

My dream is to write a great Lesbian novel — one that rings with our difficulties as well as our joys. Most writers fictionalize actual life, but given the intent of feminism (which I interpret to mean giving equal voice to all), do I have the right to only my version of events? Literature, as we know it, was created with the deliberate exclusion of many classes of people — so the concept of the "neutral third person voice" is a sham, given that for thousands of years that voice was defined exclusively by the privileged. I imagine that a dialogue is a more appropriate "voice" for our writing future, but I'm still unclear about the form. My lover & I keep a joint journal, answering back & forth, which might work as a possibility. In the past, I haven't used her name when writing about us, at her request. I've asked her permission to write about events between us which she has given. But what happens if I want to write about something that she doesn't want to reveal?

I've been relatively silent about a number of issues that concern me because I've feared alienating Native People and/or Lesbians. These issues include drug addiction, prostitution, violence between women, alcoholism, skin color prejudice & privilege, the mimicked sexism of Native men, the plague of violence among Native families, the rude racism of many Lesbians toward Native men, the full implications of being a person not really welcome in either group & what I'll call "kinky" sex. I reject the term S/M as a male-created practice—defined in the writings of the Marquis de Sade, in the same spirit that I reject Marx as being a middle-class, eurocentric, caucasian male heterosexual living in a different era & thus not very useful to us now.

What do these silences mean? How can I break out of them respectfully? In claiming my former life, as a prostitute & junkie, for instance, will I increase the prejudice about Native women in the minds of readers? I was raised to avoid discussion of female issues or sex in public, or even with close friends. In opening these areas to scrutiny, am I violating my culture? Is that culture the actual tradition or merely a mirror of colonization? No one is alive who could answer that question—all the words about us were written by foreigners until quite recently. Even our recorded speeches are translations.

How much does colonization shape my writing? My goals as a writer? Is it even possible to create a new place with words, given the repressive nature of english as a language?

As "fame" increasingly invades my life, with its own peculiar diseases, how do I maintain my balance & continue to write honestly? How much of myself do I "have to" give away in order to be respected as a writer? What do I owe my audience? The whole nature of publishing is colonial & patronizing—even when the publishing is controlled by feminists or by Native people—because it posits that "I" (or another writer) have words that are more important than another's or than everyone else's. How can we use these tools of colonization to clear our paths to a better life?

Because the historical stance of the writer is to be "the one who knows," how does one incorporate one's real fears & inadequacies into the text without seeming pitiful or weak?

Given the resistance on the part of most of the male (both straight & gay) literary establishments to the words of women & the prevalent sexism all over the world, how can one dialogue with writers who are a part of these establishments? I've felt dismissed by gay, male, caucasian writers, who are supposed to be my brothers, & have found that organizing with them is extremely painful because many of them have not even noticed feminism or any of the issues which feminism seeks to address. Thus, at the first OutWrite Conference (San Francisco, March 1990), there were only nine writers of Color (we counted); issues of inaccessibility were not considered & both keynote speakers were able-bodied caucasians. One particularly obnoxious comment was, "Well, white gays are really focused on being *gay!*"

The Words Without Borders Literary Festival at Gay Games III (Vancouver, August 1990) followed this same pattern, including completely inaccessible reading sites & the obligatory panel of writers of Color whose job was to discuss racism (which Sky Lee roundly & eloquently denounced).

Even saying these words marks me as ungrateful, rude, nasty & not on "our" side. Why am I supposed to give gay white people the benefit of the doubt after more than twenty years of organizing? I *thought* they were listening to those of us whose *lives* are these issues. If I criticize, I'm not asked back & I'm a bad sport & I don't understand. I understand very well; that's why I'm so crabby.

At the original OutWrite Conference, even though I was one of the presenters, my book wasn't for sale at the tables. My book has not been for sale at a number of conferences I've been invited to (including as Keynote speaker), so I've taken to carting it around myself, which is difficult because I have had back surgery. I always sell out. *Not Vanishing* is in its fourth printing, which is unusual for a poetry book, so it is not hard to sell. What does it mean when I can't trust the organizers of conferences I'm invited to, to make sure my book is for sale? Is this racism? Is it classism (as I'm not "educated" or academic & I despise playing ego bumper cars)? Is there something wrong with me? I'm not charming enough, that's obvious. I didn't realize charm was so much a part of surviving as a writer. Why do I even have to ask these whiny questions?

This lack of trust affects my writing. It affects how much I'm willing to give to audiences, who are primarily white, even when the readings are organized by Native Studies programs or students of Color. The writer who is white cannot possibly imagine the sense of dismay one feels as a Person of Color facing a sea of mostly white faces. I'd guess most white writers don't even notice. What would my writing be like if I faced three hundred Native Queers when I read?

What does it mean to be a sober person when most writers still drink? When conferences are organized around cocktail parties (I went to one where there was nothing else but alcohol to drink)? When having a "good time" still means getting drunk & alcohol is still romanticized as part of the starving artist malarkey? Because Twelve Step programs are not helpful to me, I find it very lonely to be sober as a writer.

What does it mean, that although I am a very good teacher, I cannot get a job anywhere teaching writing, even among feminists, because I don't have pedigree papers? I'm afraid to do all the work of going to college because I wonder if I still would not be able to get a job at the white-dominated women's studies or creative writing departments. I know I can always find work as a maid. This affects my writing as well as my outlook. It makes me irritable & not polite. It means I have very little patience for writers who work inside academia & know very little of what I persist in calling real life. You know, the drunks with no place to go; the kids with black eyes; the women working the streets with mean pimps. How can I possibly read a thesis on an Italian poet of the twelfth century, let alone write one in order to get a degree?

Last night, I was browsing through a feminist calendar in which mostly white women were addressing the issue of racism. Sort of. I was struck by the statement that they had become a white group because they developed their group through friendship circles — as though that were a legitimate excuse. If all one's friends are white, what does that mean? I've been told it's more comfortable. Comfortable is one of those terrible seductive words with no politics. I'm the sole acquaintance of Color of far too many white people already. How am I perceived as a writer by someone whose only contact with People of Color is through books or movies or records? Our art certainly becomes the exotic color & we remain tokenized, other, outsiders. When I go someplace new & all the posters are of white women in a women's center, is it ethical for me to use my "power" as a "famous writer" to shame them into something more inclusive? Will that change even a hair in whatever town I've been? As racism & anti-semitism increase in violence, what are our responsibilities as writers to end this terror?

Writing takes time & privacy, both of which continue to be rare in my life.

I give priority to political organizing & feel I have no choice about that. My writing suffers because I can't give it the full attention it deserves. Because my time is torn in so many directions, I'm impatient with long meetings in which people discuss things, such as, "Should we print & distribute this information we've spent eight months collecting, if nobody will read it anyway?" Politics are not my social club & I'm often rude to those for whom they are. I say that I'm not as good a writer as I could be & also that I'm not as good an organizer. In a culture that demands mono-attention to one aspect of life, how can I remain multi-dimensional & not go crazy?

I use writing, quite consciously, to survive. I let off steam, I celebrate, I feel less invisible when I write. Though I am published & fairly well known (in the small feminist world, not the larger literary one), I still feel disrespected, unheard. Perhaps I'm looking for the family who will take me in & allow me to be all of my selves. Looking for the place, which doesn't exist, where world peace & an end to global hunger are reality.

I write because I want to change how we relate to one another. I understand that this makes my work less literary, because my goal is not only to create interesting patterns with words or to evoke beautiful images. The definition of "good writing" is to some extent limited to these qualities which seem superficial to me. I'm running too hard, even when I have time to write, to be able to indulge myself in that way. I'm angry about that too. Why can't I write 13 Sonnets to Blackbirds? Because I don't live in that world of safety, of speculation, of distance (I'm busy noticing that two of the birds have deformed feet from traps & can't eat properly). I want to blow up every ivory tower in the world. This makes me very difficult to get along with; makes me mean & not sensitive. This means I'm most often referred to as an "angry" writer. Isn't it interesting that no one is referred to as a "passive" writer?

Who is the appropriate audience for Lesbian writers, who only comprise a small percentage of the population? Writing only to other Lesbians seems self-defeating to me, if one's goal is social change. On the other hand, I could never abandon Lesbians to further my career or agree to the closet in exchange for mainstream publishing. The majority of Lesbians are not interested in literature as anything more than vapid entertainment — no more so than the average citizen. If my goal is to write deeply, who is my support system? Only other sympathetic Lesbian writers?

The worst question (which I face by re-using all my paper, typing on backs of flyers, beginning to use recycled paper, etc.) is what am I doing writing when my sisters, the trees, are being cut down so that I can? I'd prefer forests (the unmanaged kind) to a stack of my books, but the possibility of forests is rapidly disappearing as we clear-cut our way into the future & exchange wild land for tree farms. I live near clear-cuts, see their pain regularly, so the fact of my collusion with destruction is never far from my thoughts. I was very happy that recycled paper was used for the "Shame On" broadsheet which Press Gang Publishers recently printed.[3]

I AM a colonized person, in many dimensions. I've spent most of my life attempting to unravel that damage. I expect to continue this until I keel over. How can I as a writer address colonization clearly, when I'm strangling inside of it?

How can I be most useful? Perhaps these questions are more helpful to me than to others. I'm only beginning to formulate them, so the answers, if I can find them, are in the future. I welcome dialogue with anyone who wants to address these issues openly; please write to me in care of Press Gang Publishers.

Part of my political stance is to demystify writing. So, I'll say that I wrote this on a shaky card table, eating leftovers with my hair uncombed, while my lover was out of town & I was fighting depression & resisting the lure of garbage on TV. I've been sick for over a month, while on the road, & am due out again this weekend, which I dread because I'm so tired. I wrote trivia in my journal for about an hour before I started this. The table is a mass of unanswered mail, things I have to do today, scraps of newspaper articles & cartoons. I'm avoiding working on my new manuscript, which is overdue. I don't recommend my disorganization & last minute approach to writing, but I'm learning to forgive myself for it, since when I "make time" to write, I'm often very tedious. My best work erupts & surprises me.

I long to do nothing but write, but it's a dream I probably won't realize. I always remember I'm not supposed to write at all. So every sentence is a bouquet, a relief, a song I hope reaches the next generations.

NOTES

1. *Dream On*, published by Press Gang Publishers, 1991.
2. "For Eli," in *Not Vanishing*, is a poem about a young boy beaten to death by his father, and

about other incidents of violence and abuse.

3. "Shame On," a poem about appropriation of Native spirituality, is available as a broadsheet as well as in the book *Dream On*.

SELECTED PUBLICATIONS

BOOKS

Not Vanishing. Vancouver: Press Gang Publishers, 1988.
Dream On. Vancouver: Press Gang Publishers, 1991.

ANTHOLOGIES

Poems and a drawing. In *A Gathering of Spirit: A Collection of North American Indian Women*, edited by Beth Brant. Montpelier, Vermont: Sinister Wisdom Books, 1984; Ithaca N.Y.: Firebrand Books, 1988; Toronto: The Women's Press, 1988.

Poems and prose. In *This Bridge Called My Back: Writings by Radical Women of Color*, edited by Cherríe Moraga and Gloria Anzaldúa. Watertown, Mass.: Persephone Press Inc., 1981; New York: Kitchen Table: Women of Color Press, 1984.

"Perhaps" (prose). In *Out the Other Side: Contemporary Lesbian Writing*, edited by Christian McEwen and Sue O'Sullivan. London: Virago Press, 1988; Freedom, Calif.: The Crossing Press, 1989

Excerpts from letters. In *Making Face, Making Soul/Haciendo Caras: Creative and Critical Perspectives by Feminists of Color*, edited by Gloria Anzaldúa. San Francisco: Aunt Lute Foundation, 1990.

Poems. In *Dancing on the Rim of the World: An Anthology of Contemporary Northwest Native American Writing*, edited by Andrea Lerner. Tuzcon, Ariz.: Univ. of Arizona Press, 1990.

REVIEWS AND INTERVIEWS

Celeste George and Constanza Silva. "With breathtaking clarity: Chrystos talks back." Interview (Part One). *Kinesis* (July/August 1988);

———."Good Enough to be Alive." Interview (Part Two). *Angles* (January 1989): 12-13.

Ana Terri Ortiz. "The generous poetry of Luz María Umpierre and Chrystos." Review of *Not Vanishing* and other books. *Gay Community News*, 4-10 September 1988.

Karen Claudia. "Chrystos: *Not Vanishing* & In Person." Interview and review. *off our backs* (March 1989): 19.

Jewelle Gomez. "In Review: *Not Vanishing*, by Chrystos." *Trivia* 14 (Spring 1989): 82-89.

Margaret Randall. "Many-colored poets." Review of *Not Vanishing* and other books. *Women's Review of Books* 6, no. 12 (September 1989): 29-31.

Rebecca A. Johns. "Poets weave verses of struggle." Review of *Not Vanishing* and other books. *Guardian Book Review Supplement*, (Winter 1989): 8-9.

Andrea Lerner. Review of *Not Vanishing*. *Western American Literature*, 24, no. 3, 266-67.

To(o) Queer the Writer —
Loca, escritora y chicana

GLORIA ANZALDÚA

Queer Labels and Debates

I believe that while there are lesbian perspectives, sensibilities, experiences and topics, *there are no "lesbian writers."*

For me the term lesbian *es un problemon*. As a working-class Chicana, mestiza† — a composite being, *amalgama de culturas y de lenguas* — a woman who loves women, "lesbian" is a cerebral word, white and middle class, representing an English-only dominant culture, derived from the Greek word *lesbos*. I think of lesbians as predominantly white and middle-class women and a segment of women of color who acquired the term through osmosis much the same as Chicanas and Latinas assimilated the word "Hispanic." When a "lesbian" names me the same as her she subsumes me

---

†The new mestiza queers have the ability, the flexibility, the malleability, the amorphous quality of being able to stretch this way and that way. We can add new labels, names and identities as we mix with others.

under her category. I am of her group but not as an equal, not as a whole person—my color erased, my class ignored. *Soy una puta mala*, a phrase coined by Ariban, a *tejana tortillera*. "Lesbian" doesn't name anything in my homeland. Unlike the word "queer," "lesbian" came late into some of our lives. Call me *de las otras*. Call me *loquita, jotita, marimacha, pajuelona, lambiscona, culera*—these are words I grew up hearing. I can identify with being *"una de las otras"* or a *"marimacha,"* or even a *jota* or a *loca porque*— these are the terms my home community uses. I identify most closely with the Nahuatl term *patlache*. These terms situate me in South Texas Chicano/*mexicano* culture and in my experiences and *recuerdos*. These Spanish/Chicano words resonate in my head and evoke gut feelings and meanings.

I want to be able to choose what to name myself. But if I have to pick an identity label in the English language I pick "dyke" or "queer," though these working-class words (formerly having "sick" connotations) have been taken over by white middle-class lesbian theorists in the academy. Queer is used as a false unifying umbrella which all "queers" of all races, ethnicities and classes are shoved under. At times we need this umbrella to solidify our ranks against outsiders. But even when we seek shelter under it we must not forget that it homogenizes, erases our differences. Yes, we may all love members of the same sex but we are not the same. Our ethnic communities deal differently with us. I must constantly assert my differentness, must say, This is what I think of loving women. I must stress: The difference is in my relationship to my culture; white culture may allow its lesbians to leave—mine doesn't. This is one way I avoid getting sucked into the vortex of homogenization, of getting pulled into the shelter of the queer umbrella.

What is a lesbian writer? The label in front of a writer positions her. It implies that identity is socially constructed. But only for the cultural "other." Oblivious to privilege and wrapped in arrogance, most writers from the dominant culture never specify their identity; I seldom hear them say, I am a white writer. If the writer is middle class, white and heterosexual s/he is crowned with the "writer" hat—no mitigating adjectives in front of it. They consider me a *Chicana* writer, or a lesbian Chicana writer. Adjectives are a way of constraining and controlling. "The more adjectives you have the tighter the box."[1] The adjective before writer marks, for us, the "inferior" writer, that is, the writer who doesn't write like them. Marking is always "marking down." While I advocate putting Chicana, *tejana*, working-class, dyke-feminist poet, writer-theorist in front of my name, I do so for reasons different than those of the dominant culture. Their reasons are to marginalize, confine and contain. My labeling of myself is so that the Chicana and lesbian and all the other persons in me don't get erased, omitted or killed. Naming is how I make my presence known, how I assert who and what I am and want to be known as. Naming myself is a survival tactic.

I have the same kinds of problems with the label "lesbian writer" that I do with the label "Chicana writer." *Si, soy chicana,* and therefore a Chicana writer. But when critics label me thus, they're looking not at the person but at the writing, as though the writing is Chicana writing instead of the writer being Chicana. By forcing the label on the writing they marginalize it.

I've had the legitimacy issue thrown at me by another Chicana lesbian, Cherríe Moraga. In a book review of *Borderlands/La Frontera,* she implied that I was not a real lesbian because I did not stress my lesbian identity nor did I write about sexuality. I gathered that she wanted me to focus on lesbian sexuality. Her criticism implies that there is such a thing as a lesbian writer and that a lesbian writer should only write about lesbian issues and that lesbian issues are about sexuality.[2] It is ironic that some straight Chicanas/os, seeing only sexual difference because to them it is a glaring difference, also stress lesbian and gay aspects of my identity and leave out the culture and the class aspects. Always the labeling impacts expectations. In this double bind, one reader may view the label as a positive attribute, another as a way to marginalize.

This anthology's topic, "lesbian writers writing about their own writing," assumes the existence of a "lesbian" writer. It follows the tradition in which white middle-class lesbians and gay men frame the terms of the debate. It is they who have produced queer theory and for the most part their theories make abstractions of us colored queers. They control the production of queer knowledge in the academy and in the activist communities. Higher up in the hierarchy of gay politics and gay aesthetics, they most readily get their work published and disseminated. They enter the territories of queer racial ethnic/Others and re-inscribe and recolonize. They appropriate our experiences and even our lives and "write" us up. They occupy theorizing space, and though their theories aim to enable and emancipate, they often disempower and neo-colonize. They police the queer person of color with theory. They theorize, that is, perceive, organize, classify and name specific chunks of reality by using approaches, styles and methodologies that are Anglo American or European. Their theories limit the ways we think about being queer.

Position is point of view. And whatever positions we may occupy, we are getting only one point of view: white middle-class. Theory serves those that create it. White middle-class lesbians and gays are certainly not speaking for me. Inevitably we colored dykes fall into a reactive mode, counter their terms and theories — as I am doing, as I have to do before I can even begin to write this essay. We focus on the cultural abuse of colored by white and thus fall into the trap of the colonized reader and writer forever reacting against the dominant. I feel pushed into trying to "correct" the record, to speak out against it while all the time realizing that colored queers are not responsible for educating white lesbians and gays.

What I object to about the words "lesbian" and "homosexual" is that they are terms with iron-cast molds. There are assumptions made, by both insiders and outsiders, when one identifies with these terms. The words "lesbian" and "homosexual" conjure up stereotypes of differences that are different from those evoked by the word "queer." "Queer" also provokes different assumptions and expectations. In the '60s and '70s it meant that one was from a working-class background, that one was not from genteel society. Even though today the term means other things, for me there is still more flexibility in the "queer" mold, more room to maneuver. "Lesbian" comes from a Euro-Anglo American mold and "homosexual" from a deviant, diseased mold shaped by certain psychological theories. We non-Euro-Anglo Americans are supposed to live by and up to those theories. A mestiza colored queer person is bodily shoved by both the heterosexual world and by white gays into the "lesbian" or "homosexual" mold whether s/he fits or not. *La persona está situada dentro de la idea en vez del reves.*

I struggle with naming without fragmenting, without excluding. Containing and closing off the naming is the central issue of this piece of writing. The core question is: What is the power and what is the danger of writing and reading like a "lesbian" or a queer? Can the power and danger be named and can queer writing be named? How does one give queer writing labels while holding the totality of the group and the person in one's mind? How do we maintain the balance between solidarity and separate space, between the *gueras/os* and the *morenas/os*? "Where are our alliances, with our culture or our crotch?"[3] *Envez de dejar cada parte en su región y mantener entre ellos la distancia de un silencio, mejor mantener la tensión entre nuestras quatro o seis partes/personas.*

Identity is not a bunch of little cubbyholes stuffed respectively with intellect, race, sex, class, vocation, gender. Identity flows between, over, aspects of a person. Identity is a river — a process. Contained within the river is its identity, and it needs to flow, to change to stay a river — if it stopped it would be a contained body of water such as a lake or a pond. The changes in the river are external (changes in environment — river bed, weather, animal life) and internal (within the waters). A river's contents flow within its boundaries. Changes in identity likewise are external (how others perceive one and how one perceives others and the world) and internal (how one perceives oneself, self-image). People in different regions name the parts of the river/person which they see.

La búsqueda de identidad — How Queer is Queer?

Often I am asked, "What is your primary identity, being lesbian or working class or Chicana?" In defining or separating the "lesbian" identity from other aspects of identity I am asked to separate and distinguish all aspects from one another. I am asked to bracket each, to make boundaries around each so as to articulate one particular facet of identity only. But to put each in a separate compartment is to put them in contradiction or in isolation when in actuality they are all constantly in a shifting dialogue/relationship — the ethnic is in conversation with the academic and so on. The lesbian is part of the writer, is part of a social class, is part of a gender, is part of whatever identities one has of oneself. There is no way that I can put myselves through this sieve, and say okay, I'm only going to let the "lesbian" part out, and everything else will stay in the sieve. All the multiple aspects of identities (as well as the sieve) are part of the "lesbian."

I can understand that impulse to nail things down, to have a checklist which says that for you to be a dyke, a radical lesbian, or an S/M lesbian, you must pass certain criteria. But when those criteria are applied to people who fall outside the characterizations defined by white, middle-class lesbians and gays, (such as racial ethnic/Others) it feels very totalitarian. It feels more totalitarian for dykes of color than for lesbians because the checklist and criteria come from gay white ideology, whether its proponents are white or colored.

Different lesbians and gays scrutinize the cultural/Other to see if we're correct — they police us out of fear of instability within a community, fear of not appearing united and fear of attack by non-gay outsiders. But I fear a unity that leaves out parts of me, that colonizes me, i.e., violates my

integrity, my wholeness and chips away at my autonomy. We police ourselves out of fear as well. Because of our *mestisaje*, colored queers have more
communities to deal with (ethnic, class, white lesbians, etc.) that analyze
us to determine if we "pass."

The same thing is true of the dyke community: it wants to pinpoint the
dykes who are in the closet, the lesbians who are out, the queers who are
activists, gays who are writers. You are privileged differently if you are out
there being a model of "the good lesbian." And if you're not, if you happen to
be a lesbian and you write a story in which the protagonist is male or a
straight woman, then you're criticized for supporting the patriarchy by writing traditionally, for writing about concerns that are not seen as "lesbian concerns." But yet, what these lesbian readers fail to see is that a lot of times, in
presenting traditional content or characters that the gay community thinks
support the patriarchy, they may not be "seeing" that the queer colored
writers are doing something radical or critical via the form and/or style.
The story may depict violence of men against women. The white lesbian
"reads" this as a text perpetuating the oppression of women. Often in showing "how it really is," colored dykes actually effect changes in the psyches of
their readers. Often the lesbian reader misses the subtle subversive elements
and hidden messages. Her binocular vision, focusing on the trees, misses the
forest.

Reading Them Reading Me

A strange thing happens when I attend poetry or prose readings where two
or three lesbian feminists read. Often nothing they say moves me because it
is too predictable, too "white" and racist in its ignorance of colored gay experiences. I have done a number of readings within the white lesbian community and almost always have received a very generous reception. They may
squirm when I bring up racism and class oppression, but they seem to swal-
low what I say. I've also read in the Latino/Chicano Mission community
(where I have drawn smaller crowds) and have felt they would rather I had
checked my queerness at the door. On the other hand, poems and stories
dealing with race and class are received with much fervor.

Once in the Haight district I read to an audience of white and colored hip-
pies, straight beats and non-literary people. Later in a poem I tried to express the feelings of "at-home-ness" I experienced with them. I realized that

they had been open and receptive to my work and that class had something to do with it. When I read poems dealing with colored queer or Chicana issues, the audience didn't have any preconceptions. I felt accepted, respected and valued in a more total way than I had experienced in the "lesbian" or the Mission communities in San Francisco. These feelings are central to the interaction between writer, reader and text. Class *y el conflicto de clases* is at the core of this paper, perhaps more than dealing with being "queer of color."

In the past the reader was a minor character in the triangle of author-text-reader. More and more today the reader is becoming as important if not more important than the author. Making meaning is a collaborative affair. Similar class, ethnic and sexual identity is a strong component of the bond between writer and reader. This intimate interactive relationship I have with readers has to do with a colored queer feminist mestiza identity. Not all writers experience this interaction. This interaction comes with the realization that writing is a collaborative, communal activity not done in a room of one's own. It is an act informed and supported by the books the author reads, the people s/he interacts with and the centuries of cultural history that seethe under her skin. The idea of shared writing is not yet part of the consensual reality of most writers.

A lot of my poems, stories and essays (what I call *autohistorias*) are about reading—not just reading as in the act of reading words on a page, but also "reading" reality and reflecting on that process and the process of writing in general. The Haight poem is about me reading, about other people reading me and me reading them reading me. Most of these people at the Haight reading were straight, and a lot of them were men—what you would consider chauvinist and anti-feminist—yet they were there for me in a way that the other groups such as the politically correct or the politically aware groups weren't. What was it about them that was open and receptive? They would call out encouragement, would rock and hum to my words—they were listening with their bodies and not just their intellects. They weren't "reading" me the usual way. They were "reading" my readings in front of me. Their faces were not blank nor passive. They saw me as vulnerable, a flesh and blood person and not as a symbol of representation, not as a "Chicana" writer. They saw me as I wanted to be seen then—as an embodied symbol.

Reading Like a Lesbian

Reading like a queer feminist, which includes listening like one, may be how one would distinguish dyke-feminist or feminist from non dyke/feminist. Queer readers want to interact, to repeat back or reflect or mirror, but also do more than just reflect back and mirror—to add to the dialogue. White lesbians feel that colored dykes have important things to communicate or perhaps they want to really "listen to" and "read" us better in order to mitigate and correct their ethnocentrism. And that might be why dykes of color have such a low patience with texts and public events that don't allow us to participate fully. When I attend white women's music concerts there's so little part of me that gets to interact that there's nothing there for me. When I read Emma Pérez or Terri de la Peña or watch comedians Monica Palacios and Margo Gomez perform and when I study the art of Ester Hernández I realize what is missing from white lesbian texts—colored queer rites of passage.[4]

Though the Haight-Ashbury audience responded best, (back then in 1980-81) in 1991 lesbian and gay readers and audiences (who have learned to "read" me in their classrooms) not only are beginning to reflect back my ideas but to also actively engage with me and my theories.

Queering the Writer and Reading With a Queer *Facultad*

We queers also label ourselves. It is we as well as white, middle-class heterosexuals who say, "S/he's a gay writer." The gay community wants so badly to have pride in its artists and writers; it wants to shout it from the rooftops. There is a hunger for legitimacy in queers who are always trying to "discover" gay movie stars and great writers.

Can a straight woman or a man write a lesbian story? The questions are, Are you a dyke writer because you're a dyke, or are you a lesbian writer because the concerns that you write about are lesbian concerns? In other words, Is there such a thing as a lesbian language, dyke style, lesbian terminology, dyke aesthetics, or is it all up to the individual who's writing, regardless of whether she's a dyke or a straight woman, or a man? This is the same question that theorists asked in earlier debates—can a man write as a straight woman, can a man read as a woman? *We all know that women read as men and women write as men, because that's how we were taught.* We were

trained to read as men. Little girls read the books that boys read, but the
boys never read the books with little girl heroines, and so women are taught
to read westerns and spy novels and mysteries, and the "serious" literature,[5]
but we also read "women's literature," watch soap operas, read romances,
read women's mysteries. But men aren't taught to read women. How and why
do we break with this gender socialization? Isn't the departure as significant
as establishing the criteria? Reading affects the development of female and
male identity. I, for one, define my life and construct my identities through
the process of reading and writing — dyke detective novels, cultural theory,
Latin American fiction. Can we apply this in the same way to the lesbian
readers and the lesbian writers?

A straight woman reader of dyke writings would likely not catch a lot of the
undercurrents having to do with dyke sexualities or sexual experiences (unless, of course, she has a lot of lesbian friends). Queers (including cultural
Others) can fill in the gaps in a lesbian text and reconstruct it, where a
straight woman might not. I am arguing for a lesbian sensibility, not a lesbian
aesthetic.

Reading is one way of constructing identity. When one reads something
that one is familiar with, one attaches to that familiarity, and the rest of the
text, what remains hidden, is not perceived. Even if one notices things that
are very different from oneself, that difference is used to form identity by
negation — "I'm not that, I'm different from that character. This is me, that's
you." Yet readers have an attraction to the unfamiliar, a curiosity. Which is
why straight readers read gay literature. When a straight writer writes about
us, perhaps also out of curiosity, or latent queerness or to capitalize on a
trendy forbidden lifestyle, s/he often ends up appropriating our lives,
paying them token attention and focusing on sex instead of the full complexity of our lives. So while we do write for straight readers, they don't write for
us.

Identity formation is a component in reading and writing whether through
empathy and identification or disidentification. If it's a lesbian who's reading, she will have more incentive to keep reading when she reaches a dyke-
concern-laden passage in my writing. There will be more doors and windows
through which she can access the text than if she's a non-lesbian. If she's a
working-class dyke of color, however, there are even more *entradas*, more
identity-making opportunities. If she's a Chicana lesbian she's got the
greatest possibility of finding herself represented in my writing. But some
Chicana dykes, such as urban dwellers or younger ones, may be excluded

from my writing, while others bearing other kinds of "otherness" may plug into my writing. Just as we speak in different ways, we read in different ways, write in different ways. Educational and lived experiences change the way we speak, hear, read, and write.

However, there are straight, white, academic women who sometimes "see into" and "see through" unconscious falsifying disguises by penetrating the surface and reading underneath the words and between the lines. As outsiders, they may see through what I'm trying to say better than an insider. For me then it is a question of whether the individual reader is in possession of a mode of reading that can read the subtext, and can introject her experiences into the gaps. Some conventionally trained readers do not have the flexibility (in identity) nor the patience in deciphering a "strange," that is, different, text. Reading skills may result from certain ethnic, class or sexual experiences which allow her to read in non-white ways. She looks at a piece of writing and reads it differently.

I'm also a reader of my own work. And as a reader, I usually have more in common with the Chicana dyke than I do with the white, middle-class feminist. I am in possession of both ways of reading — Chicana working-class, dyke ways of reading, and white middle-class heterosexual and male ways of reading. I have had more training in reading as a white, middle-class academic than I do reading as a Chicana. Just like we have more training reading as men.

Reading With One's Foot In One's Mouth

Learning to read is not synonymous with academic learning. Working-class and street people may go into an experience — for example an incident taking place on the street — and "read" what is taking place in a way that an academic couldn't. One always writes and reads from the place one's feet are planted, the ground one stands on, one's particular position, point of view.

When I write about different ideas, I try to flesh out and embody them rather than abstract them. But I don't always spell things out. I want the reader to deduce my conclusions or at least come up with her own. Often the working-class person or the colored dyke will automatically identify with that experience and say, "Oh, yeah, I've lived it, or my friend has told me she's lived that," or whatever. The white, middle-class academic woman might see it in terms of where the author positions herself; whether she is "rereading"

(reinterpreting) or reinscribing certain patriarchal signs; whether s/he lo-
cates herself in a specific historical period; whether she is self-reflective
about her writing. These are approaches and moves she has learned to make
as a feminist critic, and they are different from the moves that the street-wise
person utilizes. The street reader looks at an experience as something that's
alive and moving or about to move, whereas the academic looks at the flat-
tened out, abstract theory on these pages that is not connected to the actual
experience. Being queer, being of color, I consider myself standing in the
Borderlands (the actual crossroads or bridge) of these two "readings." I may
be able to read the situation in the street from the point of view of a street-
wise person, and I can look at these abstract theoretical writings and be able
to read them academically because of the schooling that I've had.

    One of the things that I've discovered about people critiquing my writing is
that they want me to flesh out more of the gaps, provide more transition. I
suppose this is so they don't have to do as much work. "In my instruction in
tutoring writing," commented Vicki Alcoset, my writing intern, who is
Chicana and Jewish, "this is the main hidden agenda that defines 'good' writing in the U.S. The point is to assume the reader is lazy, wants everything
spelled out for her/him. If the reader has to work to get meaning, the writing
is no 'good.' " Another reason that people sometimes want me to elaborate is
because they want to know my meaning as well as their own. Roz Spafford, a
college composition writing instructor at UCSC,[6] suggests that perhaps the
reader is looking for fullness and complexity, and a desire not to project their
experience/thinking onto mine, a desire to listen fully. But for me, what's
fun about reading is those gaps where I can bring my experience into the
piece of the writing and use concrete images to go off into my own experience. It makes the writing richer because I can bring more into it. But we
haven't been taught to read in that manner. We have, in fact, been taught not
to trust it. I think that I can "read" that way because I'm in my inner world,
my psychic and imaginary worlds so much that I've developed the *facultad*
to navigate such texts. The more I interact with the text the better. The more
entrances, the more access for all of us.

White Lesbian Formula Writing

    One of the things that I find very boring about some lesbian writing —
fiction and non-fiction — is an almost formulaic impression or imposition on

the writing of what lesbians should think about—a kind of politically correct way of writing that feels very sterile, very flat. One formula leads to the underlying belief that to be a lesbian writer you have to write about sexuality, and that the predominant concern of our work should be sexual relationships or sexuality. It's a given. This ideological imprint makes us view our sexuality in a preconstructed way. It tells us dykes how to think and feel about our bodies. Perhaps if we weren't supposed to write about sex so much, the writing would be more vital and vibrant. Besides, not all dykes want to write about sex or sexuality. Which brings us back to an earlier point: Is lesbian writing called such when it's not about lesbianism/sexuality but is by a lesbian?

Certain tropes that are considered lesbian properties—the coming-out story, the lesbian couple relationship, the break-up—have become formulaic. The formula is very white and mostly middle class and so prevalent that it is almost a genre. A coming-out story is different if it is written from the perspective of some "other,"—racial, cultural, class, ethnic or for whatever reason a lesbian has been "othered." A lot of cultural Others take the white lesbian patterns as models. So that whatever freshness of perspective, of presentation, of self-confrontation, encountering oneself as a lesbian and confronting one's community as a lesbian, instead of having that fresh, unique presentation of it, what we do is we copy this other model that's white middle class. It kills our writing. If it's not possible to entirely change the formula I'd at least like to see it be more representative of the diverse realities of queers, to read it and write it through other cultural lenses. I think that dykes have breached an opening in the dialogue about women connecting with our bodies. Dykes bridged some of the political, theoretical, cultural, critical concepts/beliefs with concrete experience—external/internal, sexual and corporeal. And that was really good.

A rainbow is a bridge. The word is used politically by Native Americans —it derives from Native American people symbolizing the way different people communicate and relate with each other. It's the vision that the Native Americans have of the red and the white and the black and the yellow being able to communicate and make alliances. According to the Native Americans, they were the keepers of the Earth and they were the ones that would facilitate this rich, multi-alliance, multi-bridging. A bridge excludes racial separatism. So the concept has taken a beating recently because of the reactionary times we're going through and the upsurge in racism and white supremacy. But I can see that in the '90s a rainbow *serpent* bridge composed of new mestizas/os, bi- and multi-racial queer people who are mixed and politicized will rise up and become important voices in our gay, ethnic and other communities.

WRITER'S NOTE

This essay is in progress and is excerpted from a longer piece. It started as a take-off on the transcription of my part in an interview/dialogue with Jeffner Allen. *Gracias a mis* interns Dianna Williamson, Vicki Alcoset, Audrey Berlowitz and Michelle Ueland, and also to Betsy Warland and Roz Spafford, who made comments: grammatical, stylistic and conceptual.

NOTES

1. Dianna Williamson commentary on this text, April 1991.
2. Cherríe Moraga, " '*Algo secretamente amado*': A Review of Gloria Anzaldúa's *Borderlands/La Frontera: The New Mestiza.*" *Third Woman*, (Fall 1989).
3. Dianna Williamson in her commentary on this text, April 1991.
4. See *Chicana Lesbians: The Girls Our Mothers Warned Us About*, edited by Carla Trujillo. (Berkeley: Third Woman Press, 1991).
5. The debate is not settled as to what's "serious" literature as opposed to woman-centered literature. The terms are suspicious ones to embrace. Does this imply that what women read is not "serious," i.e. not important? This piece is not the place to take on that discussion.
6. The book Spafford uses for Lit 203 at the University of California at Santa Cruz, *Facts, Artifacts and Counterfacts: Theory and Method for a Reading and Writing Course*, by David Bartholomae and Anthony Petrosky (Portsmouth, New Hampshire: Boynton Cook, 1986) suggests reading is misreading.

SELECTED PUBLICATIONS

BOOKS
Borderlands/La Frontera: The New Mestiza. San Francisco: Spinsters/Aunt Lute, 1987.

EDITED BOOKS

Making Face, Making Soul/Haciendo Caras. Creative and Critical Perspectives by Feminists of Color. San Francisco: Aunt Lute Foundation, 1990.

CO-EDITED BOOKS

With Cherríe Moraga. *This Bridge Called My Back: Writings by Radical Women of Color.* Watertown, Mass.: Persephone Press, 1981; New York: Kitchen Table: Women of Color Press, 1984.

FORTHCOMING BOOKS

Prietita Has a Friend/Prietita tiene un amigo (bilingual children's book). San Francisco: Children's Book Press, 1991.

Prieta, Auto-historias (autobiographical and fictitious narratives). San Francisco: Aunt Lute Foundation, 1992.

Lloronas, Women Who Wail: Explorations of (Self) Representation and the Production of Writing, Knowledge and Identity. 1992.

Writing mano: A Creative Writing Handbook. San Francisco: Aunt Lute Foundation, 1993.

Theory by Chicanas: An Anthology.

With Francisco Alárcon. *De las otras, de los otros: Collection of Art and Writings by Lesbians and Gay Chicanos.*

ANTHOLOGIES

"Metaphors in the Tradition of the Shaman." In *Conversant Essays: Contemporary Poets on Poetry*, edited by James McCorkle. Detroit: Wayne State Univ. Press, 1990.

"She Ate Horses — Version 1." In *Lesbian Philosophies and Cultures*, edited by Jeffner Allen. Binghamton, N.Y.: Women's Studies Series of State Univ. of N.Y. Press, 1990.

"People Should Not Die in June in South Texas." In *Daughters and Fathers*, edited by Irene Zahava. Freedom, Calif.: The Crossing Press, 1990.

"How to Tame a Wild Tongue." In *Out There: Marginalization and Contemporary Cultures*, edited by Russell Ferguson, Martha Gever, Trinh T. Minh-ha and Cornel West. New York: The New Museum of Contemporary Art, 1990.

"Bridge, Drawbridge, Sandbar or Island." In *Bridges of Power: Women's Multicultural Alliances*, edited by Lisa Albrecht and Rose M. Brewer. Philadelphia: New Society Publishers, 1990. Collection of papers from National Studies Association Conference.

"La artista cuando muchacha." In *Race and Class: An Anthology* (forthcoming), edited by Christian McEwen. Freedom, Calif.: The Crossing Press, 1992.

JOURNAL PUBLICATIONS

"La historia de una marimacho" (story). *Third Woman*, "Latina Sexuality" issue (Spring 1989).

ARTICLES AND REVIEWS

Carolyn Woodward, "Daring to Write." In *Changing Our Power: Introduction to Women's Studies*, edited by Cochran et al. Dubuque, Iowa: Kendall/Hunt, 1987.

Linda Nelson, "After Reading *Borderlands*." *Trivia* 14, (Spring 1989).

Diane P. Freedman, "Living in the Borderlands: The Poetic Prose of Gloria Anzaldúa and Susan Griffin. *Women and Language* 12, no. 1 (Spring 1989): 1-4.

Cherríe Moraga, " '*Algo secretamente amado*': A Review of Gloria Anzaldúa's *Borderlands/La Frontera: The New Mestiza*." *Third Woman* (Fall 1989).

Shelley Fishkin, "Borderlands of Culture: Writing by W.E.B. Du Bois, James Agee, Tillie Olsen and Gloria Anzaldúa." In *Literary Journalism in the Twentieth Century*, edited by Norman Sims. New York: Oxford Univ. Press, 1991.

Sonia Saldívar-Hull, "Feminism on the Border: From Gender Politics to Geopolitics." In *Chicano Literary Criticism: New Studies in Culture and Ideology*, edited by Hector Calderon and José Saldívar. Durham, N. Carolina: Duke Univ. Press, 1991.

TRANSLATORS' AUTOPORTRAIT(E)S

LOU NELSON: works as a freelance translator in Montreal. She has translated books of non-fiction, other short texts by Nicole Brossard and is currently working on a book of poetry by Anne-Marie Alonzo.

this lesbian comes to another through her writing
her reading of hope etched
in the certainty of our permanence

we will not be erased

for our senses overlap in the transposition
of sustenance
from tongue to tongue

indelible

MARLENE WILDEMAN: I came to Montreal from Vancouver in May of 1977, when Quebec was in full renaissance: all that was good about being a Quebecker was being rejuvenated and celebrated. Fueling the enthusiasm was the promise of greater things to come, now that the "politics of the collectivity" had rocketed into the collective consciousness. At the time, I was writing my first novel. My fictive characters were uniformly English Canadian, with origins that were either understood to be British, or irrelevant to the story — a character development problem for a writer whose original language and culture were themselves irrelevant, not to say dispensed with.

My parents, along with many others of their generation of Saskatchewan-born German Catholics, moved to British Columbia in the fifties looking for work. Soon, except at family gatherings when the old folks were present, there was no obvious use or advantage to speaking German. Outside the home, it provoked frank disapproval.

By the time I went to school I spoke only English, but there were foreign roots in my linguistic storehouse, and expectations about how people interact, that came from an industrious German perspective on the world. Nobody had to teach me how culture was bound up with language. I therefore set out to rid myself of anything identifiably German; before long, I could spell, read aloud, write and speak English as well as, or better than, anyone in school. Paradoxically, for most of my school years I was hobbled by a desire to be indistinguishable from everyone else.

Alas, certain things were beyond my control. Destined to stand out regardless, I was the girl that grew. At sixteen, still auditioning for the sweetheart role in the school play, I was five-foot-ten and they were calling me Amazon. Ten years later in lesbian feminism I learned what they were trying to tell me. Finally, after knocking awkwardly on a few wrong doors, and spending a few hope-filled years apprenticing writing within and without the university, I stepped into a vehicle I had been trying to catch up with all along. . . . I was loved by women, I loved language and writing, and I sensed that my home(land) would be wherever I set up my workroom. English Canadian politics on the whole lacked credibility, even with feminist change, and I needed a viable, culturally productive community where I could do some good. Quebec's women were thriving, and I had always been enamoured of French. In Montreal, I learned that I was also at home in the Jewish community, which is bilingual and cosmopolitan. By assimilating myself into lesbian life and language in Quebec, I slid into the driver's seat of my own life at last.

My first published translation was a *Vie en rose* 1982 editorial titled: *Aimons-nous les hommes?* Written by a single collective hand, in combining lesbian and heterosexual feminist theory, this text heralded a breakthrough in lesbian feminist relations. I felt compelled to relay this triumph of theory over dissension to English Canadian feminists, with the result that I was catapulted into translation print — in *Broadside* and *Kinesis*.

For ten years now I have been translating primarily lesbian and feminist literary works, notably Nicole Brossard's collected essays, *The Aerial Letter,* and *The Montreal Massacre* anthology. For the International Feminist Book Fair in Montreal in 1988, I organized Trade Days' events, including panel discussions on translation. Later that year, translating sociologist Line Chamberland's presentation for a CRIAW [Canadian Research Institute for the Advancement of Women] conference led to my decision to edit an anthology of lesbian feminist theory, for which I wrote a "seed text" designed to incite new writing by lesbians. I continue to write and publish short fiction. I have attempted a second novel, published a few critical articles, and presented at academic feminist conferences. For the next Feminist Book Fair, I am preparing a presentation on "Feminist Issues in Criticism of Literary Translations."

Language appears to be the instrument and purpose of my life. Through language I transform meaning for others, I am transformed and my life given meaning. For the past five years, I have taught English as a Second Language while taking courses to obtain my teaching certificate. I am presently studying Applied Linguistics at the Master's level. Unfortunately, when I teach, or translate, I don't write. I then torture myself by thinking I am really more a teacher, or a translator, and not really a writer. My intense involvement in whatever I am doing, teaching or translating or studying, keeps at bay any doubt about whether I'm "producing," and permits me to eclipse the time and mind-space necessary for my own attempts at writing.

Obviously, what I have left of German culture is *angst!* I may also have a heightened sense of the value of *Zeitgeist* as a tool for social change. Yet I must say I have never felt more Canadian than when I was travelling through Germany. Regardless, whenever I think I can stop and rest, a wise but iron-willed *Frau* deep inside calls out: *There must be something else you can do!*

CONTRIBUTORS

ANNE-MARIE ALONZO is a poet, fiction-writer, playwright, editor/publisher, and literary critic. She was born in Alexandria, Egypt on the thirteenth of December, 1951, and has lived in Quebec since 1963. To date, she has written fifteen books, among them *Lead Blues*, which won the Émile-Nelligan Prize in 1985. She has taught creative writing at the University of Montreal and her work has appeared in numerous anthologies and reviews in Europe, Quebec, the United States, and Canada. Co-founder and co-director of *Trois*, a review and a publishing house, in 1987 she also launched A.M.A. Productions, a company which produces books-on-cassette.

GLORIA E. ANZALDÚA is a Chicana *tejana* feminist-dyke poet-writer-theorist born in September 1942 in South Texas, and now living in Santa Cruz. In 1991 she received a National Endowment for the Arts award for fiction. Gloria has taught creative writing, Chicano Studies and Feminist Studies at numerous universities. She has been Artist-in-Residence (The Loft, Minneapolis), Writer-in-Residence (Chicano Studies, Pomona College), contributing editor of *Sinister Wisdom*, and she serves on editorial boards for various publications.

BETH BRANT is a Bay of Quinte Mohawk from Tyendinaga Mohawk Territory in Ontario, who has lived much of her life in Michigan. She is a lesbian mother and grandmother, a Taurus with Scorpio rising, a high school drop-out, a working-class woman who grew up with the sound of the factory whistle regulating the lives of her family. She began writing at the age of forty in 1981, has lectured extensively throughout North America on Native women's writing, and teaches creative writing.

Born in 1943 in Montreal where she lives, NICOLE BROSSARD is a poet, novelist and essayist. She has published more than twenty books since 1965. She co-founded the literary magazine *La Barre du Jour* (1965-1975) and the feminist newspaper *Les*

Têtes de pioche (1976-1979). She is twice winner of the Governor General Award and was awarded, in 1989, Le Grand Prix de poésie de la Fondation Les Forges. She recently co-edited with Lisette Girouard an anthology of women's poetry in Quebec (1677-1988).

ANNE CAMERON was born in Nanaimo, British Columbia, in August 1938. Raised and educated on the West Coast, she has two daughters, two sons, one step-daughter, two granddaughters, four grandsons, and is a feminist, pro-choice, environmental activist, pagan.

CHRYSTOS is a Native American born November 7, 1946 in San Francisco of a Menominee father & a Lithuanian/Alsace-Lorraine mother. She is self-educated and is an artist as well as a writer. She tours extensively throughout North America as a speaker and as an activist participating in Indigenous Land & Treaty Rights struggles, including working for the freedom of Leonard Peltier, the Diné Nation at Big Mountain, and the Mohawk Nation at Kanehsatake (Quebec). She now makes her home in Seattle.

CHERYL CLARKE (born May 16, 1947) is from Washington, D.C. and has been living in New Jersey since 1969, currently in Jersey City. She is an editor of *Conditions*, a feminist magazine of writing by women, with an emphasis on writing by lesbians. She is a member of the Board of the Center for Lesbian and Gay Studies at the City University of New York Graduate Center. She is presently working on her fourth book of poetry.

CM DONALD was born in 1950, in Derbyshire, England. She thrived in girls' schools, survived Cambridge University, came out as a lesbian and a feminist in 1976, moved to Canada in 1980, and now works in Toronto (for pay) as a freelance editor and (from conviction) with the Coalition for Lesbian and Gay Rights in Ontario.

ELANA DYKEWOMON was born in New York City in 1949 and has been looking for lesbian community since she was three; actively participating in its creation since 1971. She lives in Oakland, California, blessed with love and inspiring friendships.

GLORIA ESCOMEL was born in Montevideo, Uruguay in 1941, and has resided in Montreal since 1967. With a Ph.D. in French Literature, Gloria Escomel is a part-time lecturer at the University of Montreal and the University of Quebec at Montreal. She is a freelance journalist for *La Gazette des femmes* and a literary critic, as well as a feminist, a lesbian, a committed Free Mason, and a member of Amnesty International.

JUDY GRAHN was born in Chicago, Illinois on July 28, 1940, and grew up in New Mexico. She lives in Oakland, California where she teaches independently for LavenderRose Women's Mysteries School, which she is founding. She is currently interested in writing for tape using musical technology. Her poetry has been translated into several languages, widely performed and staged.

IRENA KLEPFISZ (born in 1941) is an activist in the lesbian/feminist and Jewish communities. She has been a founder and editor of lesbian and women's publications and has been particularly active in the last four years on the Israeli/Palestinian conflict with the Jewish Women's Committee to End the Occupation of the West Bank and Gaza (NYC). She now serves as Executive Director of New Jewish Agenda, a multi-issue activist organization. She is committed to helping develop Jewish secular consciousness in the United States, emphasizing the role of women and of lesbians in the Jewish community. She hopes to do this through further writing and teaching.

JUDITH MCDANIEL (born in November 1943) is a writer, teacher, and political activist who lives in Albany, New York. Her first lesbian romance, *Just Say Yes*, was published in 1991 by Firebrand Books. She is also the author of *Metamorphosis: Reflections on Recovery* and *Sanctuary: A Journey*.

Born in 1942, DAPHNE MARLATT lives on Salt Spring Island some five hours from Vancouver and can be identified as a lesbian feminist West Coast poet, although she also writes novels and critical theory. She is a founding co-editor of the journal *Tessera*, which publishes new Quebecoise and English-Canadian feminist theory and writing. She is currently working on a third novel, a "prequel" to *Ana Historic*.

MARY MEIGS, writer and painter, was born in Philadelphia, Pennsylvania in 1917, and grew up in Washington D.C. She received her B.A. from Bryn Mawr College in 1939, and moved to Quebec in 1975, where she lives in Montreal.

SUNITI NAMJOSHI was born in India in 1941. She has worked as an Officer in the Indian Administrative Service and in academic posts in India and Canada. Since 1972 she taught in the Department of English at the University of Toronto, and now lives and writes in Devon, England. She has published numerous books of poetry and fiction, and one children's book. Her poems, fables, articles and reviews have appeared in anthologies, collections and literary and Women's Studies journals in India, Canada, the United States and Britain.

MINNIE BRUCE PRATT was born September 12, 1946, in Selma, Alabama. She received her academic education at the University of Alabama (Tuscaloosa) and the University of North Carolina (Chapel Hill) and her actual education through grassroots organizing with women and through teaching at historically Black universities. For five years she was a member of the lesbian editorial collective of *Feminary: A Feminist Journal for the South.* In 1989, her book of poetry, *Crime Against Nature,* was chosen as the Lamont Poetry Selection by the Academy of American Poets. She lives in Washington, D.C., and teaches Women's Studies at the University of Maryland (College Park). She is the mother of two sons.

JANE RULE was born in Plainfield, New Jersey, March 28, 1931, moved to Canada in 1956 and became a Canadian citizen. After intermittent teaching at the University of British Columbia, she moved from Vancouver to Galiano Island in 1976.

SARAH SCHULMAN was born in New York City in 1958. She is the author of five novels, including *After Delores,* winner of the American Library Association Gay/Lesbian book award in 1989. *People In Trouble* was awarded The Words Project AIDS/Gregory Kolovakos Memorial Prize for fiction in 1990. Her books have been translated into German, Greek, Dutch, Japanese and are available in British editions from Sheba Press. Sarah is a long-time activist, currently a member of ACT-UP (AIDS Coalition To Unleash Power). She is co-founder (with Jim Hubbard) of The New York Lesbian and Gay Experimental Film Festival which has presented work since 1986.

LUZ MARÍA UMPIERRE ("Luzma"): I was born in Santurce, Puerto Rico, and through the immense sacrifices of my parents and numerous scholarships, I graduated from the Universidad del Sagrado Corazón and from Bryn Mawr College (Pennsylvania). I was the first openly Lesbian Puerto Rican woman to be tenured in the Spanish Department at Rutgers University (New Jersey). Because of my advocacy for Gays and Lesbians and other Minorities, I was severely persecuted at Rutgers and this has led to my filing in federal court in Newark, New Jersey an unprecedented case based on discrimination on the basis of sex, national origin, and sexual preference. In 1989 I became Head and Professor of Modern Languages and Intercultural Studies at Western Kentucky University. In 1990 I was awarded a "Life Time Achievement Award" from the Gay and Lesbian organizations in New Jersey and named "Woman of the Year" by the Women's Alliance at Western Kentucky University. I reside in Bowling Green, Kentucky.

Writer and editor BETSY WARLAND has been active in creating a feminist literary community in English Canada since 1975 when she co-founded the Toronto Women's Writing Collective. She initiated and was a co-ordinator of the first cross-Canada women's literary conference, *Women and Words / les femmes et les mots*, in Vancouver in 1983. She was born in Iowa in 1946 and immigrated to Canada in 1972, where she lives on Salt Spring Island, off the coast of Vancouver Island.

BARBARA WILSON was born in 1950 and raised in Long Beach, California. She has lived in Seattle most of her adult life, though she's also spent several years in Germany, Norway, Spain and England. In addition to being a fiction writer she is co-publisher of Seal Press, which celebrates its fifteenth anniversary in 1991. She is also the editorial director of Women in Translation, a non-profit press which publishes international women's literature.

MARG YEO is pushing 45 and has recently returned from England, where she lived for many years. Currently, she lives in Toronto, and makes her living by editing, writing and designing educational and training materials. She is working on a new book of poems and thinking hard about two very different novels.

EVE ZAREMBA was born in Poland in 1930 and still speaks the language. She immigrated to Canada in 1952 and is a graduate of the University of Toronto. Eve has worked in libraries, in advertising and marketing, and in research and business consulting. She has owned a used bookstore and a small press. A long-time feminist activist and writer, she was a founding member of *Broadside, A Feminist Review*, for which she wrote articles too ephemeral and numerous to mention. She lives happily in Toronto with her mate and partner, Ottie Lockey.

Press Gang Publishers Feminist Co-operative is committed to publishing a wide range of writing by women which explores themes of personal and political struggles for equality.

A free listing of our books is available from Press Gang Publishers, 603 Powell Street, Vancouver, B.C.   V6A 1H2   Canada